Visual QuickStart Guide

Word 6
for Windows

Stephanie Berglin

with

Catherine Howes & Suzie Wynn Jones

Webster & Associates

Peachpit Press

Word 6 for Windows: Visual Quickstart Guide
Webster & Associates

Peachpit Press, Inc.
2414 Sixth Street
Berkeley, CA 94710
(510) 548-4393
(510) 548-5991 (fax)

Notice of Liability

Trademarks

ISBN: 1-56609-110-1

Printed and bound in the United States of America

 Printed on recycled paper

Why a Visual QuickStart?

Virtually no one actually reads computer books; rather, people typically refer to them. This series of **Visual QuickStart Guides** has made that reference easier thanks to a new approach to learning computer applications.

Although conventional computer books lean towards providing extensive textual explanations, a **Visual QuickStart Guide** takes a far more visual approach—pictures literally show you what to do, and text is limited to clear, concise commentary. Learning becomes easier, because a **Visual QuickStart Guide** familiarizes you with the look and feel of your software. Learning also becomes faster, since there are no long-winded passages through which to comb.

It's a new approach to computer learning, but it's also solidly based on experience: Webster & Associates have logged thousands of hours of classroom computer training, and have authored several books on computer applications.

Chapters 1 through **18** of this Word 6 for Windows Visual QuickStart Guide provide a graphic overview of the major features. These chapters are easy to reference and use screen shots to ensure that you grasp concepts quickly.

Acknowledgments

The authors wish to acknowledge the effort and dedication of the following people:

- Sean Kelly for editing

- Carrie Webster for helping with screen shots

- Jenny Hamilton for proofing and correcting

Contents

Chapter 3. Managing Files

Chapter 4. Paragraph Formatting

Chapter 5. Document and Section Formatting

Chapter 6. Styles

Chapter 7. Templates and Wizards

Chapter 8. Document Checking Tools

Chapter 9. Page Views

Chapter 13. Long Document Capabilities

Chapter 14. Macros and AutoText

Chapter 15. Field Codes

Chapter 16. Merging Documents

THE SCREEN

THE WORD SCREEN

Figure 1. This chapter gives you an overview of the different areas and features of the Word screen covering the items indicated in this figure. It also provides details on the Help functions within Word.

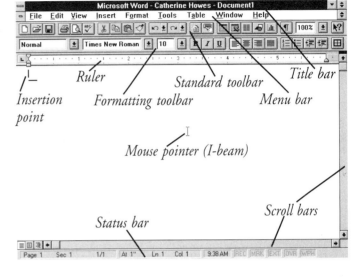

Ruler *Standard toolbar* *Title bar*
Insertion point *Formatting toolbar* *Menu bar*
Mouse pointer (I-beam)
Scroll bars
Status bar

SCREEN COMPONENTS

TITLE BAR

Figure 2. The title bar is located along the top of the window, and contains: the Application Control menu box; the name of the application—Microsoft Word; the name of the person or company the Word 6 installation disks are licensed to; the name of the active document; and the minimize and restore (maximize) buttons.

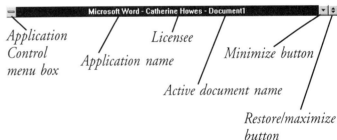

Application Control menu box *Licensee*
Application name *Minimize button*
Active document name
Restore/maximize button

Figure 3. Clicking on the Application's Control menu box displays this menu. These are the commands for closing Word, switching to other applications, and resizing and moving the Word window.

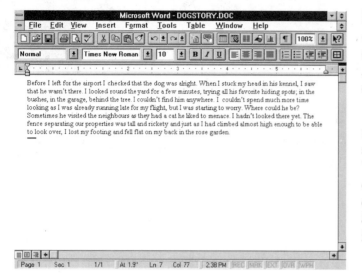

Figure 4. Once you have saved a document, Word replaces the default document name—*Document 1*—with your new choice of name.

You can name documents with up to eight characters. Word automatically adds the extension ".DOC" to your files, but you can choose your own specific extensions if you like (see the **Saving a File** section of **Chapter 3** for more information).

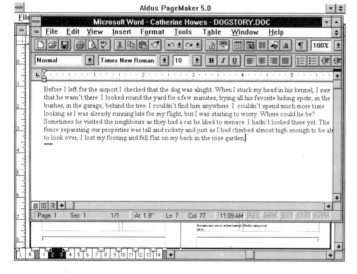

Figure 5. The restore button (Figure 2) reduces the Word window view on the screen. This allows you to see other Windows applications that you may have open behind Word.

Figure 6. To move the application window, drag the title bar (you can move a window only if you have not maximized it).

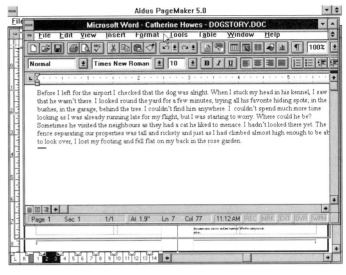

Figure 7. You can then click on the maximize button to fill the screen with the Word application window.

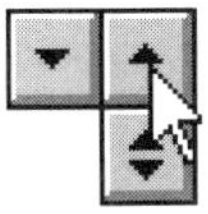

Figure 8. When you click on the application minimize button, this reduces Word to its icon. (Double-click on the icon to restore it again.)

MENU BAR

Figure 9. The menu bar is located below the title bar. It contains the Document Control menu box, Word's command menu names, and the restore button. You choose menu commands to instruct Word to carry out an action.

Figure 10. To view the commands in a menu, do one of the following:

• Click with the left mouse button on the menu name.

• Press Alt + the underlined letter in the menu name. For example, press Alt+F to see the contents of the **File** menu.

Any command in a menu followed by an ellipsis (...) produces a dialog box when activated. Commands that don't have an ellipsis produce an effect straight away.

If you select a menu by mistake, and want to deselect it, click the mouse outside the menu, or press Esc on the keyboard.

Figure 11. You select a command by clicking on that command with the mouse.

Another method of selecting menus and commands is to hold your mouse button down with the pointer on the required menu name, and move the mouse down the menu. Release the mouse on the command you want.

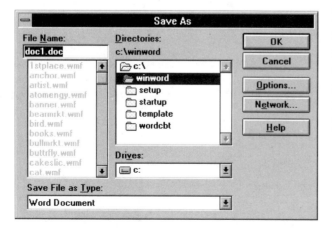

Figure 12. When you select a menu command, many of them activate a dialog box. In these dialog boxes, you can specify measurements, and choose from options that change and format your document.

Figure 13. Some dialog boxes are organized into categories. Word indicates these with tabs. To display a different category, click on the tab for the category you want to display.

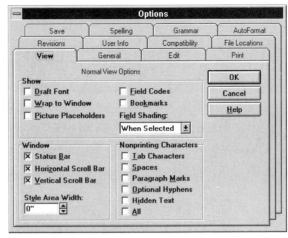

Figure 14. The menu bar also contains the Document Control menu box, and the document's restore button (see Figure 9). Click on the Document Control box to display this menu. You use these commands for sizing, moving, splitting, and closing the document window, and for moving between windows.

Figure 15. When you click on the document's restore button, this separates the active Word document from the menu bar, *Standard* toolbar, and *Formatting* toolbar. This allows you to move the document window around the screen by dragging on the document title bar.

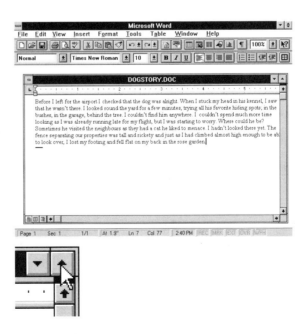

Figure 16. Click on the document's maximize button to enlarge the document window again. This returns you to the same screen layout as shown in Figure 1.

TOOLBARS

There are seven toolbars available in Word. Toolbars give you quick mouse access to many of the tools used in Word.

If necessary, you can customize the toolbars and save them with particular types of documents.

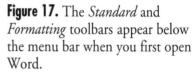

Figure 17. The *Standard* and *Formatting* toolbars appear below the menu bar when you first open Word.

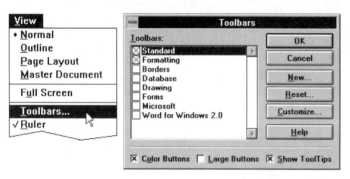

Figure 18. To display or hide toolbars, select the *Toolbars* command from the **View** menu. In the *Toolbars* dialog box select the toolbars that you want to display and deselect the toolbars you want to hide, then click on *OK*.

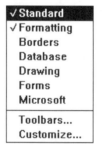

Figure 19. You can also hide and display toolbars using the toolbars shortcut menu. To display this menu, move the mouse pointer over any toolbar and click the right mouse button. To display a toolbar, select it from the list. To hide a toolbar, deselect it from the list.

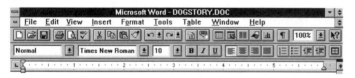

Figure 20. Toolbars can either be "anchored" or "floating." An anchored toolbar is locked into an anchor position such as under the menu bar, above the status bar or on the left or right hand side of the screen.

Figure 21. A floating toolbar is in a separate window which you can move or resize like a standard window.

Figure 22. To anchor a floating toolbar window, click down on the title bar and drag it to one of the anchor positions mentioned in Figure 20. When the border of the toolbar window changes to a long thin rectangle, release the mouse button. Alternatively, double-click on the title bar of the toolbar window.

Figure 23. You can float an anchored window by double-clicking on the background of the toolbar.

Figure 24. Word labels its tools on the toolbars. To see a description of a tool, move the mouse pointer over the tool and wait for a few seconds and a Tooltip appears on the screen.

Figure 25. Some toolbars, such as the *Formatting* toolbar, contain drop-down lists. To use a drop-down list, click on the down arrow and select a command.

RULER

Figure 26. The ruler is displayed directly above the text editing area. The ruler lets you indent paragraphs, adjust margins, change column and table widths, and set tab stops.

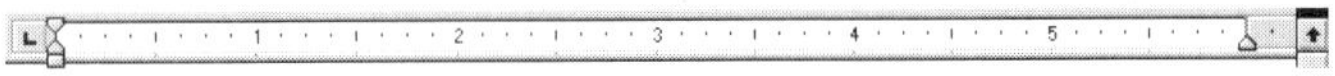

Figure 27. To hide or display the ruler choose *Ruler* from the **View** menu. The check mark beside the *Ruler* command indicates that you have selected the ruler and it is displayed on the screen.

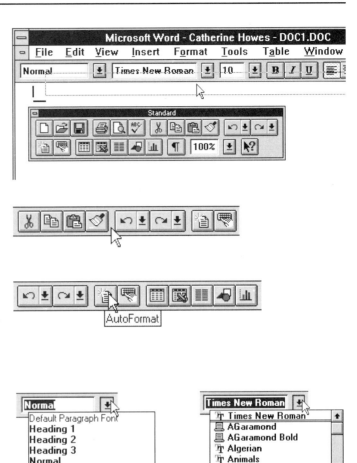

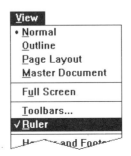

SCROLL BARS

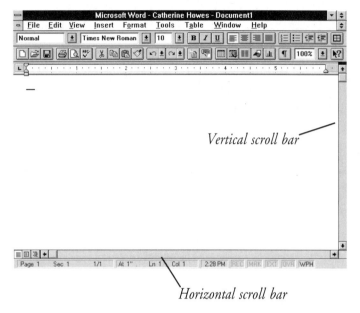

Vertical scroll bar

Horizontal scroll bar

Figure 28. The scroll bars appear at the right and bottom edges of the document window. The scroll boxes inside the scroll bars indicate your vertical and horizontal position in the document. You can drag these scroll boxes, or click on the arrows, to move to a different location in the document.

The horizontal scroll bar also contains three buttons that change your document view. See **Chapter 9** for details on different document views.

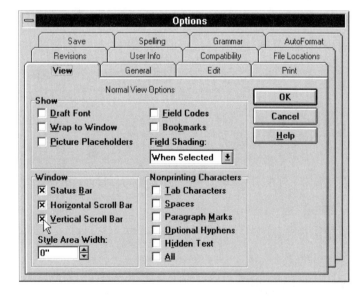

Figure 29. Because you can also use the cursor keys to move around your document, Word allows you to hide one or both of the scroll bars. Do this by selecting *Options* from the **Tools** menu and opening the *Options* dialog box.

In the *View* category tab, click on the *Horizontal* and *Vertical Scroll Bar* check boxes to deselect them.

STATUS BAR

Figure 30. The status bar is displayed at the bottom of the Word window. It provides information such as messages to help you use Word; statistics about the insertion point's position; the magnification percentage of the page; and the status of some important keys.

Figure 31. This table describes some of the information shown on the status bar.

Status bar item	Meaning
Page	Indicates the page you are viewing
Sec	Indicates the section you are viewing
2/4	Indicates the number of the page you are viewing (2) and the total pages in the document (4)
At	Indicates the distance between the insertion point and the top of the page
Ln	Indicates the number of lines from the top of the page to the insertion point
Col	Indicates the number of characters from the left margin to the insertion point.
12:00 AM	The current time as set on your computer
REC	When bold, indicates the macro recorder is active
MRK	When bold, indicates revision marking is active
EXT	When bold, indicates Extend Selection is active
OVR	When bold, indicates Overtype mode is active
WPH	When bold, indicates Help for WordPerfect users is active

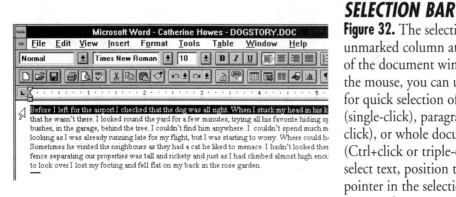

SELECTION BAR

Figure 32. The selection bar is an unmarked column at the left edge of the document window. With the mouse, you can use this area for quick selection of a line (single-click), paragraph (double-click), or whole document (Ctrl+click or triple-click). To select text, position the mouse pointer in the selection bar; the pointer changes to a right-pointing arrow. Then click the mouse.

POINTERS

There are a number of different pointers in Word. You use these to perform different tasks.

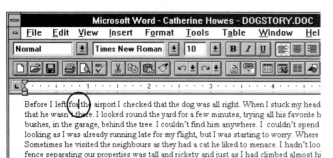

INSERTION POINT

Figure 33. The insertion point appears on the screen as a blinking vertical line. Wherever you place the insertion point is where inserted text, or a graphic, appear on the page.

You can move the insertion point around the document by pointing and clicking the mouse at a particular position, or by using the arrow keys on the keyboard.

MOUSE POINTER

Figure 34. When you position the mouse over the text area, or text boxes within dialog boxes, the mouse changes to an I-beam shaped icon.

Figure 35. When you position the mouse over a part of the screen that you use for selecting commands, such as the menu bar, toolbars, or ruler, the mouse changes to a left-pointing arrow.

HELP FUNCTIONS

Figure 36. Press the F1 key, or select *Index* from the **Help** menu, to activate Help.

Figure 37. The *Word Help* window lists the help contents. Positioning the mouse over a topic changes the pointer to a hand. Select a topic by clicking the hand on its text. Keep clicking on the relevant topics until you have all the information you need.

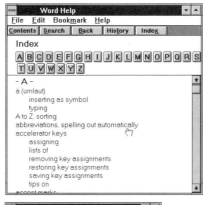

Figure 38. When you click on words that have a solid underline, Help gives you more information about that topic.

Figure 39. When you click on a word that has a dotted underline, Help gives you a definition of that word.

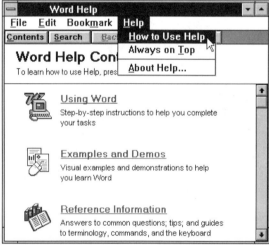

Figure 40. In the *Help Contents* window you can press F1 or select *How to Use Help* from the **Help** menu to find out how to use Help.

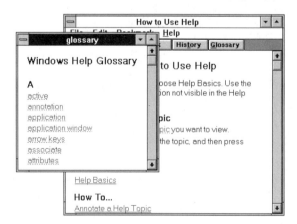

Figure 41. When you click on the *Glossary* button, in the *How to Use Help* window, Help gives you a list of terms. Click on one of the terms to display a definition of that term.

Figure 42. You can click on the *Search* button to find information about a specific topic. In the *Search* box, move up and down the list by clicking on the scroll arrows. You can also type a word into the text box at the top of the dialog box. Then, select a topic from the list, and click on the *Show Topics* button.

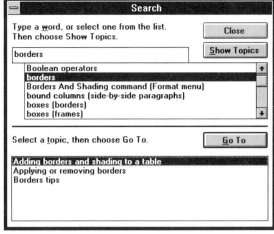

Figure 43. In the bottom box of the *Search* dialog box, choose a topic by clicking on its name. Then click on the *Go To* button to view the instructions about that topic in the *How To* dialog box.

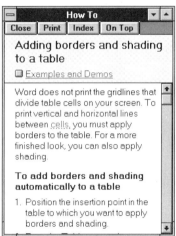

Figure 44. To close the *Help* window, choose *Exit* from the **File** menu, or double-click on the Control menu box.

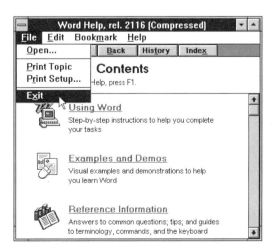

USING HELP AS YOU WORK

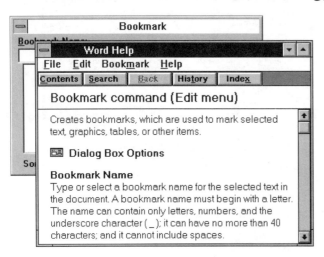

Figure 45. You can also activate Help to assist you as you work. For example, if you have opened a dialog box press the F1 key or click on the *Help* button to view information about that dialog box.

Figure 46. For easy access to Help on menu commands or parts of the screen, click on the *Help* button.

Figure 47. This adds a question mark to the pointer. Click on a command or an area on the screen and Word displays the corresponding Help information.

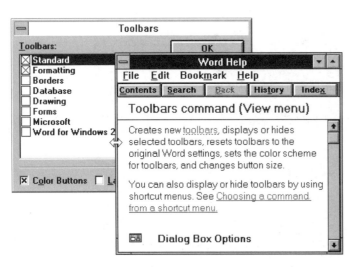

Figure 48. You can resize the *Help* window to view the instructions as you perform tasks in your document. Word displays the pointer as a double-headed arrow when you place it over the Help window's border. Drag the border to resize the window. You can also move the whole window to another location on the screen by dragging its title bar.

ENTERING AND EDITING TEXT   2

INTRODUCTION

You can edit and format Word documents in a variety of ways. Text formatting affects individual letters and words; paragraph formatting affects blocks of text; and other kinds of formatting affect the whole document.

This chapter looks at how to create a new document and how to do some simple text formatting.

CREATING A NEW DOCUMENT

Each time you start Word, it automatically opens a document with the label *Document1* on the title bar. You can start typing immediately.

TYPING TEXT

Figure 1. To begin a document, all you need to do is start to type. In a new document, the insertion point is in the top left-hand corner of the screen. Word inserts the text you type from this point.

You do not need to press Enter at the end of every line. Word adjusts line breaks automatically with a feature called *wordwrap*. Wordwrap lets you type, insert, or delete text, without having to adjust your line breaks.

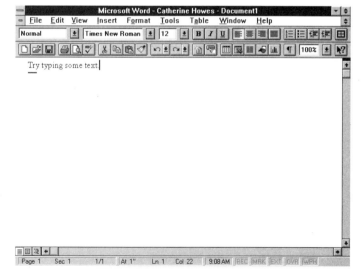

Selecting Text

In order to format text, you must first select it. You can select text using the mouse, or the keyboard.

With the Mouse

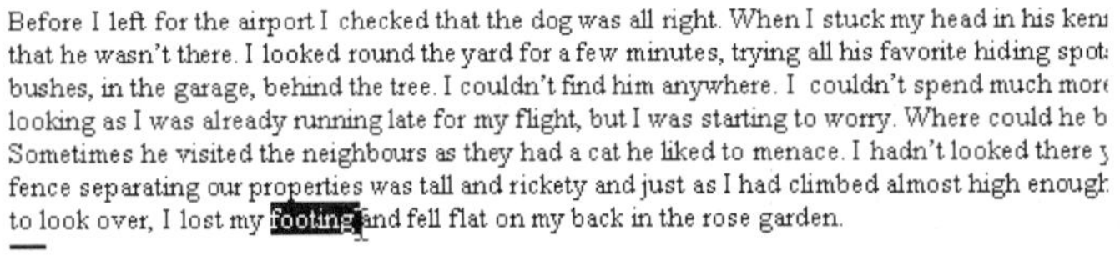

Before I left for the airport I checked that the dog was all right. When I stuck my head in his ken
that he wasn't there. I looked round the yard for a few minutes, trying all his favorite hiding spot
bushes, in the garage, behind the tree. I couldn't find him anywhere. I couldn't spend much mor
looking as I was already running late for my flight, but I was starting to worry. Where could he b
Sometimes he visited the neighbours as they had a cat he liked to menace. I hadn't looked there
fence separating our properties was tall and rickety and just as I had climbed almost high enoug
to look over, I lost my footing and fell flat on my back in the rose garden.

Figure 2. Using the mouse, place the I-beam just before the text you want to select. Then click and hold down the left mouse button, drag to the end of the text, and release the mouse. As you move the mouse along, you select the text to the left of the I-beam. Word shows selected text as white on black.

Another quick way to select text is to put the insertion point in front of the text you want to select. Then hold down the Shift key, move the I-beam to the end of the text, and click the left mouse button. Word selects all text between these points.

To select a word, position the I-beam over the word and double-click with the mouse.

Microsoft Word - Catherine Howes - DOGSTORY.DOC
File
Edit
View
Insert
Format
Tools
Table
Window
Normal
Times New Roman
10
Before I left for the airport I checked that the dog was all right. When I stuck my hea
that he wasn't there. I looked round the yard for a few minutes, trying all his favorite
bushes, in the garage, behind the tree. I couldn't find him anywhere.
I couldn't spend much more time looking as I was already running late for my flight,
worry. Where could he be? Sometimes he visited the neighbours as they had a cat he
hadn't looked there yet. The fence separating our properties was tall and rickety and j
almost high enough to be able to look over, I lost my footing and fell flat on my back

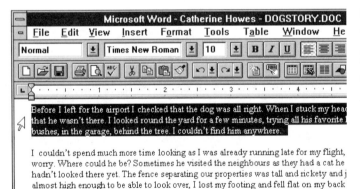

Figure 3. To select a line, move the I-beam to the left side of the screen until it becomes a pointer. This area is the selection bar. Then, click next to the line you want to select.

To select a paragraph, double-click in the selection bar, on the edge of the paragraph you want to select.

To select the whole document, hold down the Ctrl key, and click in the selection bar or triple-click.

WITH THE KEYBOARD

To select text using the keyboard, the insertion point needs to be just before the text you intend to select. Hold down the Shift key, and use the arrow keys on the keyboard to highlight text.

Figure 4. You can also select text using *Extend-Selection* mode. Pressing F8 once activates this mode, and EXT is highlighted in the status bar, at the bottom of the screen.

Figure 5. To select a word using *Extend-Selection* mode, place the insertion point in the word, and press F8 twice.

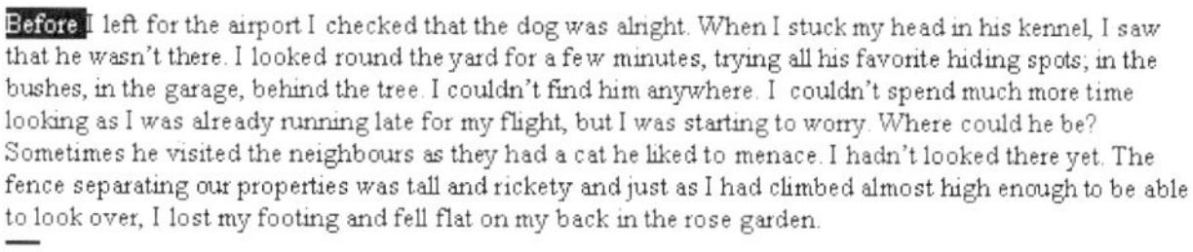

To select a sentence that contains the insertion point, press F8 three times.

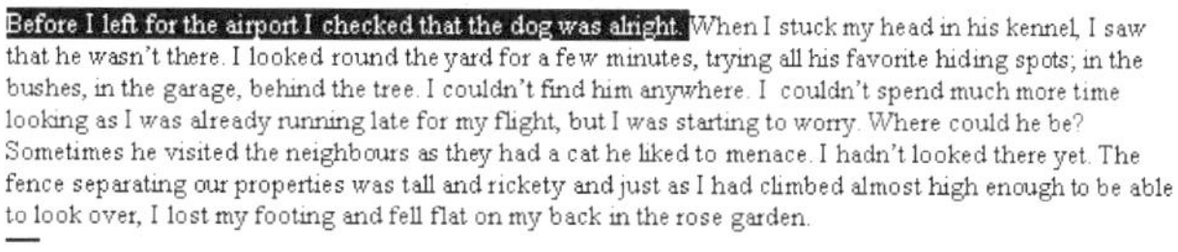

To select a paragraph containing the insertion point, press F8 four times.

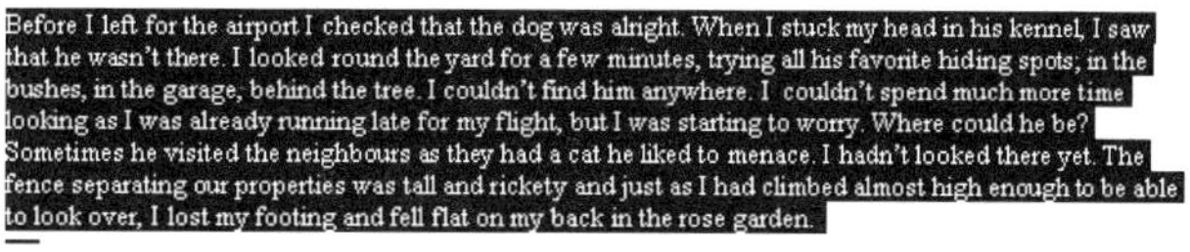

To select a section (see **Chapter 4**) that has the insertion point in it, press F8 a total of five times.

To select the whole document, press F8 five times, or six times if your document has sections.

To deselect the *Extend-Selection* mode, press Esc on the keyboard, and then click the mouse to deselect the text.

To Select...	Do This...	
	Keyboard	Mouse
A word	Place insertion point in the word and press F8 twice	Double-click on the word
A line	Place insertion point in the sentence and press F8 three times	Click in the selection bar to the left of the line
A paragraph	Place insertion point in the paragraph and press F8 four times	Double-click in the selection bar to the left of the paragraph
The whole document	Press F8 five times (six times if document has sections)	Triple-click in the selection bar

Figure 6. The adjacent table shows the major mouse and keyboard operations for selecting words, lines, paragraphs, and whole documents.

FORMATTING TEXT

Figure 7. You can change the font, size, and style of selected text using the *Formatting* toolbar. (If you don't have any text selected, it will effect the text you type next.) The *Formatting* toolbar does not contain all character formats, but contains the most common ones and is easy to access.

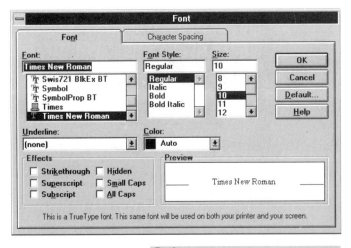

Figure 8. Alternatively, you can use the *Font* dialog box. The *Font* command in the **Format** menu activates this dialog box.

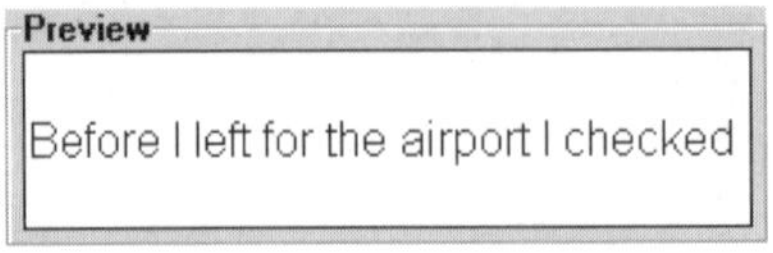

Preview

Before I left for the airport I checked

Figure 9. The *Preview* box in the *Font* dialog box shows you how the text will look when you click on *OK*.

FONT

Figure 10. The *Font* list box, in the *Font* dialog box, shows you what fonts are available. The fonts listed depend on the printer you are using and whether you have installed any downloadable fonts.

To change the font of highlighted text, or the next text you type, simply choose the name of the font you require from the *Font* list box, and click on *OK*.

Figure 11. Alternatively, you can use the *Formatting* toolbar to change fonts. Click the mouse pointer on the down arrow of the *Font* drop-down list box to display fonts. Then click on a font to select it.

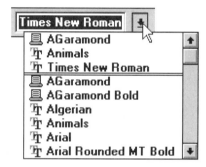

The drop-down list box is divided by a double line; the top half shows you other fonts you have used in this document. When you choose a font, the word containing the insertion point changes to that font.

FONT STYLE

Figure 12. To apply one of the options from the *Font Style* list box in the *Font* dialog box of Figure 8, click on the option you want to select.

You can also make text bold, or italic by clicking on their respective buttons through the *Formatting* toolbar. To deselect, click on the button again.

SIZE

Figure 13. Change the size of text by selecting the size you want from the *Size* list box in the *Font* dialog box, then click on *OK*.

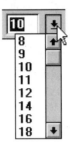

Figure 14. You can also use the *Formatting* toolbar to change text size by clicking on the *Point size* down arrow, and selecting the required size from the list.

The font sizes in the list vary according to the font selected, and are also printer dependent.

UNDERLINE

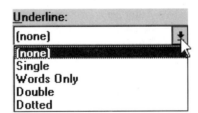

Figure 15. You can underline your text in four ways using the *Underline* drop-down list box. *Single* places a single line under all of the text you selected. *Words Only* places a single line under each word in the text. *Double* places a double line under all of the text. *Dotted* places a dotted line under all of the text.

COLOR

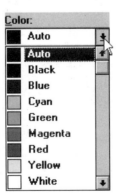

Figure 16. You can set the color of text in your document. First, select the text, then open the *Color* drop-down menu in the *Font* dialog box, and choose the color you want.

EFFECTS

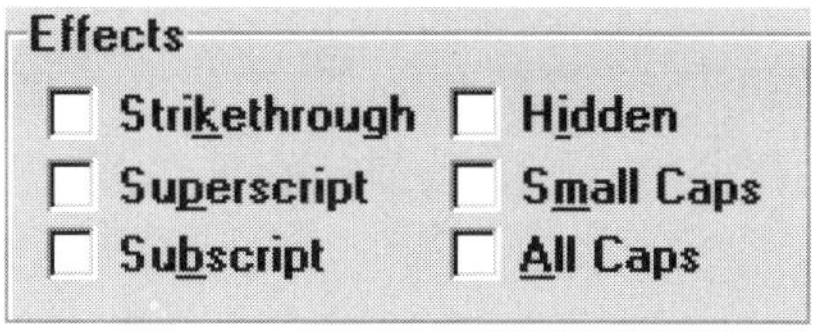

Figure 17. The *Effects* options let you apply special effects to the text you select in your document. *Strikethrough* places a line through the middle of the text. *Superscript* raises the text above the baseline. *Subscript* lowers the text below the baseline. Both also change the text size. *Hidden* hides the text on the screen and when you print it. *Small Caps* changes all of the text to capitals that are the same size as the lower case letters. *All Caps* changes the text to upper case.

Effects

☐ Stri**k**ethrough   ☐ H**i**dden
☐ Sup**e**rscript   ☐ S**m**all Caps
☐ Su**b**script   ☐ A**l**l Caps

SPACING

Figure 18. To change the spacing between characters in your text, click on the *Character Spacing* tab in the *Font* dialog box. The *Character Spacing* settings affect the amount of space between characters.

You can expand or condense text and choose the amount of space from the *By* text box next to the *Spacing* drop-down list. Click on the arrows, or type in your own spacing distance.

Choosing *Normal* resets the spacing to the default.

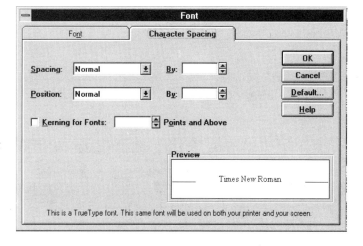

Figure 19. The *Position* options let you raise or lower text using a specific amount you enter into the *By* text box.

Figure 20. The *Kerning for Fonts* option enables you to automatically kern, or set the space between characters. You enter a point size above which Word will kern the text. You normally set this to the point size of your headings.

DEFAULT BUTTON

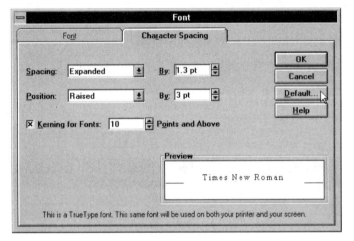

Figure 21. The *Default* button in the *Font* dialog box lets you change the default text formatting of the *Normal* template. (See **Chapter 6** for more information on using templates.)

To do this, first change the settings you want to change in the *Character* dialog box. Then, click on the *Default* button to make your settings the default settings.

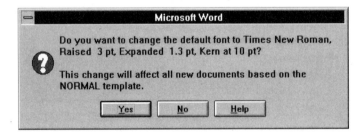

Figure 22. In the dialog box that appears, click on *Yes* to change the default font in the *Normal* template or *No* to return to the *Font* dialog box.

Word asks you if you want to save the changes you made to the default settings when you exit from Word. The changed default settings affect all new documents you create based on the *Normal* template, but not existing documents which used previous default settings.

CHARACTER FORMATTING KEYBOARD SHORTCUTS

Figure 23. The adjacent table lists the various character formatting keyboard shortcuts available.

To	Press
Change your font	Ctrl+Shift+F
Change your font size	Ctrl+Shift+P
Make your text bold	Ctrl+B
Italicize your text	Ctrl+I
Underline your text	Ctrl+U
Change the case of letters	Shift+F3
Increase the font size by 1 point	Ctrl+)
Decrease the font size by 1 point	Ctrl+(
Create all capital letters	Ctrl+Shift+A
Create small capital letters	Ctrl+Shift+K

CHANGE CASE

The *Change Case* feature lets you quickly and easily change the case of text in your document.

Figure 24. To change case, choose the letters you want to manipulate, then choose *Change Case* in the **Format** menu.

Change Case
Sentence case.
lowercase
UPPERCASE
Title Case
tOGGLE cASE
OK
Cancel
Help

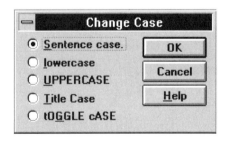

Figure 25. You have five options in the *Change Case* dialog box. Choose the option you need and click on *OK* to apply it to the selected text.

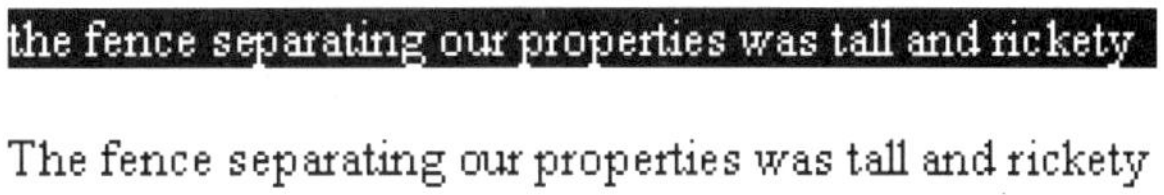

the fence separating our properties was tall and rickety
The fence separating our properties was tall and rickety

Sentence case

The fence separating our PROPERTIES was tall and rickety
The fence separating our properties was tall and rickety

Lower case

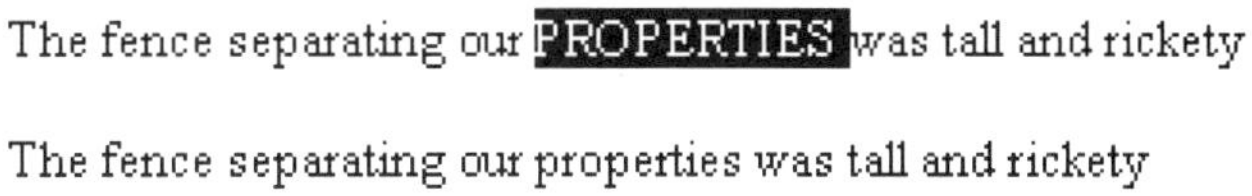

The following list outlines these options. The dialog box shows you how they look in your document.

- *Sentence case* changes the initial letter in a sentence into a capital.

The fence separating our ▓properties▓ was tall and rickety

The fence separating our PROPERTIES was tall and rickety
Upper case

The fence separating our properties was ▓tall and rickety▓

The fence separating our properties was Tall And Rickety
Titile case

The fence separating our properties was ▓Tall And Rickety▓

The fence separating our properties was tALL aND rICKETY
Toggle case

- *Lower case* changes all of the selected letters to lower case.
- *Upper case* changes all of the selected letters to upper case.
- *Title case* makes the first letter of every word in a selection upper case.
- *Toggle case* changes the lower case letters to upper case and vice versa. (Great for when you leave the Caps Lock key on accidentally!)

DROP CAP

A drop cap is a large capital letter at the beginning of a paragraph that has been dropped below the line and enlarged.

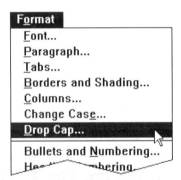

Figure 26. To create a drop cap, add the insertion point to the paragraph you want to add a drop cap to and select the *Drop Cap* command from the **Format** menu.

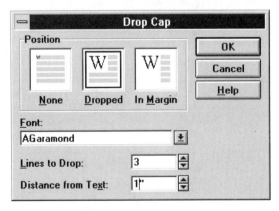

Figure 27. In the *Drop Cap* dialog box choose the type of format you want: *Dropped,* or *In Margin.* You use *None* to remove drop caps.

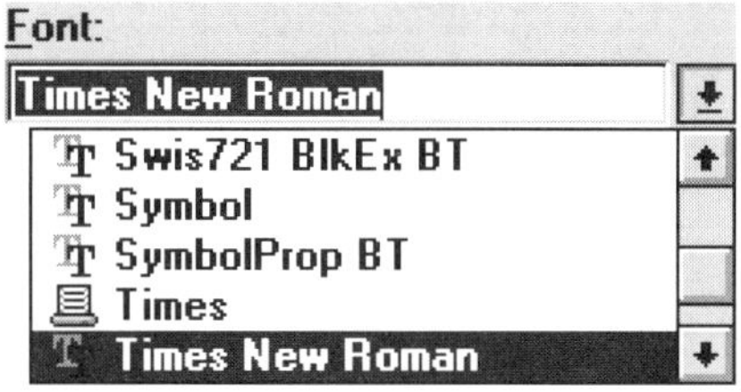

Figure 28. You can specify the font using the *Font* drop-down list box. To specify the size of the drop cap enter a value in the *Lines to Drop* text box. Use the *Distance from Text* text box to insert the amount of space you want between the drop cap and the paragraph.

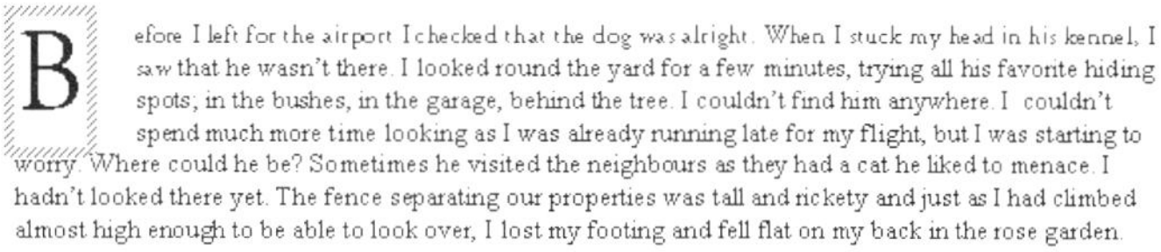

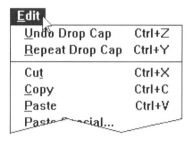

Figure 29. When you click on *OK* in the *Drop Cap* dialog box, Word creates a drop cap with the first letter in the paragraph.

CUT, COPY, AND PASTE

Figure 30. The *Cut*, *Copy*, and *Paste* commands in the **Edit** menu enable you to move text and graphics around in the current document, into other Word documents, and even to and from other Windows applications.

Figure 31. After selecting text, either use *Cut* to remove it from the screen and place it in the Windows clipboard; or use *Copy* to place selected text in the clipboard, without removing the original selection from the screen.

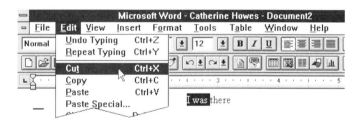

Figure 32. Then, choose *Paste* to retrieve the contents of the clipboard and insert it into your document. Do this by putting the insertion point where you want to insert the clipboard contents, then select *Paste*.

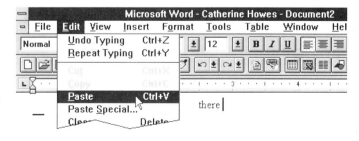

Figure 33. The text you selected to cut or copy is pasted into the new location.

Figure 34. You can also select *Cut, Copy,* and *Paste* from the toolbar with your mouse.

Figure 35. To cut text with the *Standard* toolbar, highlight the text and click on the toolbar *Cut* icon.

Figure 36. To paste text, put the insertion point where you want the text, and click on the toolbar *Paste* icon. This reinserts the text back into the document as shown.

SHORTCUT MENUS

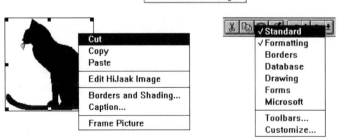

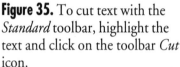

Figure 37. Word displays shortcut menus for items in your document when you click the right mouse button on them. This gives you quick access to formatting commands that are specific to that selected item. Use these menus and select commands the same way you do with menus on the menu bar.

You can display shortcut menus for toolbars, text, clipart, frames, equations, graphs, pictures, WordArt, and items you have imported into Word (such as a CorelDRAW! graphic).

MOVING AND COPYING TEXT

USING THE KEYBOARD

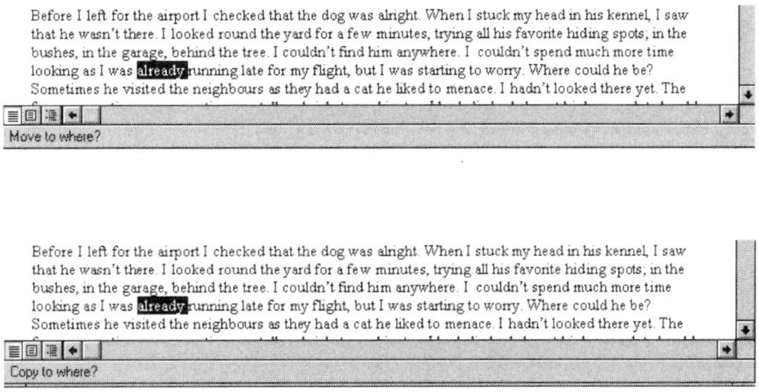

Figure 38. You can use the *Move Text* and *Copy Text* keyboard options to move text around in the document.

The first step is highlight the text you want to move or copy then press F2 to move text or Shift+F2 to copy text.

For the *Move* option, Word displays a message *Move from where?* on the left end of the status bar. For the *Copy* option, it displays *Copy from where?*.

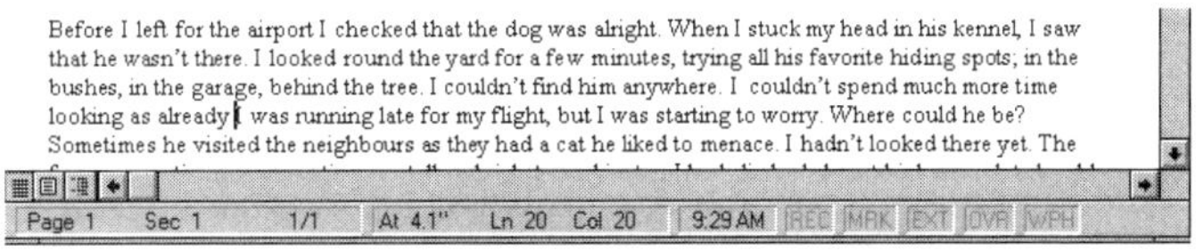

Figure 39. Now position the insertion point where you want to insert the text and press Enter. Word inserts the data you cut or copied into the document.

USING THE MOUSE

Figure 40. You can use the mouse to move text by dragging. To do this, put the mouse pointer over the highlighted text so that it becomes an arrow. Hold the left mouse button down and drag the text to the new position.

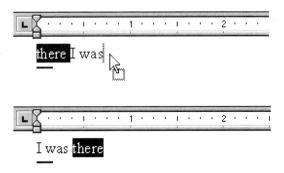

The text appears at the new insertion point when you release the mouse button.

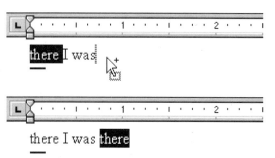

Figure 41. To copy text to a different position, do the same as for moving text by dragging, except hold down Ctrl while dragging the text. Word adds a plus sign (+) to the arrow when you hold down the Ctrl key.

USING THE SPIKE

The Spike is a multiple cut-and-paste tool that you can use if you want to remove several items from documents and then insert them as a group in a location.

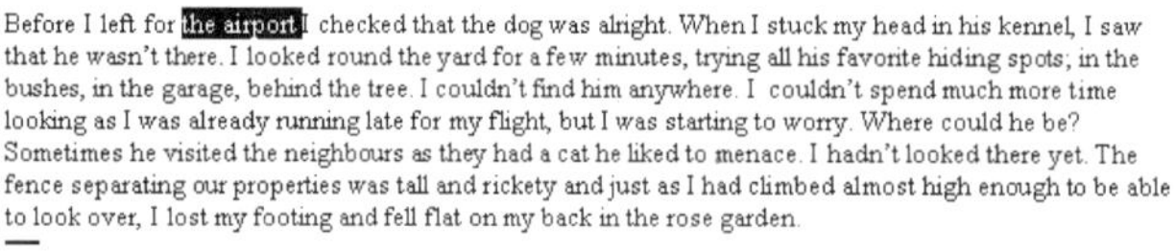

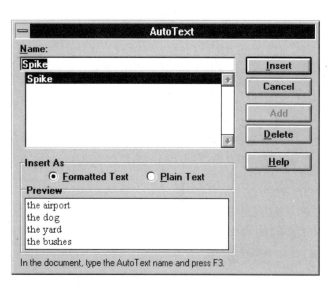

Before I left for the airport I checked that the dog was alright. When I stuck my head in his kennel, I saw that he wasn't there. I looked round the yard for a few minutes, trying all his favorite hiding spots; in the bushes, in the garage, behind the tree. I couldn't find him anywhere. I couldn't spend much more time looking as I was already running late for my flight, but I was starting to worry. Where could he be? Sometimes he visited the neighbours as they had a cat he liked to menace. I hadn't looked there yet. The fence separating our properties was tall and rickety and just as I had climbed almost high enough to be able to look over, I lost my footing and fell flat on my back in the rose garden.

Figure 42. Select the text or graphic you want to move to the Spike, and press Ctrl+F3. Word removes the selected item and adds it to the Spike. Repeat these steps for each item you want to add to the Spike.

Figure 43. To view the Spike's contents, choose *AutoText* from the **Edit** menu, and highlight Spike from the list box in the *AutoText* dialog box. Word shows the contents in the *Preview* box.

Figure 44. To insert the contents and clear the Spike, put the insertion point in your document and press Ctrl+Shift+F3.

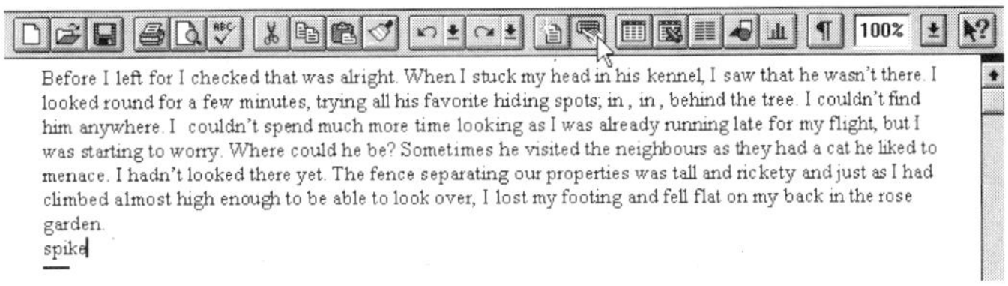

To insert the contents without clearing the Spike, type "spike" where you want to insert the contents. Then click on the *Insert AutoText* button on the *Standard* toolbar (or press F3).

Figure 45. Word inserts the Spike's contents in the same order that you added them to the Spike and each entry appears in a separate paragraph.

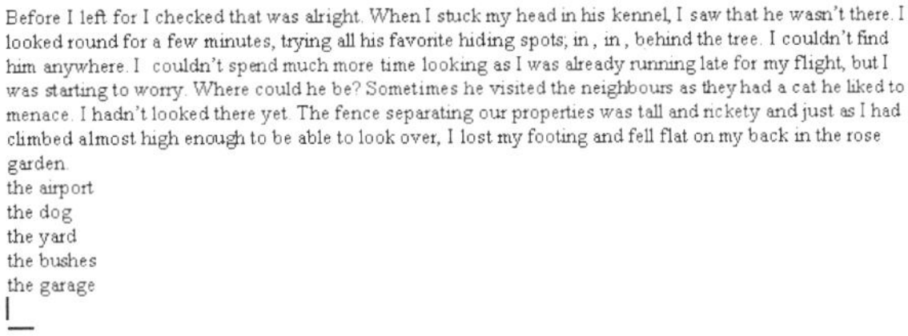

REPEAT FORMATTING

Figure 46. To reapply the most recent formatting options you selected from the *Font* dialog box, choose *Repeat Formatting* from the **Edit** menu. Using this command saves you opening the *Font* dialog box to make the same changes.

If you selected multiple options from the *Font* dialog box, this command repeats every option you set.

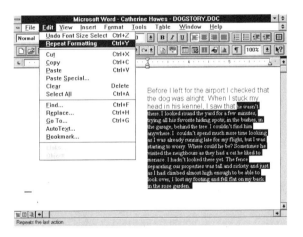

Figure 47. When you format with the *Formatting* toolbar, the *Repeat* command only repeats the last option you selected.

The *Repeat* command indicates what the last action was. For example, if you just italicized text, Word displays the *Repeat Italic* command.

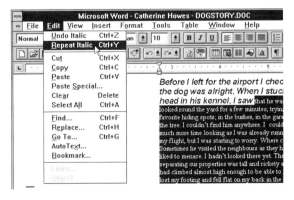

COPY FORMATTING

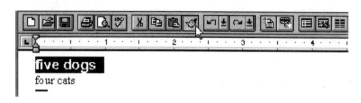

Figure 48. To copy formatting options from one piece of text to another, select the text that contains the format you want to copy. Then click on the *Format Painter* tool on the *Standard* toolbar.

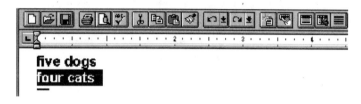

Figure 49. Word adds a paintbrush to the I-beam. To apply the format to different text drag the I-beam over the text where you want to copy the formatting options.

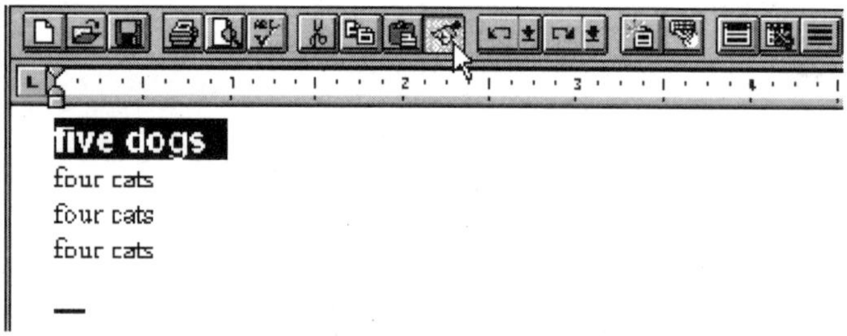

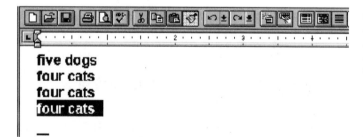

Figure 50. To copy the format to more than one position, double-click on the *Format Painter* tool.

Figure 51. Apply the format to all the text you want, then click on the *Format Painter* tool when you have finished pasting the format.

UNDO AND REDO BUTTONS

Figure 52. To undo or redo your last editing or formatting action, click on the *Undo* or *Redo* button on the *Standard* toolbar.

Figure 53. You can also undo and redo multiple actions. Click on the arrow next to the *Undo* or *Redo* button to display a drop-down list box. From the list, select the actions you want to undo or redo.

The Undo drop-down list

Note: If an action you want to undo or redo is not the first in the list, all the actions that occurred previously to the one you want to undo or redo also are undone or redone.

FIND FUNCTION

Using the *Find* command, you can search text to find all occurrences of a specified combination of characters. Possible combinations include upper case and lower case characters, whole words, or parts of words.

Figure 54. Select *Find* from the **Edit** menu to open the *Find* dialog box.

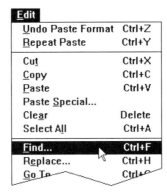

Figure 55. Type the text you want to find in the *Find What* text box.

Option	Result
Up	Searches the document from the insertion point to the beginning of the document or selection
Down	Searches the document from the insertion point to the end of the document or selection
Match Case	Searches for occurrences with specific combinations of upper and lowercase letters
Find Whole Words Only	Searches only for whole words, not sections of words
Sounds Like	Searches for words that sound the same as the search text but are spelled differently
Special	Searches for a specific character

Figure 56. You may want to restrict the search. This table summarizes the different functions available in the *Find* dialog box.

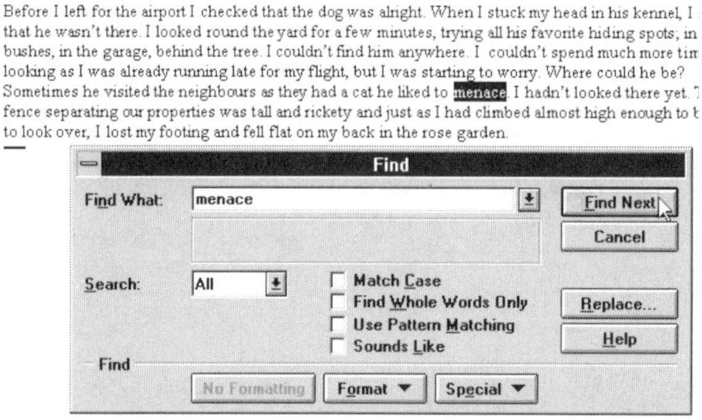

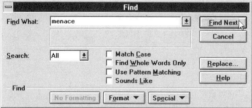

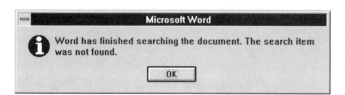

Figure 57. Click on the *Find Next* button in the *Find* dialog box to start the search. In the document, Word highlights the next occurrence of the *Find What* text. To continue searching click on *Find Next* again.

Figure 58. If Word cannot find the *Find What* text, the dialog box in this figure appears. Click on *OK* to return to the *Find* dialog box.

Figure 59. If you want to find formatted text, choose the *Format* button and then select the formats or styles you want to search for in the dialog box that appears.

The format you select appears below the *Format* box. To cancel the formats you selected, click on the *No Formatting* button.

Figure 60. To search for a special character, select an option from the *Special* drop-down menu.

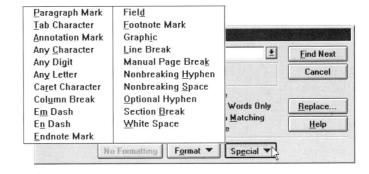

REPLACE FUNCTION

Figure 61. With the *Replace* command, you can find text and replace it with something different.

Choose *Replace* from the **Edit** menu to activate the *Replace* dialog box.

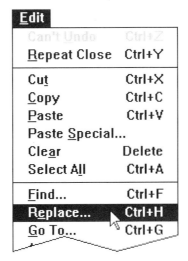

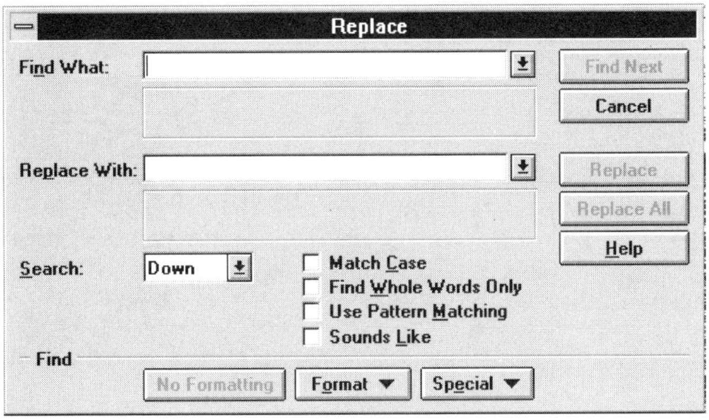

Figure 62. If you have opened the *Find* dialog box, click on the *Replace* button to display the *Replace* dialog box.

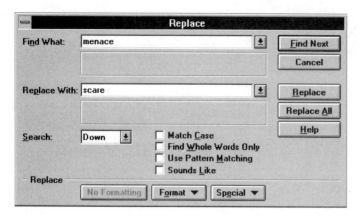

Figure 63. Type the text you want to replace into the *Find What* text box and the new text into the *Replace With* text box.

You can use the search options to restrict the search (see the table in Figure 56). In addition, you can search for formats and special characters and replace them with an alternative using the *Format* and *Special* buttons (see Figures 59 and 60).

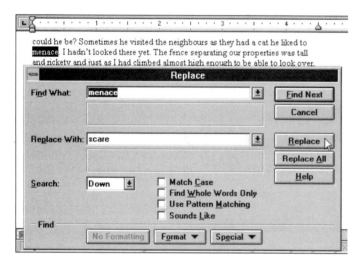

Figure 64. You can automatically replace all occurrences of the found text, or selectively replace only certain instances. To selectively replace, click first on the *Find Next* button. Then, if you want to replace the text which appears highlighted in your document, click on the *Replace* button. If you do not want to replace the highlighted text, continue the search by clicking on the *Find Next* button.

If you want to replace all instances of the text in the *Find What* text box, with the text in the *Replace With* text box click on the *Replace All* button.

AutoCorrect

You can use the *AutoCorrect* command to correct and insert items in your document. You can customize AutoCorrect to change your regular typing mistakes and expand abbreviations automatically, as you type.

Figure 65. Choose *AutoCorrect* from the **Tools** menu.

Figure 66. Word opens the *AutoCorrect* dialog box. Check marks indicate which options are active.

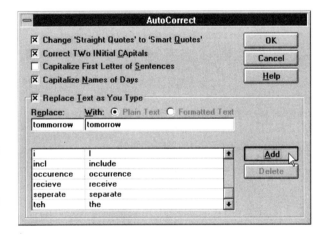

In the *Replace Text as You Type* section, type an AutoCorrect entry in the *Replace* text box—for example, the abbreviated text. (An entry can have up to 31 characters, but must not contain spaces.) In the *With* text box, type the text you want Word to automatically replace the text in the *Replace* text box. Then click on the *Add* button.

Figure 67. Word adds your entry to the list box. (Word has default AutoCorrect entries already in the list box.) Click on *OK* to close the dialog box.

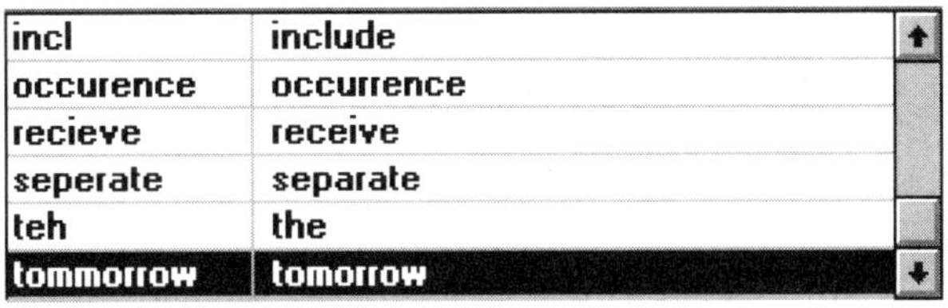

incl	include
occurence	occurrence
recieve	receive
seperate	separate
teh	the
tommorrow	tomorrow

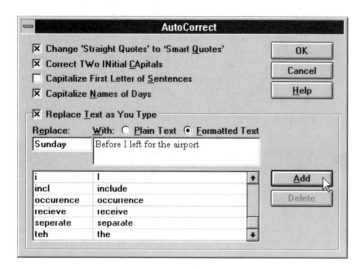

Figure 68. If you want to create an entry for formatted text, a graphic, or a large section of text, insert it into your document and select it (make sure you select the paragraph mark as well if you want to include the formatting), then open the *AutoCorrect* dialog box. Your selection appears in the *With* text box.

Type a name in the *Replace* text box. Choose the *Formatted Text* radio button if you want to save the text formatting. Now click on the *Add* button to add the entry to the list box.

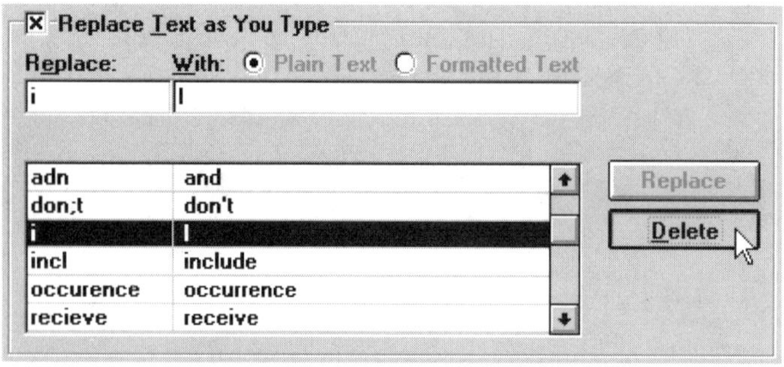

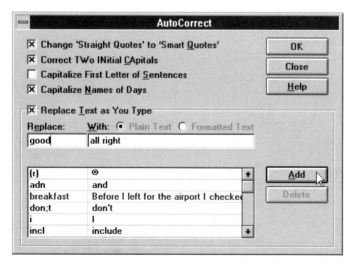

Figure 69. If you want to delete an AutoCorrect entry, select it from the list box and click on the *Delete* button.

Figure 70. You can change an AutoCorrect entry's name. Select the entry from the list box and click on the *Delete* button. Then type a new name in the *Replace* text box and click on the *Add* button to insert the entry back in the list box.

Figure 71. To change the contents of an entry that is stored as plain text, select the entry from the list box. Then type the new entry in the *With* text box and click on the *Replace* button.

If you want to change formatted text, a graphic, or a long passage of text, make the changes in your document. Select the revised text (or graphic). Then in the *AutoCorrect* dialog box, type the existing AutoCorrect name in the *Replace* text box and click on *Replace*.

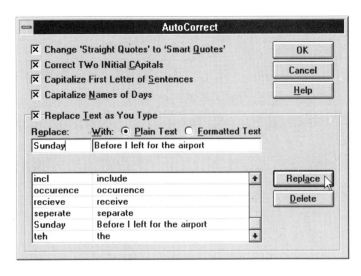

Figure 72. Word asks you if you want to redefine the entry. Choose *Yes*.

You can also add AutoCorrect entries to the list box when you are spell checking your document (see the **Spell Checker** section of **Chapter 8**).

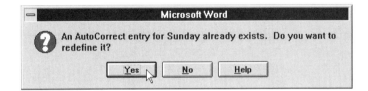

MANAGING FILES 3

MANAGING YOUR FILES

This chapter shows you how to manage your files in Word. This includes creating a new file, opening one or more existing files, closing and saving a file, using the document summary, searching for a specific file, and exiting from Word.

CREATING A NEW FILE

Figure 1. When you start Word, it automatically opens a blank document (*Document1*) based on the default template. Select the *New* command in the **File** menu to create a new file.

Figure 2. In the *New* dialog box that appears, you can select the template that you want to base the new file on. **Chapter 7** has more information on templates.

If you are creating a new document, and not a template, make sure that *Document* is selected in the *New* options. Click on *OK*.

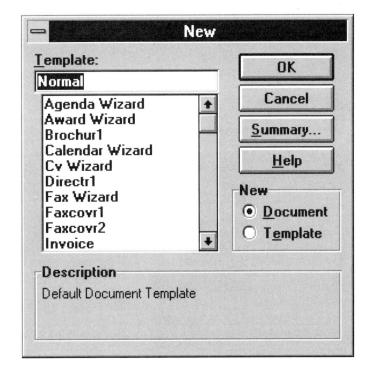

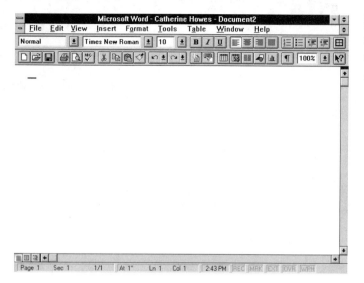

Figure 3. Word places the document in a new window and calls it *Document#* (in this case, *Document 2*).

Figure 4. You can also create a new document by clicking on the *New* button on the *Standard* toolbar. This creates a new file based on the default *Normal* template.

OPENING AN EXISTING FILE

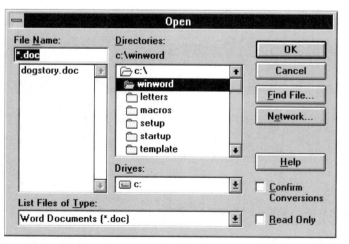

Figure 5. The *Open* command in the **File** menu and the *Open* button on the *Standard* toolbar display the *Open* dialog box. You can use this dialog box to open an existing file.

By default, Word displays all of the Word files in the current directory in the *File Name* list box. To open one of these, choose the file you want and click on *OK*.

Figure 6. The *List Files of Type* drop-down list box determines the type of files Word lists in the *File Names* list box. To change the type of files listed, choose a different option.

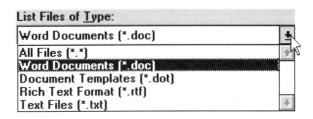

Figure 7. The *Directories* list box represents directories with folders. Open directories appear as open folders and closed directories as closed folders.

  To change directories, double-click on the open and closed folders. As you open different folders the list of files changes in the *File Name* list box. You can open these files as outlined in Figure 5.

Figure 8. To change to a different drive, choose from the options in the *Drives* drop-down list box.

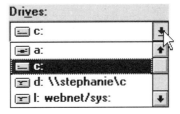

Figure 9. Select the *Confirm Conversions* option if you choose to open a file that is in a different format to a Word file, and you want to confirm the type of conversion Word proposes.

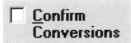

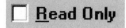

Figure 10. To open the file in *Read Only* format, choose the *Read Only* check box. *Read Only* means that you can only view the document; you cannot make changes to it.

If you don't know the name or location of the file you want to open, click on the *Find File* button in the *Open* dialog box (Figure 5). This opens the *Search* dialog box (see the **Find File** section later in this chapter).

Figure 11. The **File** menu lists the last files you have opened. You can open one of these by choosing it from the list of files at the bottom of this menu. By default, Word lists the last four files opened—you can list up to nine files (see the **Option Dialog Box** section later in this chapter).

FIND FILE

You can use the *Find File* command to find, preview, open, print, and delete documents.

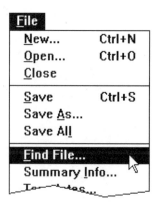

Figure 12. To look for a file, choose *Find File* from the **File** menu (or click on *Find File* in the *Open* dialog box).

Figure 13. If you haven't used this command before, Word opens the *Search* dialog box for you to specify the search criteria (see Figure 14).

Otherwise, Word uses the last search criteria and opens the *Find File* dialog box. From here you can open, print, preview, delete, and copy files as well as do other file management. Word displays the files from selected directories in the *Listed Files* list box. Click on the *Search* button in the *Find File* dialog box to view files from another directory.

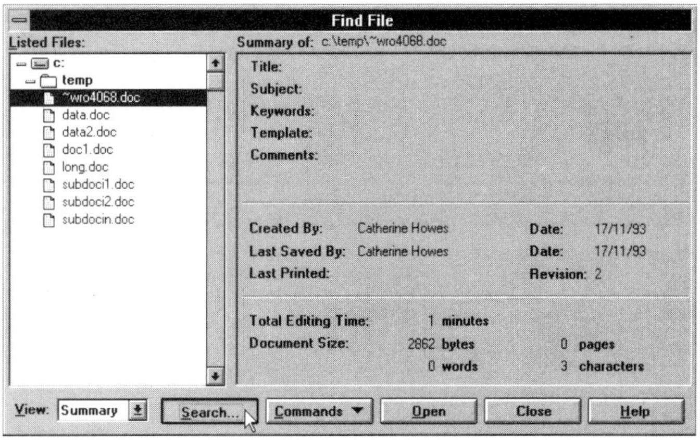

Figure 14. In the *Search* dialog box, you can change the type of file you are looking for and the path you want to search. Type a filename in the *File Name* text box in the *Search For* section, or choose from the drop-down list box.

Figure 15. Select a drive you want to search from the *Location* drop-down list box, or type the paths in the text box. Use semicolons to separate path names if you want to search multiple paths.

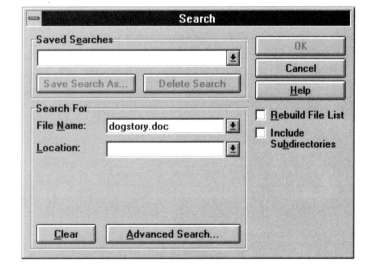

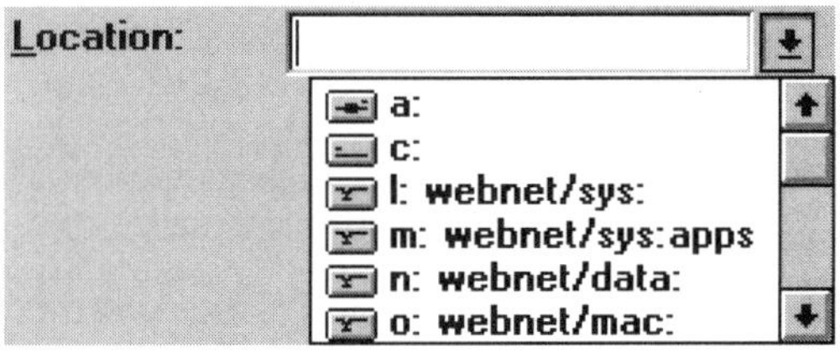

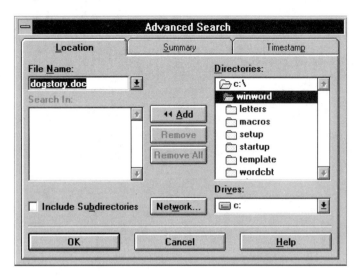

Figure 16. Clicking on the *Advanced Search* button opens the *Advanced Search* dialog box. Here you can specify search criteria using the options on the *Location*, *Summary*, and *Timestamp* tabs.

Figure 17. Clicking on *OK* returns you to the *Find File* dialog box, displaying the search criteria. Click on the *Commands* button in the *Find File* dialog box to display these options. You can open as read only, print, edit the summary information for, delete, or copy the highlighted file in the *Listed Files* list box.

(Hold down the Shift key to select consecutive files, or use the Ctrl key to select multiple files that are not together.)

Figure 18. The *Sorting* option opens this dialog box which lets you decide how the files are sorted in the *Listed Files* list box.

Figure 19. The *View* drop-down
list box in the *Find Files* dialog
box lets you choose what you
want to view about the selected

file. *Preview* shows you the document in the *Preview of* box,
File Info gives you information about the files in the *Listed
File* list box, and *Summary* lets you view information and
statistics about the file.

WORKING WITH MULTIPLE FILES

You can have multiple documents open at a time and display
several on the screen at the same time.

SWITCHING BETWEEN FILES

Figure 20. In the top-right of your
screen are the application and
document restore and minimize
buttons.

Figure 21. Click on the document
restore button to separate the
document window from the
application window. The
document window then shows
maximize and minimize buttons.

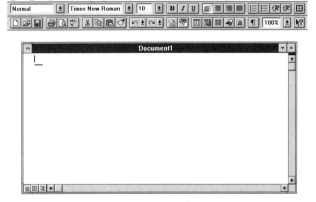

Figure 22. Click on a minimize
button to shrink the document or
application to its icon. Double-
click the icon to open it again.

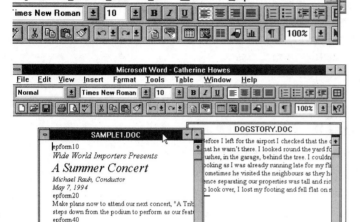

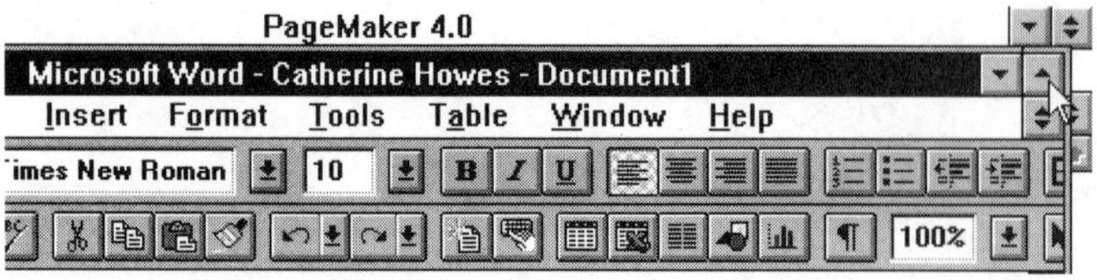

Figure 23. Click on a maximize button to enlarge the document or application window to its full size.

Figure 24. If you have more than one document open, having their windows separated from the application window lets you move the document windows around the screen by dragging the title bar. This lets you see more than one document at a time.

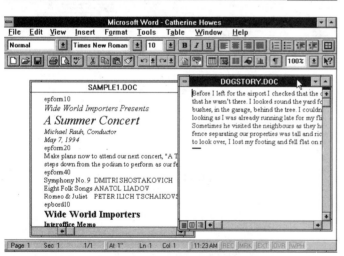

Figure 25. This also means that you can click on a document window to select it and make it active.

Figure 26. Alternatively, to make an open document active, you can select its name from the **Window** menu.

Figure 27. Also in the **Window** menu, the *New Window* command displays the active document in another window.

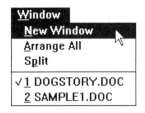

Figure 28. *Arrange All* displays all active documents on screen so you can view them all at once and click on any document window to make it active.

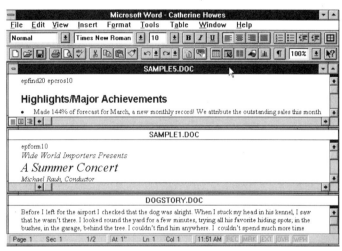

Figure 29. Choosing the *Split* command from the **Window** menu turns your mouse pointer into a vertical two-headed arrow with a gray line extending across the screen.

Figure 30. When you click the mouse, Word splits the screen with another window with its own scroll bars and ruler. This allows you to view two parts of the active document at the same time.

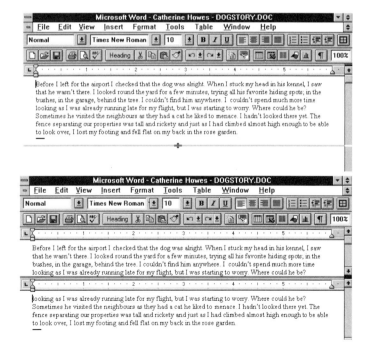

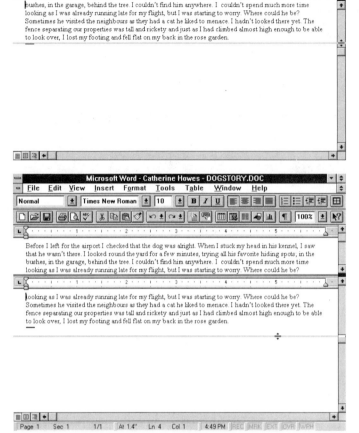

Figure 31. Alternatively, you can click the mouse pointer in the black box at the top of the vertical scroll bar. When it becomes a two-headed arrow pointer, drag it down the screen and release the mouse button where you want to split the window.

Figure 32. To adjust the size of this second window, place the mouse pointer on the top of the second ruler until it becomes the two-headed arrow. Then click and drag the window. When you release the mouse button, Word changes the window size.

Figure 33. To get rid of the split, choose *Remove Split* from the **Window** menu, drag the second window up to the top of the screen and release the mouse, or double-click in the black box on the vertical scroll bar.

SAVING A FILE

To store your Word document and retain any changes you make to an existing document, you need to save the document to disk.

Figure 34. To save a new, unnamed document, click on the *Save* button on the *Standard* toolbar.

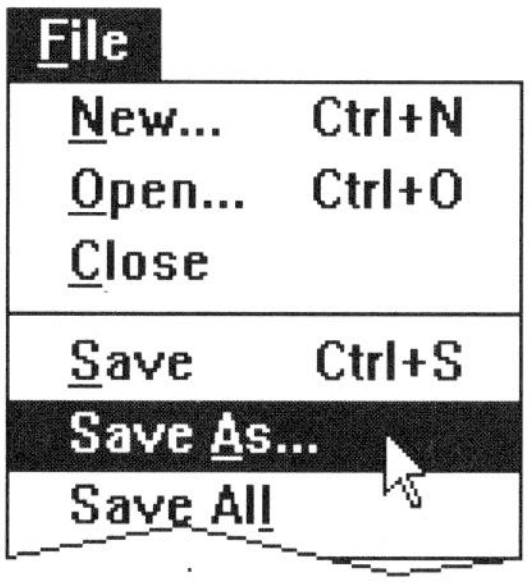

Figure 35. You can also choose *Save As* from the **File** menu. (If you want to rename an existing document, you should also choose *Save As*.)

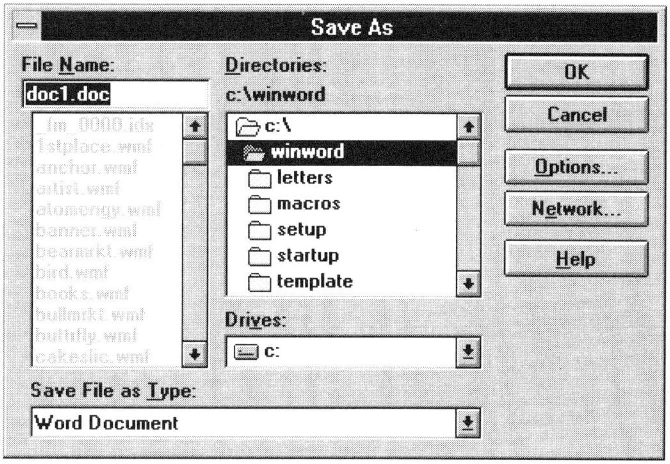

Figure 36. Both these methods open the *Save As* dialog box. Type a name in the *File Name* text box. Filenames can be one to eight characters long with a one to three character extension. If you don't type an extension, Word adds a *.doc* extension by default.

You cannot use ; : = < > [ ] { } \ / . ? or spaces as part of the name.

Figure 37. If you want to save it to a different drive and directory, use the *Directories* list box and *Drives* drop-down list box.

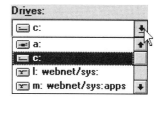

Figure 38. The *Save File as Type* drop-down list box lets you choose what format you want to save the document in. Then click on *OK*.

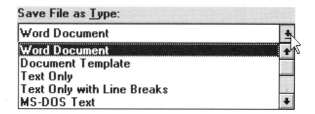

Figure 39. To save an existing document, click on the *Save* button on the *Standard* toolbar (Figure 34), or choose *Save* from the **File** menu.

Figure 40. Word saves all open documents if you choose *Save All* from the **File** menu.

If you haven't named any of the documents, Word displays the *Save As* dialog box.

DOCUMENT SUMMARY

Figure 41. If you have the *Prompt for Summary Info* check box selected on the *Save* tab of the *Options* dialog box (see Figure 55 in the **Options Dialog Box** section later in this chapter), or if you select *Summary Info* from the File menu, Word displays this *Summary Info* dialog box after you first save a document. It lets you record information about the document and provides you with statistics about the document when you click on the *Statistics* button.

Summary Info

File Name:	DOGSTORY.DOC
Directory:	C:\WINWORD
Title:	Looking for the dog
Subject:	
Author:	Catherine Howes
Keywords:	
Comments:	

OK
Cancel
Statistics...
Help

CLOSING A FILE

Figure 42. To close an active document, choose *Close* from the File menu.

File	
New...	Ctrl+N
Open...	Ctrl+O
Close	
Save	Ctrl+S

Figure 43. Alternatively, double-click on the document's Control menu box.

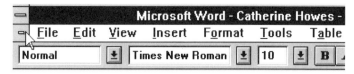

Figure 44. If you haven't saved changes, Word prompts you to do so. If you click on *Yes* and you haven't named the document, Word opens the *Save As* dialog box (see Figure 36).

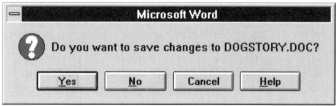

OPTIONS DIALOG BOX

The options on these different category tabs let you specify default settings for Word and customize how you want Word to best work for you.

Figure 45. Select *Options* from the **Tools** menu to open the *Options* dialog box.

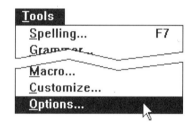

VIEW OPTIONS

Figure 46. The options on the *View* tab change slightly depending on what document view you are in when you open the *Options* dialog box (see **Chapter 9** for information about viewing documents). A check mark indicates the option is selected.

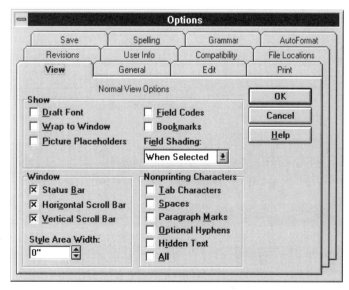

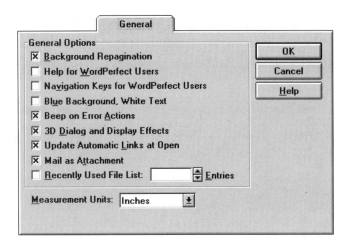

GENERAL OPTIONS

Figure 47. To change the number of documents listed at the bottom of the **File** menu, type or select the number of documents you want in the *Recently Used File List # Entries* text box. You can list up to nine documents in the **File** menu.

From the *Measurement Units* drop-down list box you can choose what you want Word to measure in.

EDIT OPTIONS

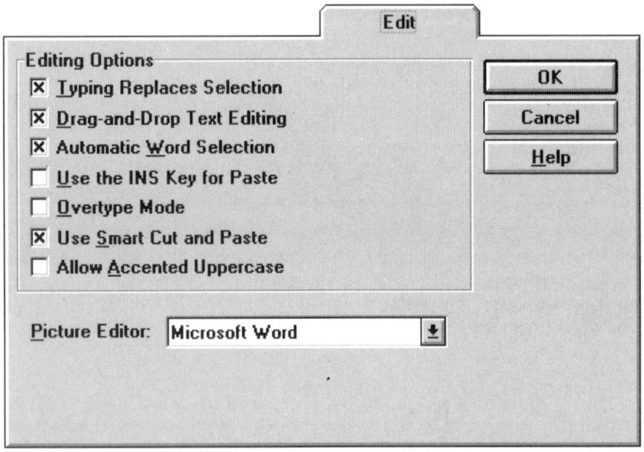

Figure 48. These options control the editing functions in Word. See **Chapter 2** for information about editing your Word document.

PRINT OPTIONS

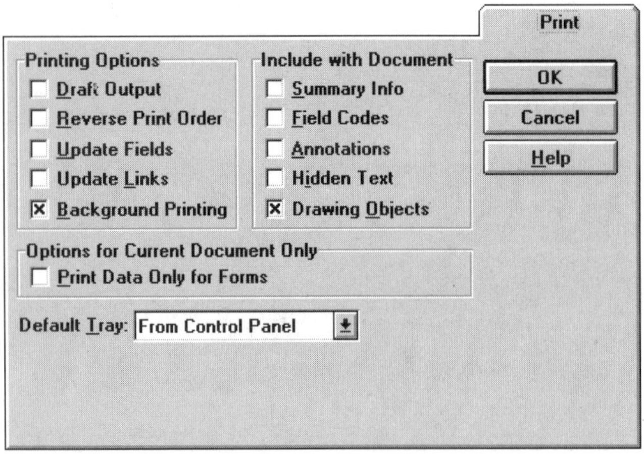

Figure 49. The *Printing* tab lets you control what you print, by default, with your documents (see **Chapter 9**).

REVISIONS OPTIONS

Figure 50. You use revision marks to indicate changes that you or other people make to a document. Word uses underline and strikethrough characters to show where text and graphics have been added, deleted or moved. This tab in the *Options* dialog box lets you customize the formatting of the revision marks.

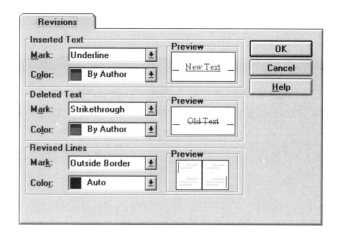

USER INFO OPTIONS

Figure 51. Here you can fill in your name and address that Word uses for the default return address when merging envelopes and mailing labels.

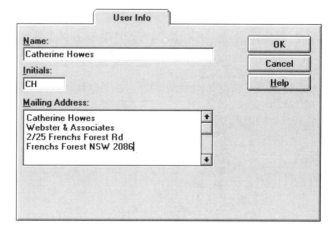

COMPATIBILITY OPTIONS

Figure 52. You can select or deselect these options to alter Word's behavior when converting documents, so that it more closely matches the behavior of another application.

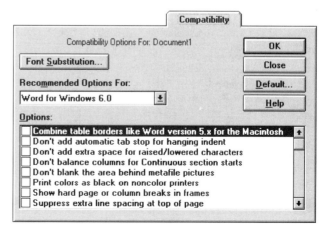

FILE LOCATIONS OPTIONS

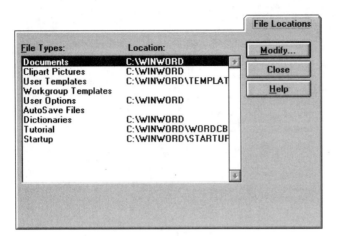

Figure 53. This tab lets you change the directories where Word saves and stores certain types of files by default. Choose from the list box, then click on the *Modify* button.

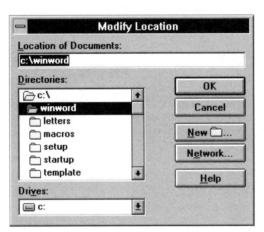

Figure 54. In the *Modify Location* dialog box, type a new path in the *Location of Document* text box, or select from the *Directories* and *Drives* list boxes. Alternatively, create a new directory by clicking on the *New* button.

SAVE OPTIONS

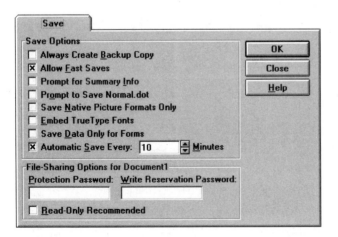

Figure 55. The save options determine how Word saves documents and whether it saves other information with the file. *Allow Fast Saves*, saves only the changes to a document. If you select *Always Create Backup Copy*, Word deselects the *Allow Fast Saves* option because backups are created only with full saves (full saves also take up less disk space).

Select the *Prompt for Summary Info* check box to have Word display the *Summary Info* dialog box when you first save a document (see **Document Summary** section earlier in this chapter).

When you select the *Automatic Save Every # Minutes* check box, Word saves a temporary copy of the document as often as you specify in the text box. But you still need to save your document normally (see **Saving a File** previously in this chapter). If you have a power failure or other problem, Word automatically displays the document next time you start Word. You lose only the changes you made after the last automatic save.

Type a password in the *Protection Password* text box to prevent others from opening the document. To prevent others from saving changes to a document, type a password in the *Write Reservation Password* text box. Passwords can be 15 characters and are case-sensitive. Word displays asterisks as you type.

Figure 56. When you click on *OK*, Word asks you to confirm the password.

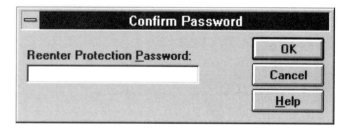

SPELLING OPTIONS

Figure 57. Set options for the spelling checker from the *Spelling* tab. See **Chapter 8** for information about the spelling checker.

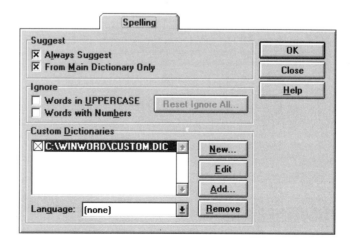

GRAMMAR OPTIONS

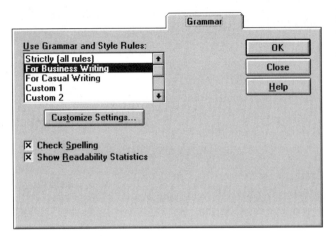

Figure 58. You can customize how the grammar checker checks your document using these options. See **Chapter 8** for information about the grammar checker.

AUTOFORMAT OPTIONS

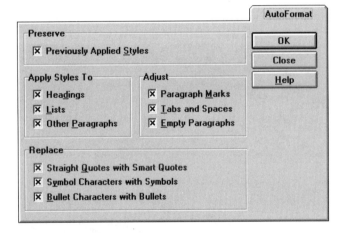

Figure 59. This tab lets you adjust the *AutoFormat* command (see **Chapter 6** for information about using *AutoFormat*).

EXITING FROM WORD

Figure 60. To shut down Word, choose *Exit* from the **File** menu.

Figure 61. Alternatively, you can double-click on the Word application's Control menu box.

Figure 62. If you haven't saved changes to any of the open documents, Word prompts you to do so.

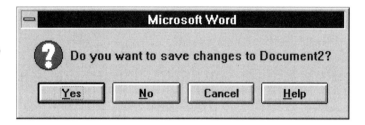

PARAGRAPH FORMATTING 4

INTRODUCTION

To Word, a paragraph is an amount of text, graphics, or other item followed by a paragraph mark (¶). It also considers a paragraph mark on a blank line as a paragraph. Pressing Enter inserts a paragraph mark, and Word carries over the preceding paragraph's formatting to the new paragraph. Paragraph formatting affects selected paragraphs, or the paragraph containing the text cursor. There are a number of paragraph formats, including text alignment, spacing, and tabs.

Figure 1. Click the mouse pointer on the *Show/Hide ¶* button on the *Standard* toolbar, to display all paragraph marks, tabs, spaces, and other non-printing characters on the screen. To deselect this option, click on the button again.

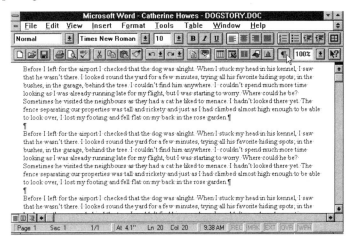

Figure 2. The paragraph mark stores the formatting information of the paragraph. So, if you delete a paragraph mark, the text of that paragraph takes on the formatting of the next paragraph in your document.

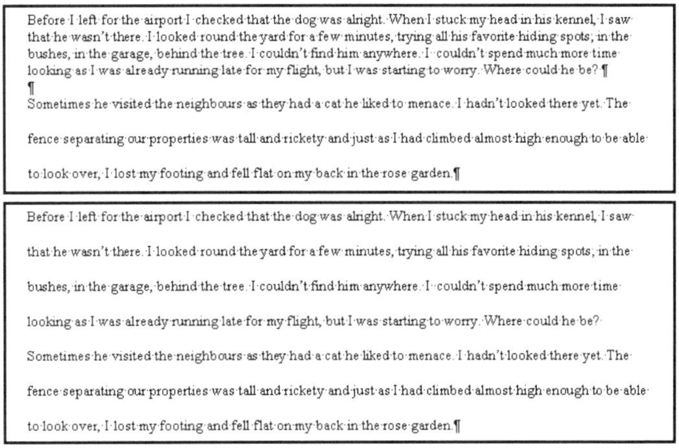

PARAGRAPH DIALOG BOX

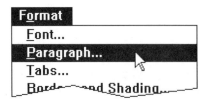

Figure 3. The *Paragraph* command in the **Format** menu opens the *Paragraph* dialog box.

Figure 4. A quick way to open the *Paragraph* dialog box is to double-click on one of the indent or margin markers on the ruler.

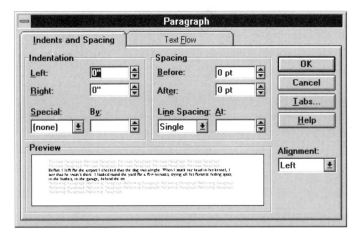

Figure 5. The *Paragraph* dialog box contains paragraph formatting options that affect how your paragraphs look. There are two categories: *Indents and Spacing* and *Text Flow*.

The *Indents and Spacing* category allows you to indent paragraphs from the margins, apply different line spacing, and change the alignment of text in a paragraph.

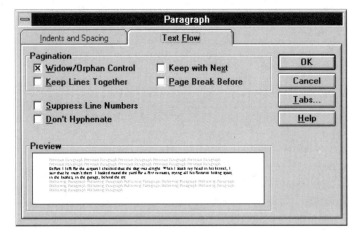

Figure 6. The *Text Flow* category allows you to control page breaks, line numbers and hyphenation.

Figure 7. You can also use the *Standard* and *Formatting* toolbars, and ruler to apply paragraph formatting to your document.

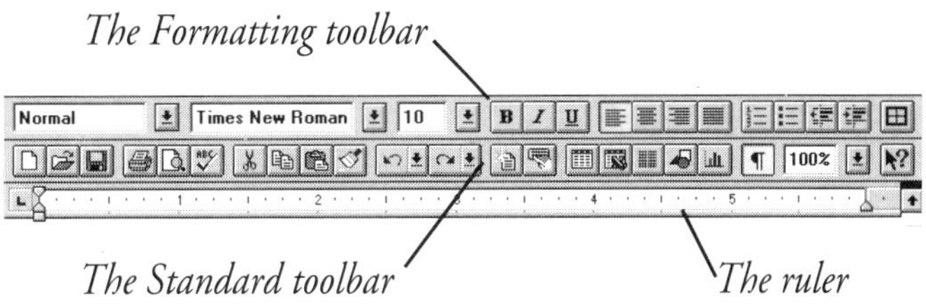

The Formatting toolbar

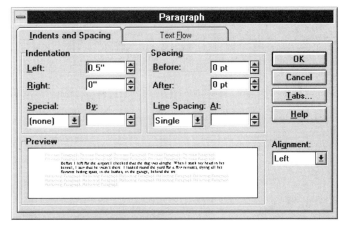

The Standard toolbar   *The ruler*

INDENTATION

You can use the *Indentation* options in the *Indents and Spacing* category in the *Paragraph* dialog box to customize the indentation of your text.

Figure 8. You can indent a paragraph from the left margin using the *Left* option. Type in or select the distance you want to indent the paragraph from the left margin.

The sample in *Preview* shows you how the paragraph formatting will look.

Figure 9. To indent a paragraph from the right margin, type in the distance that you want to indent the paragraph from the right margin into the *Right* option or select the distance using the up and down arrows.

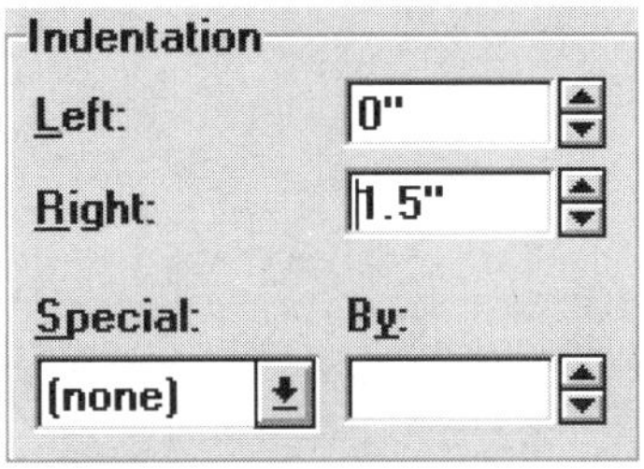

Figure 10. The *Special* options enable you to remove indentation, add a hanging indent, or indent the first line from the left margin.

To remove indentation, choose the *(none)* option.

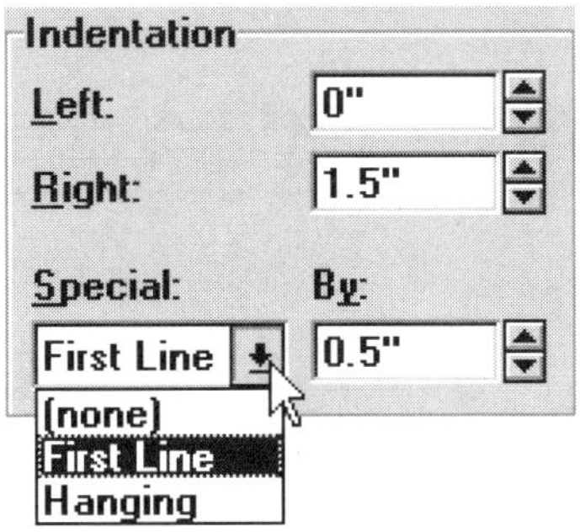

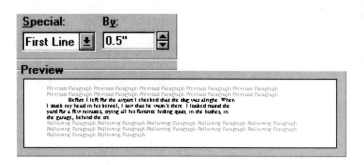

Figure 11. *First line* indents the first line in a paragraph by the amount you specify in the *By* text box.

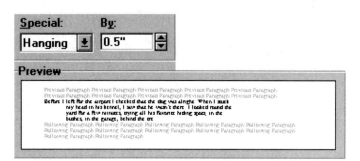

Figure 12. A hanging indent indents the lines after the first line by the amount you specify. You use hanging indents for numbered or bulleted lists. When you are typing a paragraph for numbering or bullets, insert a tab after the number or bullet. To create a hanging indent, choose the *Hanging* option. Enter the same amount as the tab into the *By* text box.

USING THE RULER

Figure 13. You can also use the ruler to indent paragraphs. To change the left indent, move the markers on the left side of the ruler to your new indent position. Do this by dragging the square marker to a new position.

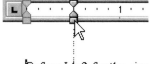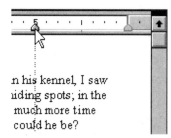

Or drag the marker on the right side of the ruler to change the right indent.

Figure 14. You can move the top of the marker on the left of the ruler independently of the bottom of the marker. This changes the first line indent of a paragraph.

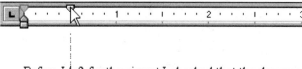

Figure 15. To create a hanging indent, drag the bottom marker to the new indent position.

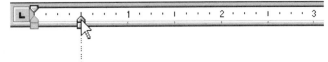

1
2
3
Before I left for the airport I checked that the dog was al
that he wasn't there. I looked round the yard for a few m
bushes, in the garage, behind the tree. I couldn't find hin
looking as I was already running late for my flight, but I

Figure 16. You can also click on the *Decrease Indent* and *Increase Indent* buttons on the *Formatting* toolbar to indent text.

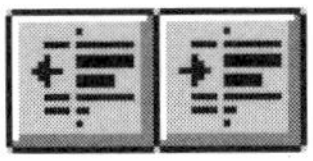

PARAGRAPH SPACING

You can set the spacing before and after each of your paragraphs. This is useful if you want to make headings stand out, or leave space for things like signatures, graphics, and tables.

By setting paragraph spacing, you can have the exact amount of white space you want. Whereas if you just press Enter, Word inserts the default amount of space.

Figure 17. To increase or decrease the space above or below a paragraph, first select the paragraph then open the *Paragraph* dialog box (see Figures 3 and 4).

Spacing
Before:
6 pt
After:
6 pt
Line Spacing:
At:
Single

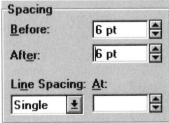

Type values into the *Before* and *After* text boxes in the *Spacing* section in the *Paragraph* dialog box. You can also select measurements by clicking on the up and down arrows.

Figure 18. Spacing is measured in points by default. Word also lets you enter a spacing distance into the text boxes in inches or centimeters (cm), for example.

Spacing
Before:
1 cm
After:
1 cm

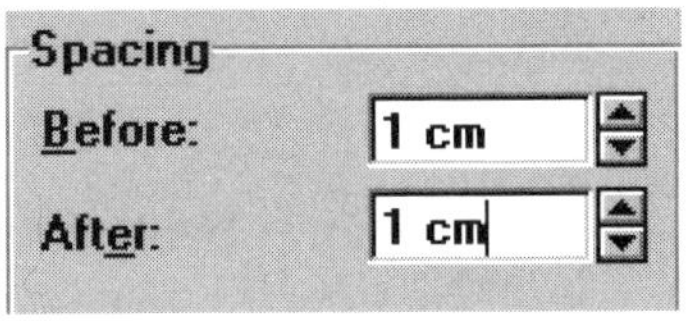

Spacing
Before:
0 pt
After:
0 pt
Line Spacing: At:
Single
Single
1.5 Lines
Double
At Least
Exactly
Multiple

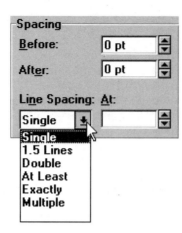

Figure 19. By default, Word single-spaces lines of text. Word measures line spacing in points; there are 72 points in an inch. To expand or contract the line spacing, select the text and use the *Line Spacing* options in the *Paragraph* dialog box.

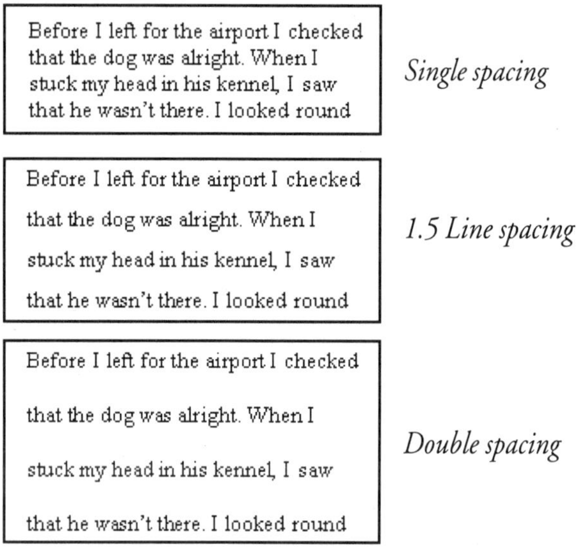

Before I left for the airport I checked that the dog was alright. When I stuck my head in his kennel, I saw that he wasn't there. I looked round
Single spacing
Before I left for the airport I checked that the dog was alright. When I stuck my head in his kennel, I saw that he wasn't there. I looked round
1.5 Line spacing
Before I left for the airport I checked that the dog was alright. When I stuck my head in his kennel, I saw that he wasn't there. I looked round
Double spacing

Figure 20. This figure displays the different examples of line spacing.

Line Spacing: At:
Multiple
.25"

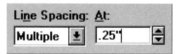

Figure 21. You can type your own line spacing measurement in the *At* text box. When you do, Word automatically selects the *Multiple* option in the *Line Spacing* text box. The *At Least* option sets a minimum spacing, which Word can adjust to accommodate larger fonts and graphics.

If you don't want Word to adjust the line height, select the *Exactly* option in the *Line Spacing* drop-down list.

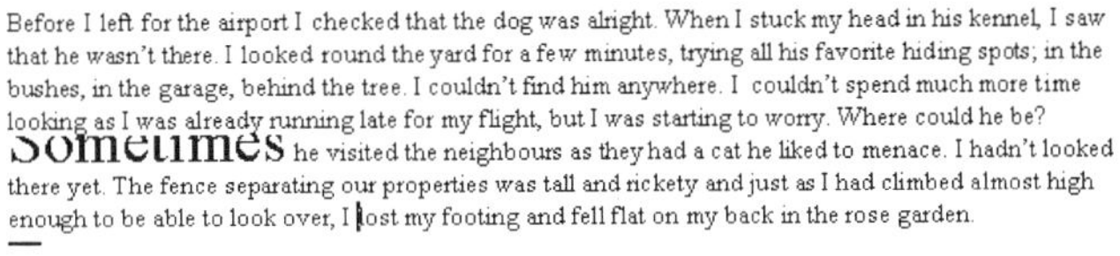

Figure 22. *Exactly* is the only *Line Spacing* option that Word does not adjust to accommodate larger fonts.

Before I left for the airport I checked that the dog was alright. When I stuck my head in his kennel, I saw that he wasn't there. I looked round the yard for a few minutes, trying all his favorite hiding spots; in the bushes, in the garage, behind the tree. I couldn't find him anywhere. I couldn't spend much more time looking as I was already running late for my flight, but I was starting to worry. Where could he be? Sometimes he visited the neighbours as they had a cat he liked to menace. I hadn't looked there yet. The fence separating our properties was tall and rickety and just as I had climbed almost high enough to be able to look over, I lost my footing and fell flat on my back in the rose garden.

In this example the line spacing has been set on *Exactly* and *12pt* and the font for the word "Sometimes" is set at 18 pt. Notice that the line spacing does not adjust to fit this word.

ALIGNING TEXT

Figure 23. The choices in the *Alignment* drop-down list are *Left*, *Centered*, *Right*, and *Justified*. You can also select these *Alignment* options directly from the *Formatting* toolbar (see Figure 7).

Figure 24. This figure displays the four different paragraph alignment options.

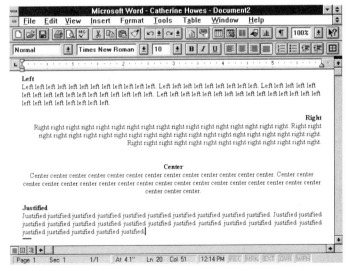

CONTROLLING PAGE BREAKS

You can control where Word inserts automatic page breaks using the *Pagination* options on the *Text Flow* category tab in the *Paragraph* dialog box. This is useful, for example, to ensure headings stay with the paragraphs that follow, and that certain paragraphs start on a new page.

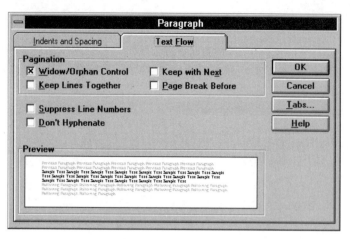

Figure 25. A "widow" is the last line of a paragraph separated on top of a new page or column. An "orphan" is the first line of a paragraph on the previous page or column. *Widow/Orphan Control* prevents widows and orphans in your document. This option is active by default.

Keep Lines Together option selected

Figure 26. The *Keep Lines Together* option ensures that selected lines of text remain together; Word does not separate these lines by column or page breaks. If a page break or column break falls in the middle of a paragraph with this option selected, Word moves the whole paragraph to the next page or column.

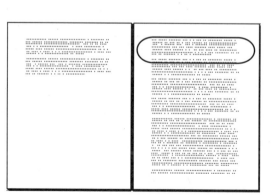

Page Break Before option selected

Figure 27. Choose the *Page Break Before* option to force a page break before the selected paragraph. Use this when you want a particular paragraph to always appear at the top of a new page.

Figure 28. Choose the *Keep With Next* option to ensure that Word does not separate the selected paragraph, and the one following, by column or page breaks. If a page break or column break falls between these paragraphs, with this option selected, Word moves both to the next page or column to keep them together.

Inserting your own page break using Ctrl+Enter overrides both the *Keep With Next* and *Keep Lines Together* commands.

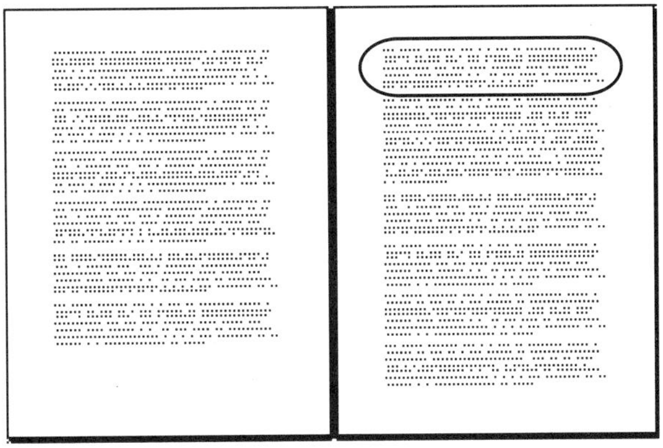

The Keep With Next option selected

PARAGRAPH FORMATTING KEYBOARD SHORTCUTS

Figure 29. This table outlines some of the paragraph formatting commands you can access with keystrokes.

Press...	To...
Ctrl+1	Single-space selected lines of text
Ctrl+2	Double-space selected lines of text
Ctrl+E	Center align
Ctrl+J	Justify
Ctrl+R	Right align
Ctrl+L	Left align

TABS

Tab stops are set positions across the document that help you to align text. You can set paragraph indents and create custom tab stops.

Word sets the default tab stops to one every half an inch; you can change these settings using the *Tabs* dialog box or the ruler. The changes you make affect the paragraph containing the insertion point, or the paragraphs currently selected.

To activate the tab stops after you have set them with the ruler or the *Tab* dialog box, press the Tab key.

SETTING TABS WITH THE TABS DIALOG BOX

Figure 30. To activate the *Tabs* dialog box, select the *Tabs* option from the **Format** menu.

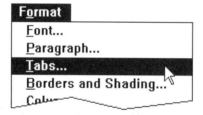

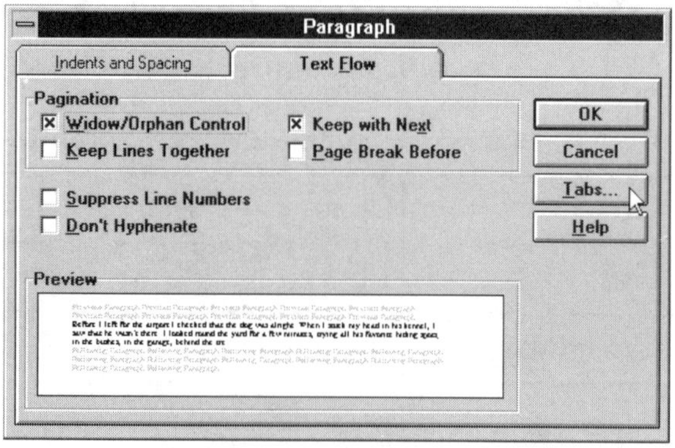

Figure 31. You can also click on the *Tabs* button in the *Paragraph* dialog box to open the *Tabs* dialog box.

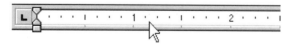

Figure 32. Alternatively, double-click on the bottom half of the ruler to open the *Tabs* dialog box. However, this also places a tab on the ruler. To remove it, click on *Clear* in the *Tabs* dialog box.

Figure 33. To change the default tabs in a document, enter a different measurement into the *Default Tab Stops* text box.

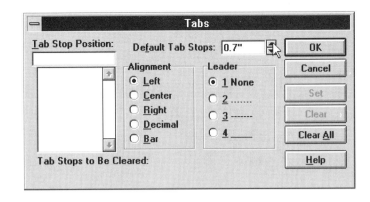

Figure 34. To create a new tab stop, type the new position into the *Tab Stop Position* text box.

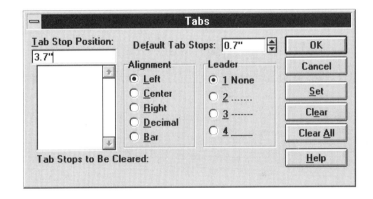

Figure 35. You then click on the alignment option you want. The *Alignment* options, *Left*, *Center*, *Right*, and *Decimal*, determine how Word arranges the text in relation to the tab stop. The *Bar* option inserts a vertical line at the tab position. You can use this to separate items in a tabular list. See the examples in this figure.

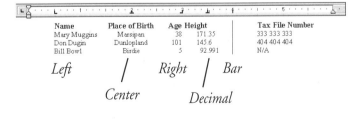

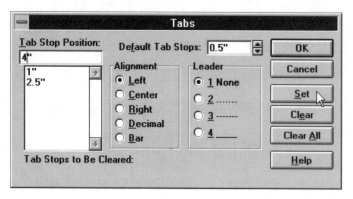

Figure 36. You use the *Leader* options in the *Tabs* dialog box to insert dotted, dashed, or solid lines between tab stops. Leaders are useful in table of contents, for example. To insert a leader, select from the *Leader* options after you have typed the tab.

To set the tab, click on the *Set* button. This inserts the tab position into the list box below the *Tab Stop Position* text box. Repeat this process for every new tab stop and display the new tab positions in the list box.

Figure 37. This figure shows you how the leaders appear in your document.

SETTING A TAB WITH THE RULER

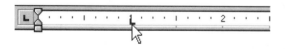

Figure 38. You can also use the ruler to set tabs. To do this, click on the *Tab* button to select the tab alignment you want.

Figure 39. You then click on the ruler wherever you want the tab stop.

If you want the same tab settings to apply to the whole document, set them up before you start typing. Each time you create a new paragraph, the tab settings continue from the previous paragraph. By deleting or adding tabs, you change your original tab settings. The original settings no longer apply when typing your document.

REMOVING A TAB

Figure 40. To remove a tab stop with the *Tabs* dialog box, first select the tab position in the *Tab Stop Position* list box, then click on the *Clear* button. To remove all the tab stops from the list box, click on the *Clear All* button.

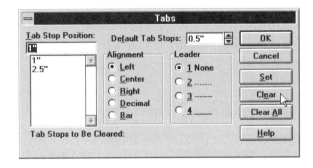

Figure 41. To remove a tab stop from the ruler, drag the tab stop marker down below the ruler, then release the mouse button.

BULLETED, NUMBERED, AND MULTILEVEL LISTS

You can use Word to automatically create bulleted, numbered and multilevel paragraphs. You can either create these in your document after you have typed the text, or when you are typing.

Figure 42. To apply these lists to existing text, select the text you want to change then choose *Bullets and Numbering* from the **Format** menu. This displays the *Bullets and Numbering* dialog box.

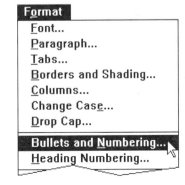

BULLETS

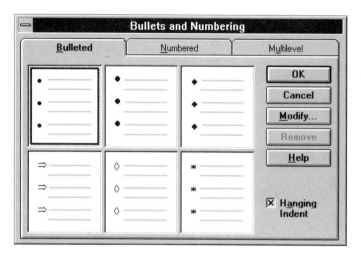

Figure 43. The *Bullets and Numbering* dialog box displays the *Bulleted* category by default. Choose one of the six bulleted list styles.

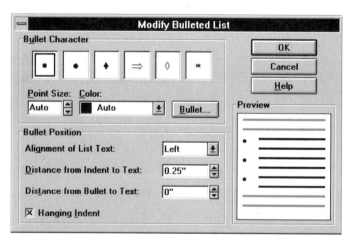

Figure 44. To change the bullet, click on the *Modify* button and select the options you want from the *Modify Bulleted List* dialog box that appears.

You can use this dialog box to change the style, color, and size of the bullet as well as the bullet position.

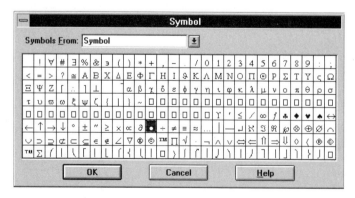

Figure 45. If you want to see more bullets, click on the *Bullet* button. This opens the *Symbol* dialog box.

Figure 46. When you add bullets to a list, Word adds a hanging indent to each bulleted paragraph. You can override this by deselecting the *Hanging Indent* option.

> • take the lawnmower to be serviced and pick up
>   some petrol on the way home
>
> • buy a cake for Justin and Matthew's joint
>   birthday party
>
> • arrange for council to pick up refuse on porch by
>   Thursday

Hanging indent

If you deselect the *Hanging Indent* option, Word inserts a space after the bullet or number, instead of an indent. A paragraph that already has a hanging indent does not affect the *Hanging Indent* option.

> • take the lawnmower to be serviced and pick up
> some petrol on the way home
>
> • buy a cake for Justin and Matthew's joint
> birthday party
>
> • arrange for council to pick up refuse on porch by
> Thursday

Non-hanging indent

Figure 47. Click on *OK* to apply the bullet to the selected paragraphs or the text you type.

> Things to do on the weekend:
>
> • take the lawnmower to be serviced and pick up
>   some petrol on the way home
>
> • buy a cake for Justin and Matthew's joint
>   birthday party
>
> • arrange for council to pick up refuse on porch by
>   Thursday

NUMBERING

Figure 48. To create an ordered list, display the *Bullets and Numbering* dialog box and click on the *Numbered* category tab. Choose a numbering style from the options displayed.

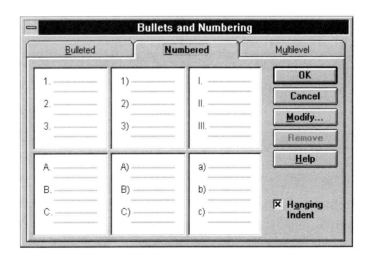

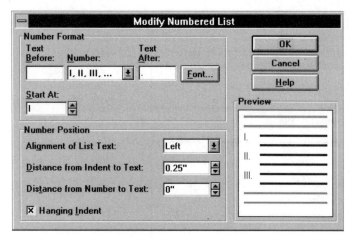

Figure 49. To change the style of the numbered list, click on the *Modify* button and select the options you want from the *Modify Numbered List* dialog box that appears.

You can use this dialog box to change the number format and the starting number of the paragraph list. You can also change the position of the number in the list.

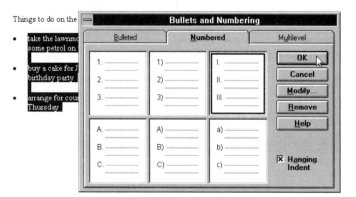

Figure 50. To convert bullets to numbers, or vice versa, first select the text and activate the *Bullets and Numbering* dialog box. Choose the option which you want to convert your text to and click on *OK*.

CREATING BULLETED AND NUMBERED LISTS WITH THE FORMATTING TOOLBAR

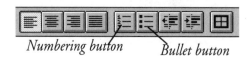

Numbering button   *Bullet button*

Figure 51. You can also add bullets and numbers directly from the *Formatting* toolbar with the *Bullet* and *Numbering* buttons.

When you select bulleting or numbering from the *Formatting* toolbar, Word uses either the default settings, or the previous settings you selected in the *Bullets and Numbering* dialog box.

To add numbering and bulleting directly from the toolbar, first select the text you want to change, then click on the appropriate button on the *Formatting* toolbar.

Figure 52. You can also use these buttons as you enter text. Word adds the bullets and numbers during this process.

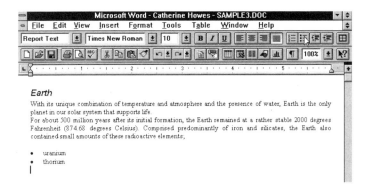

MULTILEVEL

Figure 53. You can create multilevel lists with the *Multilevel* category tab in the *Bullets and Numbering* dialog box. You can create a list with up to nine levels.

To apply a multilevel list, choose the style from one of the options displayed.

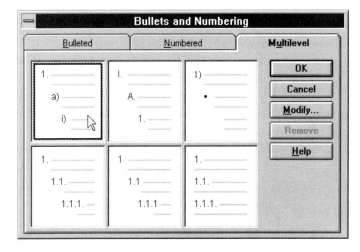

Figure 54. To change the style of the multilevel list, click on the *Modify* button and select the options you want from the *Modify Multilevel List* dialog box that appears.

You can change the format of the bullets or numbers and, if appropriate, the starting number. In addition, you can change the position of the bullet or number and the hanging indent.

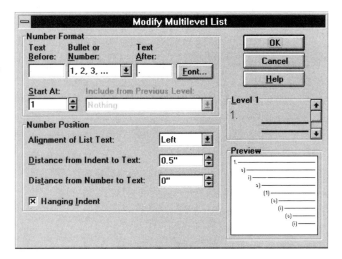

Figure 55. To see the formats of a particular paragraph, click on the *Help* button on the *Standard* toolbar (or press Shift+F1). A question mark appears with the mouse pointer. Click the mouse pointer on the text you want to check.

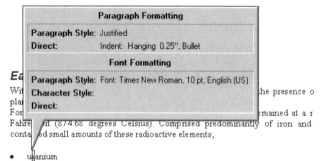

Figure 56. Word displays information about the paragraph.

Click on the *Help* button again, or press Esc, to remove the information callout box.

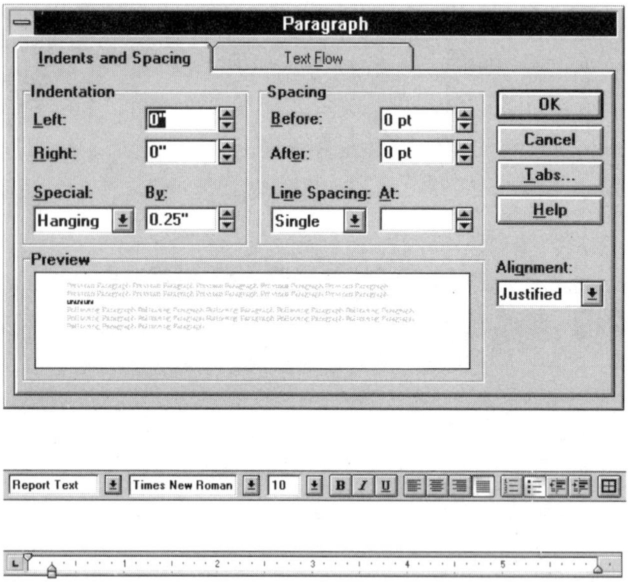

Figure 57. You can also see paragraph formats by selecting a paragraph and looking at the settings on the *Formatting* toolbar, ruler, and in the *Paragraph* dialog box.

Figure 58. If you select several paragraphs with different formatting, Word can't indicate the different formats at the same time; dialog box settings appear blank or dimmed, and dimmed markers on the ruler are settings for the first highlighted paragraph.

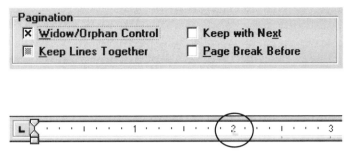

You can still apply and adjust formatting to the selected paragraphs, even though they have different formats, using the ruler, toolbar buttons, and *Paragraph* dialog box.

BORDERS AND SHADING

Figure 58. You can apply borders and shading to selected text.

Company Notices

So what has been happening around the office lately? The editor hasn't had much help this month scooping up the news and gossip. But here's the latest...

Congratulations!

Wedding fever has hit Webster & Associates this month. It must be the Christmas atmosphere! Congratulations to the happy couples.

Figure 58. Choose *Borders and Shading* from the **Format** menu and use the options in the *Paragraph Borders and Shading* dialog box.

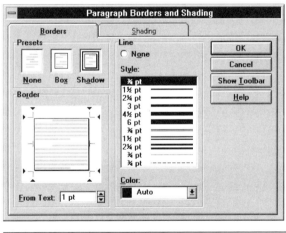

Figure 58. Alternatively, you can use the *Borders* toolbar.

For more information about applying borders and shading, and using the option in the *Paragraph Borders and Shading* dialog box and on the *Borders* toolbar, see **Chapter 11**.

DOCUMENT AND SECTION FORMATTING 5

INTRODUCTION

You can format your whole document using columns, margins, and line numbering, or you can break the document into sections, allowing you to format each section independently.

When you open Word, or create a new document, Word bases the document on the *Normal* template, unless you select a different template (see **Chapter** 7 for more about templates).

The *Normal* template in Word consists of page settings which are the default settings for each new document you create. You can change these settings for a document to suit your needs.

PAGE SETUP

There are a number of ways that you can change the setup of a page. These include changing the margins, the paper size, and the layout. You can choose whether to apply the changes you make to the whole document, or a section or part of that document.

MARGINS

There are three ways you can change margins. The first is using the *Page Setup* command in the **File** menu; the second is in *Print Preview;* and the third is by adjusting the margins on the ruler.

PAGE SETUP DIALOG BOX

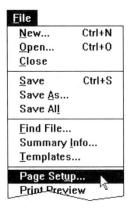

Figure 1. You can change margins in the *Page Setup* dialog box. To open this dialog box first select *Page Setup* from the **File** menu, then click on the *Margins* option at the top of the dialog box.

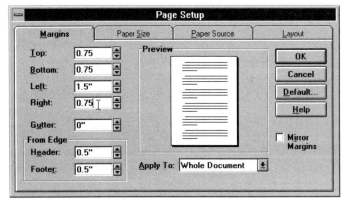

Figure 2. Enter the margin sizes you want for *Top, Bottom, Left,* and *Right* margins in the corresponding text boxes. You can also click on the up and down arrows to change the measurements.

Use the *Gutter* adjustment to create extra space in the margin to allow for the binding edge of a book, or a double-sided document.

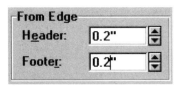

Figure 3. Use the *From Edge* options to specify the distance that you want the header and footer to be from the edge of the page.

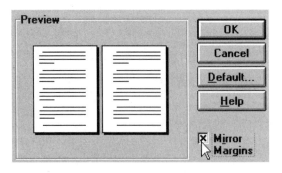

Figure 4. Set your document for double-sided printing by clicking on the *Mirror Margins* check box in the *Page Setup* dialog box.

Figure 5. You can apply the page settings to either the whole document or a part of it. To apply them to the whole document, choose *Whole Document* from the *Apply To* drop-down list. To apply the settings from the insertion point choose *This Point Forward.* If you are working in a section, the *This Section* option appears.

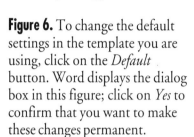
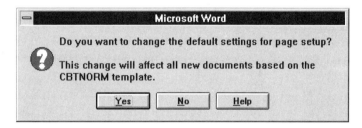

Figure 6. To change the default settings in the template you are using, click on the *Default* button. Word displays the dialog box in this figure; click on *Yes* to confirm that you want to make these changes permanent.

Figure 7. The *Preview* window shows you how the document will appear when you print it with the margins you have selected.

When you have made the changes you want in the *Page Setup* dialog box, click on *OK* to apply them to your document.

RULER

Figure 8. You can only adjust the left and right margins of selected text using the ruler. To change the margins, drag the margin marker indicated in this figure. As you drag, a guideline appears on the page to show you the position of the margin.

PRINT PREVIEW

Figure 9. To adjust margins in *Print Preview*, first select the *Print Preview* command from the **File** menu or click on the *Print Preview* button on the *Standard* toolbar.

View Ruler button

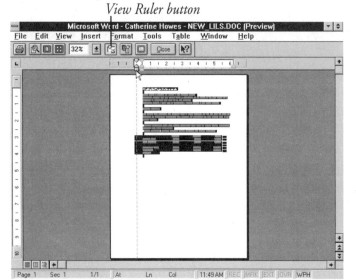

Figure 10. You can now view your pages as they would appear when printed. Turn the rulers on by clicking on the *View Ruler* button. You can then drag the margin markers on the ruler to adjust the margin settings of selected text. (Select the text as you would normally in editing mode.) You can only adjust the left and right margins in *Print Preview*.

Click on the *Close* button to return to normal editing mode.

PAPER SIZE

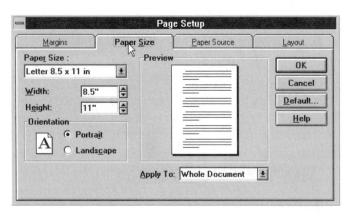

Figure 11. You can change the paper size through the *Page Setup* dialog box. Select *Page Setup* from the **File** menu to open this dialog box. To access the paper size options, click on the *Paper Size* tab.

Figure 12. You can change the paper size by choosing an option from the *Paper Size* drop-down list box. This displays standard paper sizes.

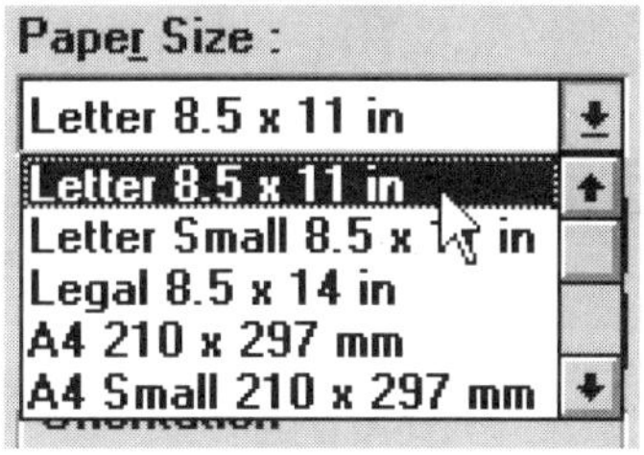

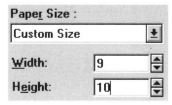

Figure 13. To create a custom paper size, insert the dimensions of the page into the *Width* and *Height* text boxes.

Figure 14. Choose the page orientation you want by clicking on either the *Portrait* or the *Landscape* radio button.

Figure 15. The *Preview* window shows you how your document will look with these settings.

Figure 16. You can make your size and orientation settings the defaults by clicking on the *Default* button in the *Page Setup* dialog box. Word then prompts you to confirm this decision. If you select *Yes*, your size and orientation settings become the settings for the template you have chosen for your current document.

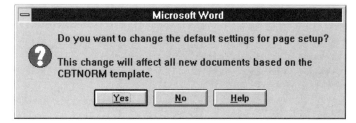

Figure 17. You can apply these changes to the whole document or a section using the *Apply To* options.

CREATING SECTIONS

You can divide your document into any number of sections and format each section differently. For example, you can make a section as short as a single paragraph for a headline in a newsletter. You can make it as long as an entire document. You can also set one section of your document to have three columns, and another section can have one.

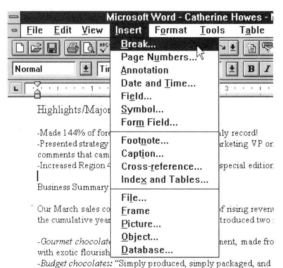

Figure 18. To insert a section break, position the insertion point where you want the new section to start then choose *Break* from the **Insert** menu.

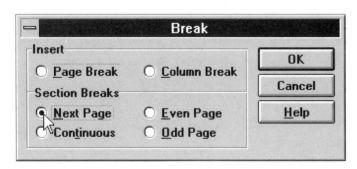

Figure 19. Under *Section Breaks*, in the *Break* dialog box that appears, select an option for where you want the new section to begin.

The options are:

• *Next Page* starts the next section on the next page.

• *Continuous* flows the text on, into the next section.

• *Even Page* starts the text of the next section on the next even-numbered page. If the section break falls on an even-numbered page, Word leaves the next odd-numbered page blank.

• *Odd Page* starts the next section on the next odd-numbered page. If the section break falls on an odd-numbered page, Word leaves the next even-numbered page blank.

Click on *OK* when you have made your choice.

Figure 20. Word shows the section break on the screen with dotted lines and the words "End of Section."

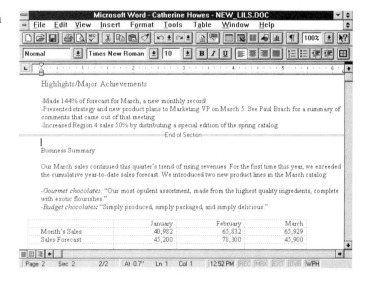

Figure 21. To remove a section break, position the insertion point on the section mark and press Delete.

Word stores all section formatting in this section mark. When you delete a section mark, you delete the formatting for the section before it. The text then becomes part of the next section, and assumes the formatting characteristics of that section.

If you accidentally delete a section mark, choose *Undo* from the **Edit** menu before doing anything else. This restores the section mark and the section formatting.

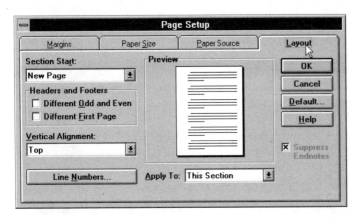

Figure 22. The *Layout* tab in the *Page Setup* dialog box gives you options to change where the section starts.

CREATING MULTIPLE COLUMNS

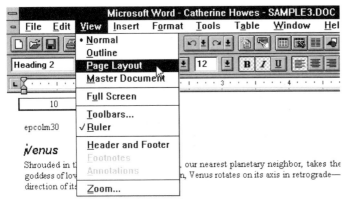

Figure 23. To create multiple columns, first put the insertion point on the line of text where you want the columns to start. If you only want text to form columns in a certain part of the document, you should create a section first (see **Creating Sections** earlier in this chapter).

Then, select *Page Layout* in the **View** menu, so you can view the columns side by side.

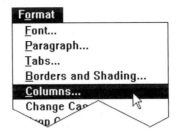

Figure 24. Choose the *Columns* command from the **Format** menu.

Figure 25. The *Columns* command activates the *Columns* dialog box.

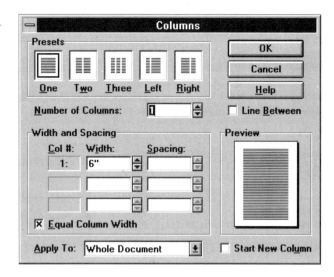

Figure 26. Choose one of the options in the *Presets* section. Alternatively, type in the number of columns you want in the *Number of Columns* text box or click the pointer on the up and down arrows to change the value.

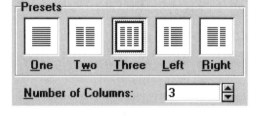

Figure 27. You can select the *Line Between* check box to place a vertical line between the columns. This line is visible only in *Print Preview.*

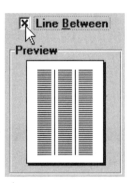

Figure 28. To manipulate the width and space between individual columns, you first need to deselect the *Equal Column Width* check box. You can then enter into the *Width* text box the specific width you need for each column.

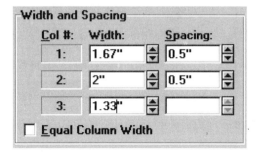

Also, type in the space you want between columns in the *Spacing* text box. The default spacing is 0.5 inches. You can also use centimeters (cm), points (pt), or picas (pi).

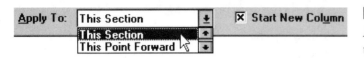

Figure 29. You can select the *Start New Column* check box to force the section you are formatting to start a new column.

Use the *Apply To* drop-down list to make column settings apply to either: the *Whole Document*; *This Point Forward*, if you have the insertion point in the text; or *This Section*, if you have created a section break.

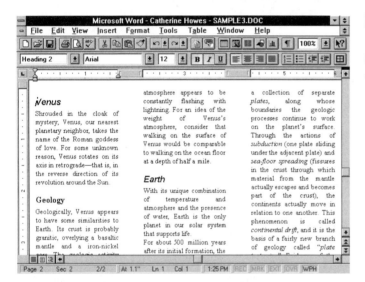

Figure 30. Click on *OK* in the *Columns* dialog box to apply your selections. The screen displays the columns.

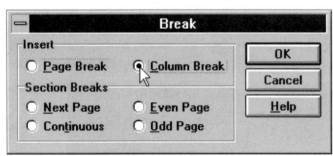

Figure 31. Word automatically breaks columns so they fit on the page, but you can specify where the columns break. First, place the insertion point where you want the columns to break, then open the *Break* dialog box by choosing *Break* from the **Insert** menu. Under *Insert,* choose *Column Break* to begin text in a new column; or choose *Page Break* to start text on a new page.

Figure 32. The status bar at the bottom of the screen shows the page and section of your document where you have positioned the insertion point.

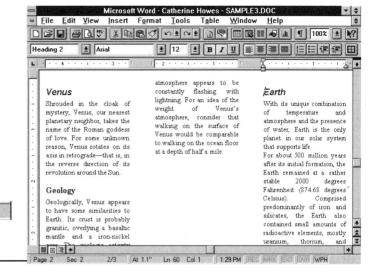

VIEWING MULTIPLE COLUMNS

Figure 33. *Normal* view is faster if you want to enter text. It shows section marks and accurate column widths. You can zoom (**View** menu or *Standard* toolbar) in or out for a close-up or overview look in *Normal* view, but it does not display columns side by side.

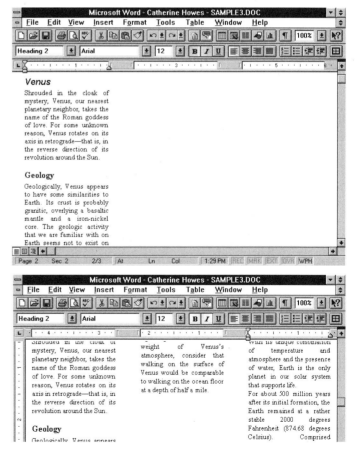

Figure 34. *Page Layout* view shows columns side by side, with framed items, such as graphics, in their correct location. This view is good for final editing, manually inserting column breaks, and adjusting column width. You can also zoom in or out in *Page Layout* view.

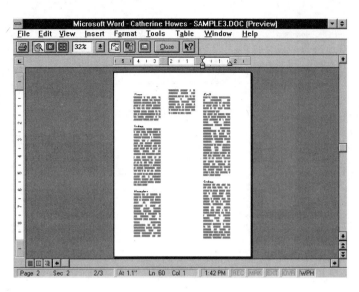

Figure 35. *Print Preview* shows the overall page layout, and indicates how the document looks on the printed page. This view is good for final adjustments to margins and page breaks.

You can use the horizontal ruler in *Print Preview* to change the width of columns and the spacing between them.

For more information about viewing your document, see **Chapter 8**.

CREATING COLUMNS USING THE STANDARD TOOLBAR

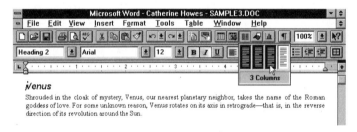

Figure 36. To create columns using the *Standard* toolbar, click in the section of the text you want to format.

If you haven't inserted sections in your document and you only want columns in part of the document, either create a section or highlight the desired text. If you don't, the *Columns* command applies to the whole document, or the section containing the insertion point.

Click on the *Column* button on the toolbar and drag the mouse to the right to select the number of columns you want. You can insert up to three columns. When you release the mouse, Word formats your text into columns.

CHANGING BACK TO ONE COLUMN

Figure 37. To change back to one column, position the insertion point in the section that you want to change to a single column section and select *Columns* from the **Format** menu.

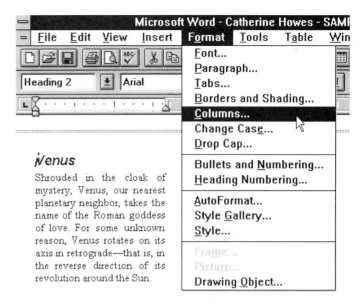

Figure 38. In the *Columns* dialog box, change the column setting in the *Number of Columns* text box to 1.

Set the *Apply To* drop-down list to either *This Section,* or *This Point Forward.*

Click on *OK.* The document now has a new section with only one column.

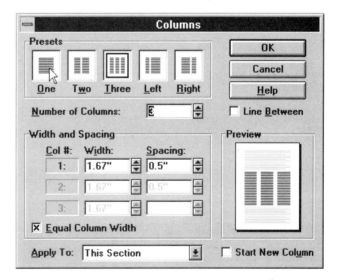

CHANGING THE WIDTH OF COLUMNS WITH THE RULER

Figure 39. You can use the ruler to change the widths of multiple columns. To view columns side by side, choose *Page Layout* from the **View** menu. Then, put the insertion point in one of the columns. The ruler shows the margins of each column.

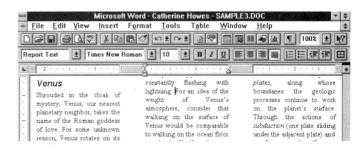

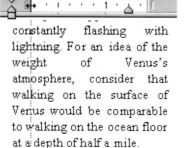

constantly flashing with lightning. For an idea of the weight of Venus's atmosphere, consider that walking on the surface of Venus would be comparable to walking on the ocean floor at a depth of half a mile.

Figure 40. Place the mouse pointer in the position shown in this figure. The pointer changes to a double-sided arrow. Drag the column boundary to a new position and release the mouse button to change the width of the column. Word automatically adjusts all columns and space between columns to equal widths.

ALTERING SECTION LAYOUTS

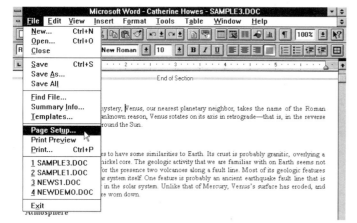

Figure 41. You can adjust the section break settings. First, position the insertion point anywhere in the section, and select *Page Setup* from the **File** menu.

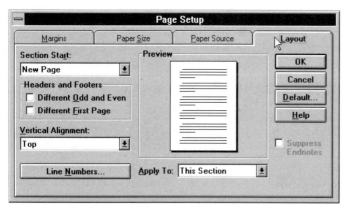

Figure 42. In the *Page Setup* dialog box, choose the *Layout* tab. Here, you can change the way the section flows on from the previous section, by choosing the appropriate option from the *Section Start* drop-down list. The effects of these options (*New Page, Continuous, Even Page, Odd Page,* and *New Column*) are explained under **Creating Sections**, earlier in this chapter.

Figure 43. The *Headers and Footers* options let you manipulate headers and footers in a section.

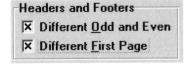

Figure 44. The options in the *Vertical Alignment* drop-down list box affect the vertical position of text in a section:

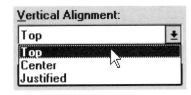

- *Top* aligns the top line with the top section margin.

- *Center* centers the text between the top and bottom margins.

- *Justified* spreads the text between the top and bottom margins by adding space between paragraphs.

Figure 45. Use the *Apply To* options to specify how you want to apply these changes.

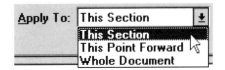

Click on *OK* to apply your choices.

LINE NUMBERING

You can use line numbering in publications, such as legal documents and scripts, to make it is easier to refer to specific lines within the document.

Line numbers appear in *Page Layout* and *Print Preview* views and are printed in the margin or between columns.

You can choose whether to include line numbers to different sections of your document. If your document contains only one section, the line numbering command affects the whole document.

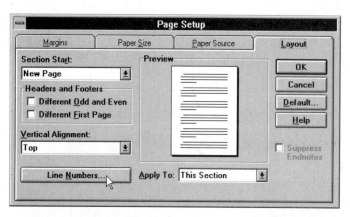

Figure 46. Put the insertion point in the section of the document that you want to number. Choose *Page Setup* from the **File** menu, then click on the *Layout* tab.

Click on the *Line Numbers* button.

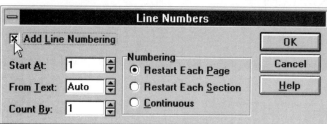

Figure 47. Click on the *Add Line Numbering* check box to activate the *Line Numbers* dialog box.

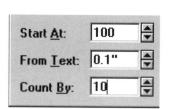

Figure 48. In the *Start At* text box enter the starting number for the numbering sequence.

Set the distance you want between the numbers and the left margin of the text in the *From Text* text box. The default option, *Auto*, is 0.25 inches for a single column, and 0.13 inches for newspaper-style columns.

You can choose how often the numbers appear. For example, every 10 lines. Type your choice in the *Count By* text box, or click on the up and down arrows.

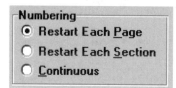

Figure 49. The *Numbering* options specify where you want to restart line numbering. *Restart Each Page* restarts the numbering after each page. *Restart Each Section* restarts the numbering after each section.

Continuous continues the line numbering from one section to the
next.

To apply your choices to the document, click on *OK* in the *Line
Numbers* dialog box then in the *Page Setup* dialog box.

Figure 50. To remove line
numbers from a section of a
document, put the insertion point
in the section. Choose *Page Setup*
from the **File** menu, then the *Line
Numbers* button from the *Layout*
tab. Deselect the *Add Line
Numbering* check box in the *Line
Numbers* dialog box and click on
OK. Click again on *OK* in the
Page Layout dialog box and when
you return to the page, the line
numbers from this section are
gone.

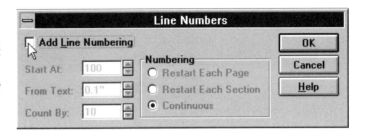

Figure 51. To suppress line
numbering for certain paragraphs,
such as headings or empty
paragraphs, select the required
paragraphs.

Open the *Paragraph* dialog box
by choosing *Paragraph* from the
Format menu.

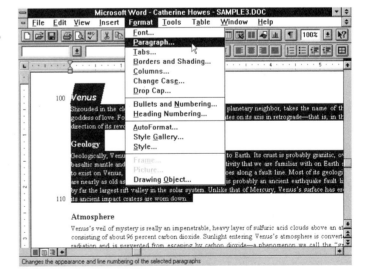

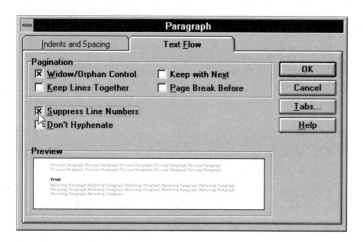

Figure 52. In the *Paragraph* dialog box, click on the *Text Flow* tab, then select the *Suppress Line Numbers* option.

STYLES 6

USING STYLES

All new text that you type into a document is, by default, assigned the *Normal* style. You can see the characteristics of the *Normal* style on the *Formatting* toolbar—Times New Roman, 10 point, left aligned, with single spacing.

A style is a set of paragraph and character format options that you name and store. Word comes with a number of pre-determined styles. Using styles can make document formatting faster and more consistent. You can apply a style to any amount of text—from a single word to the whole document. You can save styles with a document, and you can also use them in other documents.

AUTOFORMAT

You can automatically format a document using the *AutoFormat* command. Word analyzes the document and determines the characteristics of the text, then applies appropriate styles. By default, Word preserves any styles you apply to text yourself.

Figure 1. You can control the formatting changes AutoFormat makes through the options on the *AutoFormat* tab in the *Options* dialog box. (Open this dialog box by selecting *Options* from the **Tools** menu.)

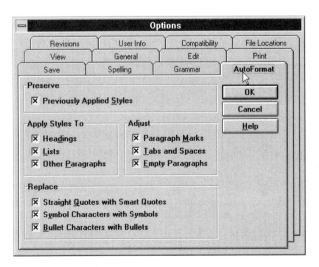

REVIEWING CHANGES

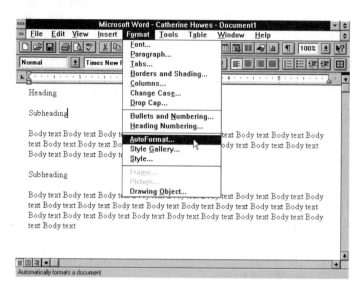

Figure 2. Place the insertion point anywhere in your document to format it, or select the part of the document you want to format. Then choose *AutoFormat* from the **Format** menu.

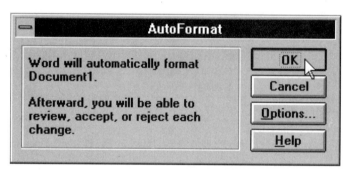

Figure 3. Click on *OK* in the first *AutoFormat* dialog box.

Figure 4. Word applies styles from the attached template and displays the second *AutoFormat* dialog box.

Figure 5. To review and reject changes, select *Review Changes* to open the *Review AutoFormat Changes* dialog box.

Figure 6. Word inserts temporary revision marks and color to indicate the changed text formatting.

You can use the scroll bars to move through your document and select a specific paragraph you want to review. If you need to move the dialog box, drag its title bar.

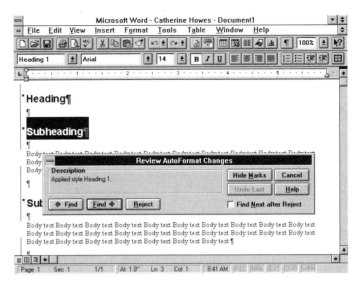

Figure 7. You can apply a different style to the text by selecting another style from the *Style* dropdown list box on the *Formatting* toolbar.

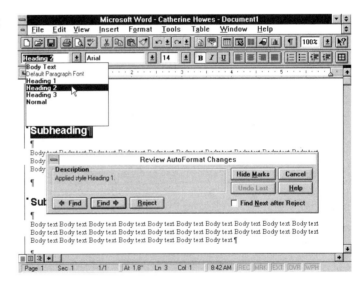

Figure 8. To review changes one by one, click on the *Find* buttons.

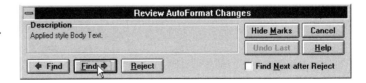

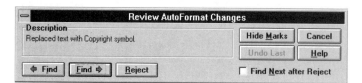

Figure 9. To undo the selected change, choose the *Reject* button. Undo the last rejected change by clicking on *Undo Last*.

Select the *Find Next after Reject* check box to have Word undo the highlighted change and move on to select the next one straight away (so you don't have to click on the *Next* button).

If you want to display the document without the revision marks so you can see what it will look like if you accepted the remaining changes, click on the *Hide Marks* button.

After reviewing your document, close the *Review AutoFormat Changes* dialog box.

Figure 10. In the *AutoFormat* dialog box, choose *Reject All* to cancel the formatting changes; or *Accept* to accept the formatting changes.

The *Style Gallery* button opens the *Style Gallery* dialog box. For an explanation, see the **Style Gallery** section later in this chapter.

(You can select the *Undo* button on the *Standard* toolbar to undo all the changes if you selected the *Accept All* button in the *AutoFormat* dialog box.)

WITHOUT REVIEWING CHANGES

Figure 11. Place the insertion point anywhere in the document, or select the part of the document you want to format. Then click on the *AutoFormat* button on the *Standard* toolbar.

Word formats the text according to the options selected on the *AutoFormat* tab in the *Options* dialog box (see Figure 1).

STYLES

The styles that are available in your active document depend on what template you chose to base the document on (see **Chapter** 7 for information about templates).

Styles let you apply a group of formats, such as font, size, alignment, and spacing, in one step. If you modify the style to apply different formatting, Word reformats all text in that style.

Figure 12. You can use two types of styles: a paragraph style (appears in bold in the *Styles* list box); and a character style (not bold). A paragraph style controls all aspects of a paragraph's appearance—font, size, spacing, alignment, tabs, borders. A character style applies formats of the *Font* command such as font, size, and effects (see **Formatting Text** in **Chapter 2**).

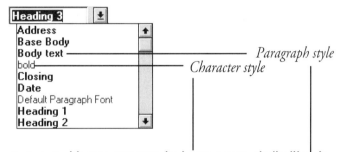

Geologically, **Venus appears to have some similarities to Earth**. Its crust is probably granitic, overlying a basaltic mantle and a iron-nickel core. The geologic activity that we are familiar with on Earth seems not to exist on Venus, except for the presence two volcanoes along a fault line. Most of its geologic features are nearly as old as the solar system itself. One feature is probably an ancient earthquake fault line that is by far the largest rift valley in the solar system. Unlike that of Mercury, Venus's surface has eroded, and its ancient impact craters are worn down.

Paragraph and character styles do not affect each other. When you apply a character style to selected text, its formats are added to those of the paragraph style applied to the text. If you change the paragraph style of a paragraph that you used a character style in, the character is not affected.

APPLYING STYLES

USING THE FORMATTING TOOLBAR

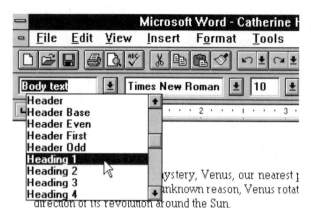

Figure 13. To apply a style to text, first select the text you want to affect. To apply a paragraph style to a single paragraph, place the insertion point anywhere in the paragraph or select any amount of text in the paragraph. Even if you only select a few words in the paragraph, the command still affects the whole paragraph. Alternatively you can select the number of paragraphs you want to affect. To apply a character style, highlight the text you want to format.

Activate the *Styles* drop-down list box by clicking on its arrow on the *Formatting* toolbar and choose the style you want to apply.

If the style you want is not displayed in the list, hold down the Shift key and click on the arrow next to the *Styles* text box.

Repeat this procedure for any non-sequential paragraphs you want to apply styles to.

Figure 14. When you apply a style to a paragraph, you can then select the other paragraphs you want to change, and choose *Repeat Style* from the **Edit** menu to apply the style. You can also press the F4 key to activate the *Repeat Style* command or press Ctrl+Y.

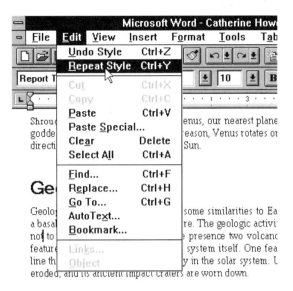

USING THE STYLE COMMAND

Figure 15. The *Style* command also applies styles to text. After selecting text you want to apply a style to, choose *Style* from the **Format** menu.

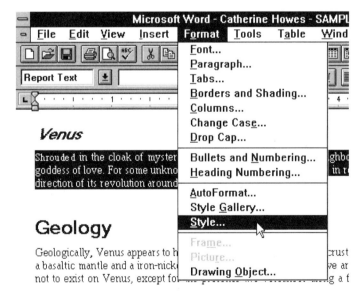

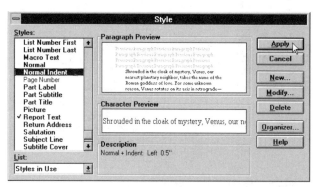

Figure 16. In the *Style* dialog box, highlight a style from the list box and click on *Apply*.

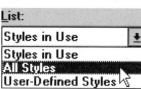

Figure 17. If the style is not listed, you can select another category from the *List* drop-down list box.

COPYING STYLES USING THE FORMAT PAINTER BUTTON

Figure 18. First select some text, highlight the paragraph mark at the end of a paragraph, or put the insertion point in the paragraph containing the style you want to copy.

Then click on the *Format Painter* button on the *Standard* toolbar.

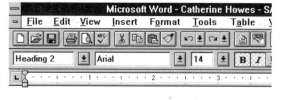

Figure 19. When you move the mouse into the text, the mouse pointer changes to an I-beam with a paint brush. Select the text you want to format (for a character style), or click in the paragraph you want to format (for a paragraph style).

To copy the style multiple times, double-click on the *Format Painter* button. Then you can select text that you want to copy the formatting to. When you have finished, click on the *Format Painter* button again.

SHORTCUT KEYS

If you use a particular style often or prefer to work without the *Formatting* toolbar, you may want to assign a shortcut key so that you can apply the style more easily.

Figure 20. Choose *Style* from the **Format** menu. In the *Style* dialog box, select a style from the list box. Then click on the *Modify* button.

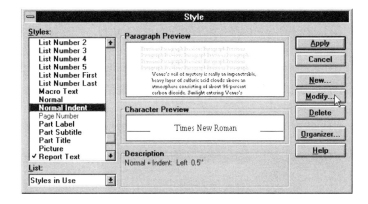

Figure 21. Then choose the *Shortcut Key* button in the *Modify Style* dialog box.

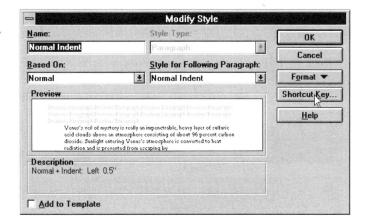

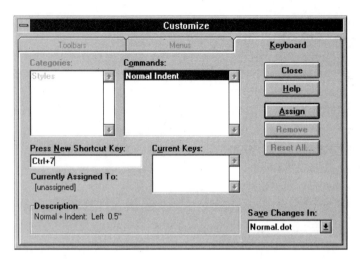

Figure 22. On the *Keyboard* tab of the *Customize* dialog box, type the shortcut keys in the *Press New Shortcut Key* text box.

The *Currently Assigned To* text tells you if your key combination already activates a command. If so, delete the text and try another combination.

Click on the *Assign* button, and close the *Customize* dialog box. Then choose *OK* in the *Modify Style* dialog box and *Close* in the *Style* dialog box.

In your document, you can press the shortcut keys to apply the style to selected text.

MODIFYING STYLES

The quickest and most consistent way of changing text in your document is to modify the style you applied. This way, Word updates all text formatted with that style throughout the document.

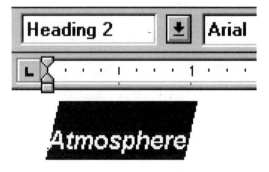

USING EXISTING TEXT

Figure 23. To modify a paragraph style, select a paragraph formatted with that style. To modify a character style, select at least one character formatted with that style. The name of the style you want to change should be displayed in the *Styles* text box on the *Formatting* toolbar.

Figure 24. Then change the text or paragraph formatting of the style in the usual way. Now click in the *Styles* text box (Word highlights the style name), and press Enter.

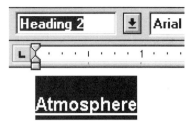

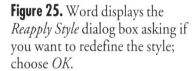

Figure 25. Word displays the *Reapply Style* dialog box asking if you want to redefine the style; choose *OK*.

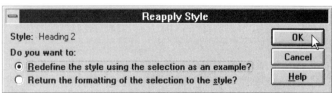

When you return to the document, Word updates and reformats any text with that style applied.

USING THE STYLE COMMAND

Figure 26. Choose *Style* from the **Format** menu, and select the style you want to modify from the list box in the *Style* dialog box. If the style you want is not listed, select another category from the *List* drop-down list box. Then click on the *Modify* button.

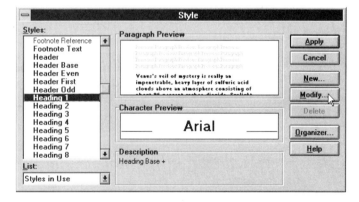

Figure 27. In the *Modify Style* dialog box, click on the *Format* button. Choose an option to activate its dialog box and make formatting changes to the style.

If you want to add the modified style to your active document's template, select the *Add to Template* check box. This style is now available for all new documents you base on that template.

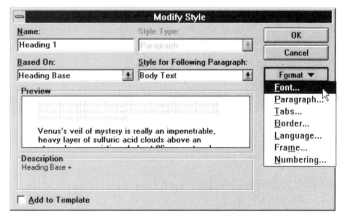

Click on *OK* to redefine the style. Then close the *Style* dialog box.

Text formatted with the modified style is updated throughout the active document.

REDEFINING THE DEFAULT (NORMAL) STYLE

You modify the formats of the *Normal* style as you do with any paragraph style. To use the modified *Normal* style in all new documents, you add the modified style to the template.

Open a document that is based on the template you use for new documents. Then follow the procedure from Figure 26, under **Using the Style Command**.

CHANGING WHAT THE STYLE IS BASED ON

Related text elements, such as headings, can share certain formats. Use the *Based On* option, in the *Modify Style* dialog box, to define a base style for a style. This allows you to update the formatting of groups of styles by redefining the formats of the style on which they are based.

For example, if you change the font of the *Normal* style, this also changes the font of other styles that are based on the *Normal* style. By having a base style, your document will have a consistent format, and therefore a consistent appearance.

Documents based on the *Normal* template have styles that are based on the *Normal* style. For other templates, paragraph styles for related elements are also based on a common "base style." These styles are also based on the *Normal* style. So, all styles are based, either directly or indirectly, on the *Normal* style.

Figure 28. When you create a new style from existing text (see **Modifying Styles, Using Existing Text**), Word bases the new style on the style you have applied to the paragraph. To specify a base style when creating a new style or to change a style's current base style, choose *Style* from the **Format** menu.

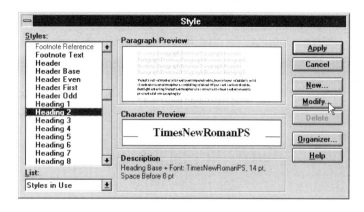

Select the style whose base style you want to change from the list box in the *Style* dialog box. Then click on *Modify.*

Figure 29. This opens the *Modify Style* dialog box. From the *Based On* drop-down list, select the style you want as the base style. If you don't want the selected style to have a base style and be affected by changes to other styles, choose *(no style)* from the drop-down list.

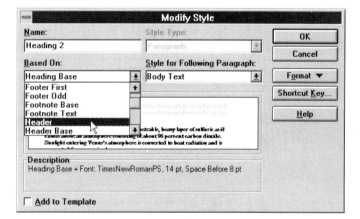

Then close the dialog box by clicking on *OK.*

CHANGING THE NEXT STYLE

In the *Modify Style* dialog box you can set the *Style for Following Paragraph* option. You use this option to define what style will follow a paragraph formatted with a particular style. For example, you can have *Normal* style text follow a *Heading* style.

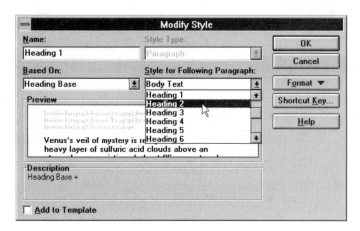

Figure 30. To do this, choose the style you want for the paragraph following the selected style from the *Style for Following Paragraph* drop-down list box. Then click on *OK*, and close the *Style* dialog box.

CREATING NEW STYLES

USING EXISTING TEXT

Figure 31. To create a paragraph style, select the paragraph and format it. Then click in the *Style* text box on the *Formatting* toolbar.

Figure 32. Delete the style name and type a new name. Then press Enter.

You have now created a style based on the format options of the paragraph that you selected. Word assigns your new style to the *Style* drop-down list box.

USING THE STYLE COMMAND

Figure 33. To create a paragraph or character style, first select *Style* from the **Format** menu to open the *Style* dialog box. Choose the *New* button.

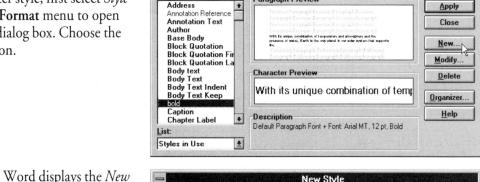

Figure 34. Word displays the *New Style* dialog box. Type a name for the new style in the *Name* text box and select the type of style you want to create from the *Style Type* drop-down list box.

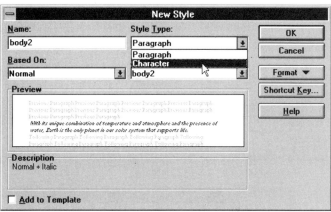

To base the new style on another, choose from the *Based On* drop-down list box. To apply a different style to the paragraph that follows the new style, select a style from the *Style for Following Paragraph* drop-down list box. (See **Changing the Next Style** for more information about these options.)

Figure 35. Click on the *Format* button and choose any formats you want applied to the style. Do this by choosing options from the dialog boxes that Word opens when you choose commands in this drop-down list.

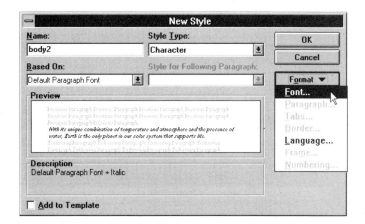

Choose *OK* to define the style and close the *New Style* dialog box. Then close the *Style* dialog box. Word adds this style to the *Style* drop-down list box on the *Formatting* toolbar.

NAMING STYLES

When you name styles, each style name in a document must be unique. Names can be up to 253 characters long, including commas and spaces. You can't use backslashes (/), braces ({}), or semicolons (;) in the name. Style names are also case sensitive; for example, "line" and "Line" would be two different styles.

RENAMING AND DELETING STYLES

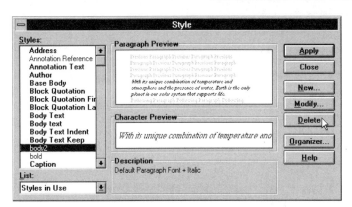

Figure 36. Activate the *Style* dialog box from the **Format** menu. Select the style you want to delete from the *Styles* list box. Then click on *Delete*.

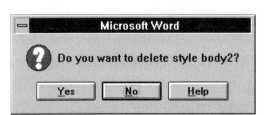

Figure 37. Confirm this decision, by choosing *Yes* in the prompt dialog box.

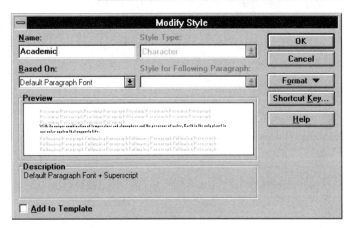

Figure 38. To rename a style, select it from the list box in the *Style* dialog box and click on the *Modify* button.

Type a new name for the style in the *Name* text box of the *Modify Style* dialog box. Then choose *OK*, and close the *Style* dialog box.

DISPLAYING STYLE NAMES IN DOCUMENT WINDOWS

To see the paragraph styles you have applied throughout the document, you can display the style names at the left hand side of the document window. You can't do this in *Page Layout* or *Print Preview* views.

Figure 39. Choose *Options* from the **Tools** menu.

Select the *View* tab of the *Options* dialog box. In the *Style Area Width* text box in the *Window* section, specify a value greater than zero to display the style names (or type '0' to hide the names from the document window).

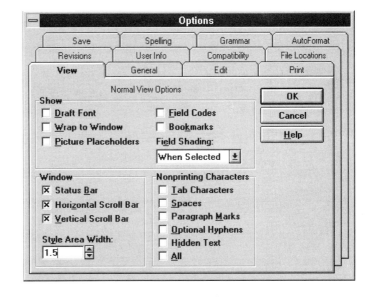

Figure 40. Word displays style names next to the document text. You can drag the style area boundary to the left and out of the window to hide the style names.

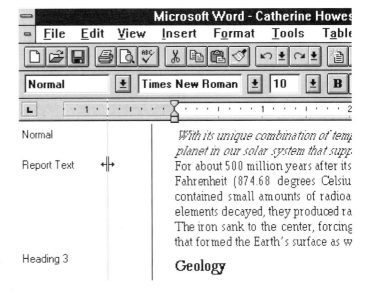

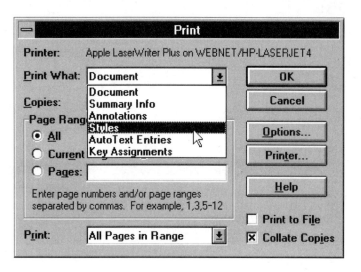

Figure 41. You can print a list of the styles in your document by selecting *Styles* from the *Print What* drop-down list box in the *Print* dialog box. For more information about printing, see Chapter 10.

STYLE GALLERY

After you have applied styles to your document, you can use the *Style Gallery* command to preview and change the document's overall appearance.

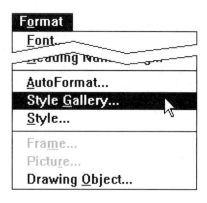

Figure 42. To use styles from a different template, choose *Style Gallery* from the **Format** menu (or click on the *Style Gallery* button in the *AutoFormat* dialog box of Figure 10).

Figure 43. In the *Template* list box of the *Style Gallery* dialog box, highlight a template. Choose an option from the *Preview* section.

Document displays the active document in the *Preview of* list box with the styles from the selected template applied to it.

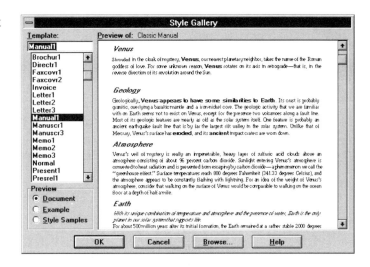

Figure 44. *Example* previews a sample document that is formatted with the selected template's styles.

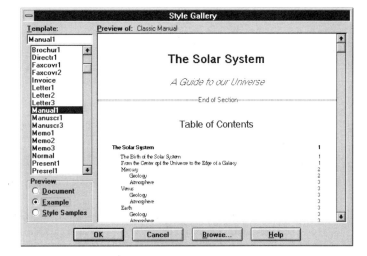

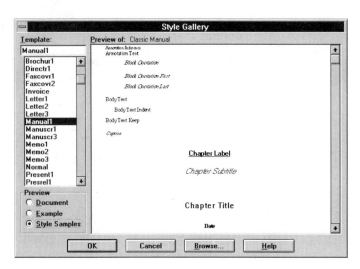

Figure 45. Choose *Style Samples* to show sample text of all the styles in the highlighted template.

Choose *OK* to copy styles from the selected template to your active document.

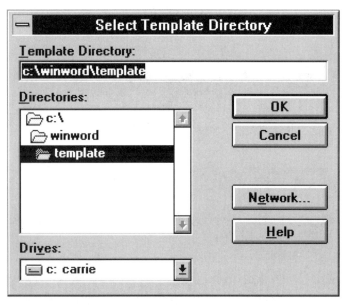

Figure 46. The *Browse* button in the *Style Gallery* dialog box activates the *Select Template Directory* dialog box if you want to preview templates that are saved in another location.

See **Chapter 7** for more information about templates.

TEMPLATES AND WIZARDS 7

INTRODUCTION

Templates are specially preformatted documents, or blueprints, which you can use to save time and effort when creating new documents. A template can include anything you would put into a normal document—it stores styles, macros, and AutoText entries. The only difference between a template and normal document is the way you save it. Word provides templates for documents such as memos and business letters.

Wizards are like templates but Word does more work for you by taking you through the creation process step by step.

TEMPLATES

Figure 1. If you need to create similar documents on a regular basis (a newsletter for example), you can create a template with the required formatting that you can re-use.

Word comes with a number of predefined templates that you can modify in any way you like. You need to base each new document created in Word on a template.

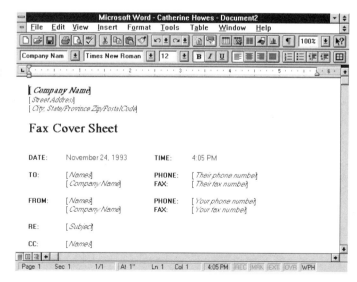

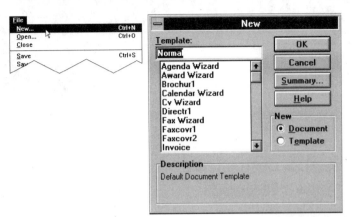

Figure 2. By default, you base every new document created in Word on the *Normal* template. When you select *New* from the **File** menu, the *New* dialog box appears. You can select which template to base the new document on, then click on *OK*.

Figure 3. If you click on the *New* button on the *Standard* toolbar, the *New* dialog box doesn't appear; Word automatically opens a new document based on the default (*Normal*) template.

USING BUILT-IN TEMPLATES AND WIZARDS

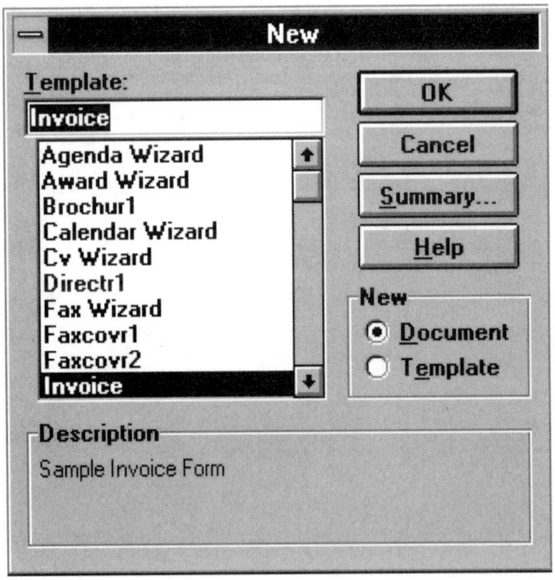

Figure 4. Word provides a wide range of document templates. Clicking on a template in the *New* dialog box *Template* list provides a brief summary of the highlighted template in the *Description* box. In the *New* section of the *New* dialog box, the *Document* radio button is selected by default. Word copies information from a selected template and attaches it to the new document. Select a template or a wizard from the *Template* list box and click on *OK*.

Figure 5. If you choose a wizard, Word bases the document on the *Normal* template, but the styles reflect the formatting you choose when working through the wizard.

Figure 6. After you click on *OK* with a wizard selected, Word displays a series of dialog boxes that lead you through laying out your document.

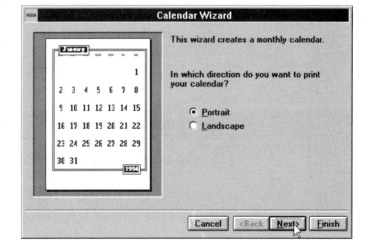

PREVIEWING TEMPLATES

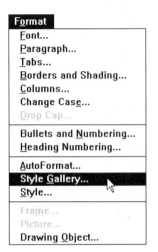

Figure 7. You can look at the formatting of a template before you choose it by choosing *Style Gallery* from the **Format** menu.

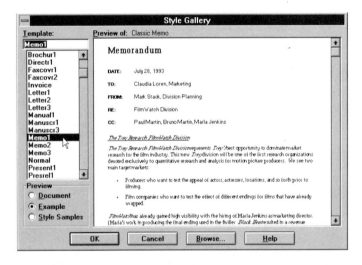

Figure 8. In the *Style Gallery* dialog box, select the *Example* radio button. In the *Template* list box, highlight a template.

Word displays sample text formatted with that template's styles in the *Preview of* list box.

CREATING TEMPLATES

You can create a new template in three ways: you can create your own; convert your current document into a template; or you can modify an existing template.

CREATING YOUR OWN

Figure 9. To create your own template, select *New* from the **File** menu. In the *New* dialog box, select the *Template* radio button and click on *OK*.

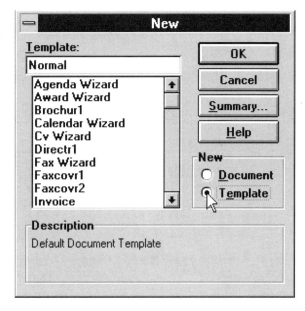

In the template document window, you can now set up the template in any way you like. You can include text and graphics, create styles, and include any item you would put in any Word document.

Figure 10. To save the template, select *Save* from the **File** menu. In the *Save As* dialog box, type the new name of your template. Because you are creating a template, the *Save As* dialog box is slightly different. You cannot change the *Save File as Type* selection, or change the directory path. By default, you must save all templates into the *winword\template* directory. Click on *OK*.

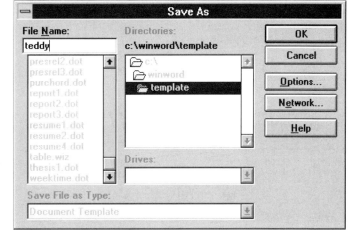

Word saves this with a *.dot* extension, as it does for all templates.

USING AN EXISTING DOCUMENT

Open an existing document that you want to save as a template. Then select *Save As* from the **File** menu.

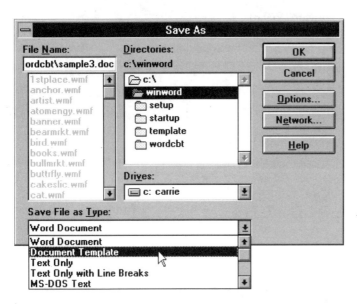

Figure 11. In the *Save As* dialog box, change the *Save File as Type* to *Document Template.* This automatically changes the directory path to the *winword\template* directory. You can type in a new name for the template, and then select *OK.*

After making the changes you want in the template document window, choose *Save* from the **File** menu to save changes to the new template.

MODIFYING AN EXISTING TEMPLATE

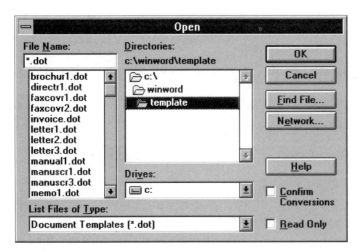

Figure 12. To change an existing template, you must first open it by selecting *Open* from the **File** menu.

In the *Open* dialog box, change the *List Files of Type* option to *Document Templates (*.dot).* You may need to change to the *winword\template* directory to list all the template files; it does not happen automatically.

Figure 13. Find and select the template you want to edit, and click on *OK*.

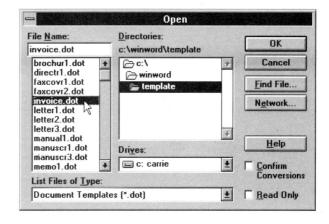

After making the necessary changes to the open template, choose *Save* from the **File** menu to update these changes.

CHANGING A DOCUMENT'S TEMPLATE

The template you use to create a document remains attached to that document, but you can change it. This changes the working environment of the document, but the formatting and the styles do not change, even if the new template has different styles. Any text in the newly attached template does not appear either. Any changes you have made to the page setup are also unaffected when you attach a new template.

Use the *Templates* command to copy items to a template from other templates and documents, attach a different template to a document, and attach extra templates so you can use items from that template.

COPYING ITEMS TO A TEMPLATE

Figure 14. To copy items between templates, first choose *Templates* from the **File** menu, and in the *Templates and Add-ins* dialog box click on the *Organizer* button.

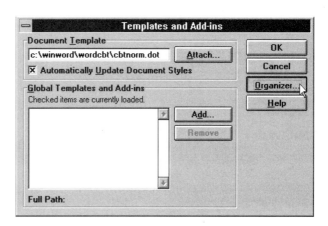

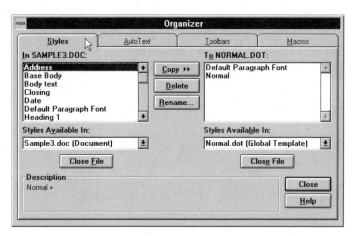

Figure 15. In the *Organizer* dialog box, select the tab for the items you want to copy—either *Styles, AutoText, Toolbars,* or *Macros.*

The list box on the left shows the items stored in the active document's template, and the items stored in the *Normal* template are in the list box on the right.

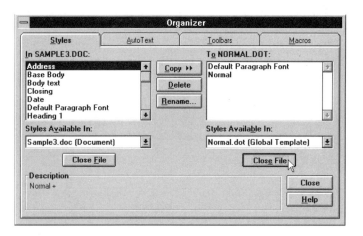

Figure 16. To copy items to or from a different template or document, choose the *Close File* button below the appropriate list box.

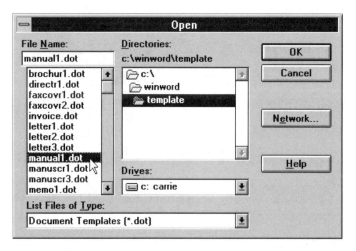

Figure 17. An *Open File* button appears in place of the *Close File* button. Click on it to open the template or document you want to copy items from.

This displays the *Open* dialog box. Select *Word Documents* or *Document Templates* in the *List Files of Type* drop-down list box to find the file. Click on *OK.*

Figure 18. Back in the *Organizer* dialog box, highlight items in the list box that you want to copy and choose the *Copy* button.

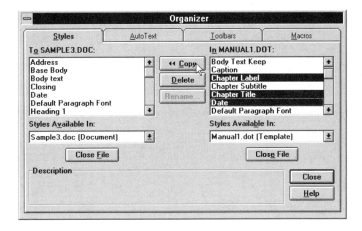

Figure 19. Word copies these items over to the selected template or document.

If you copy an item to a template that already contains an item with the same name, Word asks you to confirm that you want to replace the existing item.

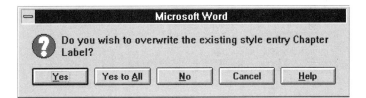

ATTACHING A DIFFERENT TEMPLATE TO A DOCUMENT

When you create a new document based on a template, that template remains attached to the document until you attach a different one. If you attach a different template that is better suited to your document, customized items such as macros and menu settings reflect the items stored in the new template. Items from the original template are no longer available to that document, unless the original was the *Normal* template.

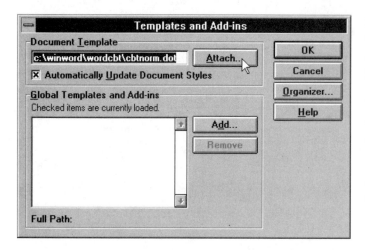

Figure 20. To attach a new template to a document, open the document and select *Templates* from the **File** menu.

This activates the *Templates and Add-ins* dialog box. Click on the *Attach* button.

(Alternatively, type in the name of the template you want and click on *OK*.)

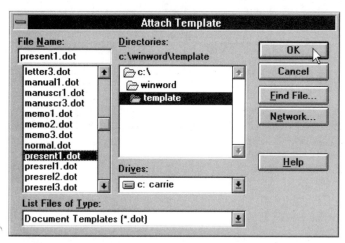

Figure 21. Choose a template from the *File Name* list box in the *Attach Template* dialog box, then choose *OK*.

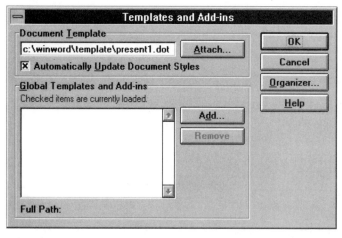

Figure 22. The *Document Template* text box in the *Templates and Add-ins* dialog box displays the name of the template. Click on *OK*.

After you change the template, the contents and document formatting of the document remain. Styles and text formatting change if you select the *Automatically Update Document Styles* check box in the *Templates and Add-ins* dialog box.

ATTACHING EXTRA TEMPLATES

If you don't want to attach a different template to the document, but you want to use items from another template, load the template as a global template. You can then use this template's macros, AutoText and customized settings in all documents. Styles in additional global templates are not added to your document.

Figure 23. Choose *Templates* from the **File** menu. Word opens the *Templates and Add-ins* dialog box. The *Global Templates and Add-ins* section displays the templates that are already available. Select the template's check box that you want to make globally available.

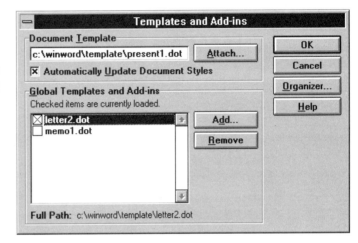

Figure 24. If the template you want is not displayed, click *Add* to activate the *Add Template* dialog box and find the template. Choose a template and click on *OK*.

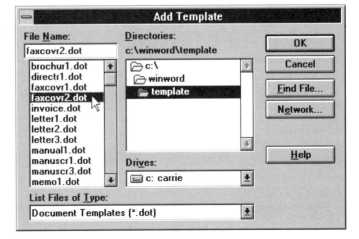

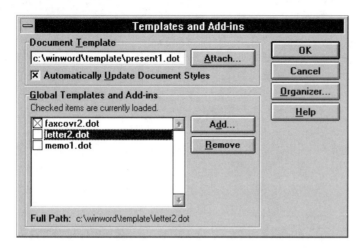

Figure 25. Word adds the template name to the *Global Templates and Add-ins* list box in the *Templates and Add-ins* dialog box, and selects it for global use (indicated by the check mark).

Repeat this process for all templates you want to make global. To close a template but keep it listed, deselect its check box. To close a template and remove it from the list, select it and click on the *Remove* button.

To load the selected templates, choose *OK*.

When you are using global templates, customized settings may conflict. Word resolves these conflicts with this order of priorities: the template attached to the active document; the *Normal* template; and additional global templates in alphabetical order.

DOCUMENT CHECKING TOOLS 8

WORD TOOLS

Microsoft Word provides a number of tools in the **Tools** menu that can assist you when working on a document. This chapter looks at the spelling checker, grammar checker, thesaurus, hyphenation, language, and word count.

CHOOSING A DICTIONARY

Figure 1. Click on the *Language* command from the **Tools** menu to select a language dictionary to use with the document checking tools.

Figure 2. In the *Language* dialog box, select the dictionary that you want, and click on *OK*. You may need to load your selected dictionary onto your PC through Word Setup if it is not on the hard disk.

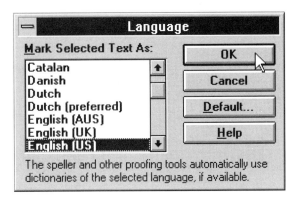

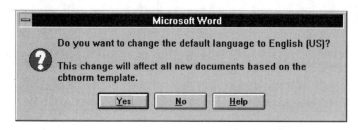

Figure 3. If you want to change the default dictionary, click on the *Default* button in the *Language* dialog box. Word displays this dialog box. Click on *Yes* to return to the document and change the default dictionary.

SPELLING CHECKER

The spelling checker in Word allows you to check your spelling in any document. You can also check a specified part of your document, or skip specific formatted parts (such as tables) during a spell check.

ACTIVATING THE SPELLING CHECKER

Figure 4. Select the *Spelling* icon (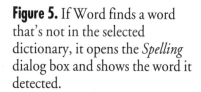) from the *Standard* toolbar, or the *Spelling* command from the Tools menu.

Word can also check selected text if you want to check only part of the document (see Figure 8).

Figure 5. If Word finds a word that's not in the selected dictionary, it opens the *Spelling* dialog box and shows the word it detected.

Word displays a list of suggested alternatives in the *Suggestions* list. To choose one of these, highlight it and click on the *Change* button. To ignore this error, click on *Ignore,* or *Ignore All* to ignore the word for the rest of the document check. If it is a name that you use frequently, you can click on the *Add* button to add it to the user dictionary.

Figure 6. After making a selection for the previous unknown word, the *Spelling* dialog box displays the next spelling error it detects. If the suggestion is the correct substitute, click on the *Change* or the *Change All* button. Click on the *Undo Last* button to undo and return to the previous detected word.

The *Options* button takes you to the *Options* dialog box (see Figure 10). To add a misspelled word and its correct spelling to the *AutoCorrect* entry list box during the spell check, click on the *AutoCorrect* button.

(See the **AutoCorrect** section of **Chapter 2** for more information about the AutoCorrect feature.)

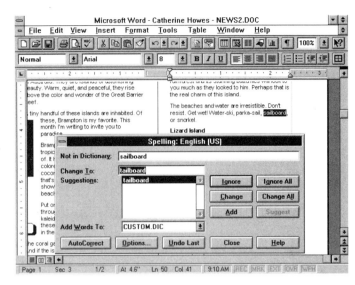

Figure 7. When Word completes the spelling check, it displays this dialog box. Click on *OK* to return to your spelling error free document.

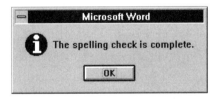

CHECKING SELECTED TEXT

Figure 8. To check specific text, select it before activating the spelling checker, and Word checks this section only. You can also check single words using this method.

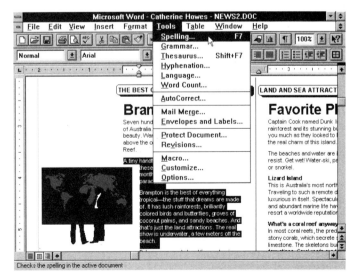

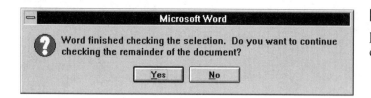

Figure 9. Word then displays this prompt box asking if you want to check the rest of the document.

SPELL CHECKING OPTIONS

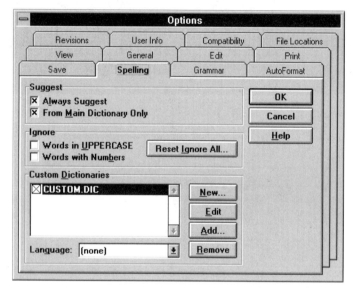

Figure 10. Selecting the *Options* button in the *Spelling* dialog box (Figure 6) opens the *Options* dialog box. Here you can customize how the spelling checker operates and what custom dictionaries it uses.

GRAMMAR CHECKER

Figure 11. To use the grammar checker, put the insertion point at the beginning of the section you would like checked; then select *Grammar* from the **Tools** menu.

By default, the grammar checker checks both grammar and spelling. If it detects a spelling error, it activates the *Spelling* dialog box (Figure 6). When you have changed or ignored the error, Word opens either the *Spelling* dialog box or the *Grammar* dialog box, depending on what error it detects next.

Figure 12. The *Grammar* dialog box displays a sentence, and also a suggestion as to why Word has selected this sentence.

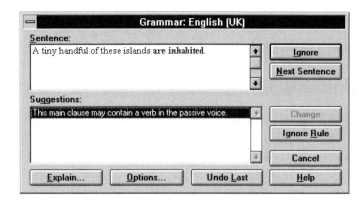

Figure 13. Click on the *Explain* button if you need a more detailed explanation. The *Grammar Explanation* dialog box explains more precisely what Word thinks is wrong with the sentence to give you a better idea of how to fix it.

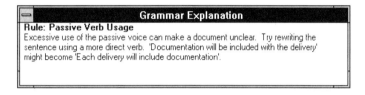

When you have read through the explanation, double-click on the Control menu box to close the dialog box.

Figure 14. Click on the *Ignore* button to ignore the suggestion and move on. Click on the *Next Sentence* button after making any corrections, so Word moves through the document and onto the next problem. You can also click on *Change* to change the problem with Word's suggestion and move through the document.

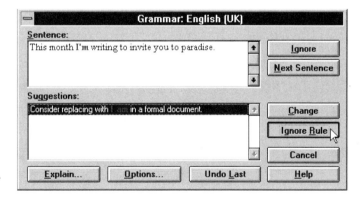

Click on the *Ignore Rule* button if you don't want to change the problem or have Word detect the same type of error again in the current check.

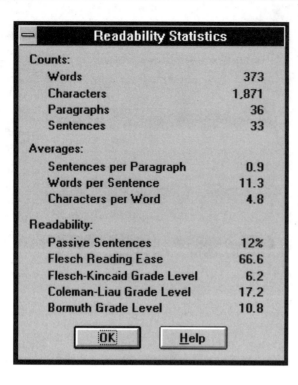

Figure 15. When you have reached the end of the document Word displays this dialog box (if you have *Show Readability Statistics* checked in the *Grammar* tab of the *Options* dialog box in the **Tools** menu—see Figure 16).

The *Counts* and *Averages* statistics are self-explanatory.

The *Readability* section shows how easy or difficult your document is to read, based on different grading levels. *Passive Sentences* displays percentage of sentences containing passive voice, rather than active voice. The other statistics give you values that are based on some widely used readability formulas.

GRAMMAR OPTIONS

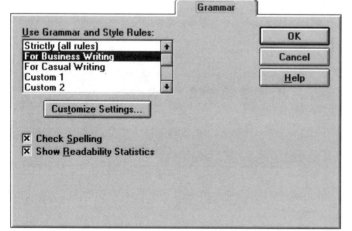

Figure 16. You can display the *Grammar* tab in the *Options* dialog box through the *Options* button in the *Grammar* dialog box, or choose *Options* from the **Tools** menu.

From here, you can set the rules Word uses to check the grammar and style of a document.

Figure 17. Click on the *Customize Settings* button on the *Grammar* tab to activate this dialog box and customize the options for the grammar and style rules.

Click on the *Explain* button and Word will show you an explanation of the selected rule. The *Reset All* button restores the default checking rules for the currently selected set of grammar rules. Once you are happy with your selection, click on *OK*.

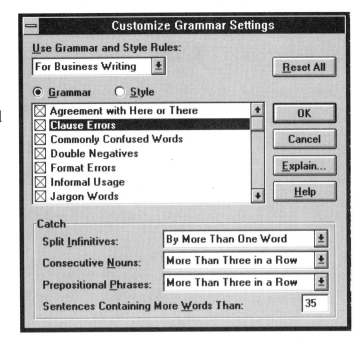

GRAMMAR CHECKING SELECTED TEXT

Figure 18. You can select parts of your document for grammar checking. Highlight the required section, then select *Grammar* from the **Tools** menu.

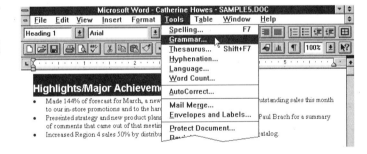

Figure 19. After Word has checked your selection, a prompt box asks if you want to check the rest of the document. The *Readability Statistics* dialog box (Figure 15) then appears showing the facts for the selected text.

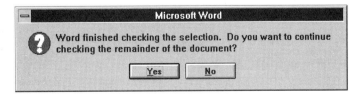

THESAURUS

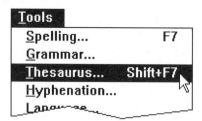

Figure 20. You can use the thesaurus to find synonyms for a selected word in your document. Highlight a word from your document or put the insertion point in it, and select *Thesaurus* from the **Tools** menu.

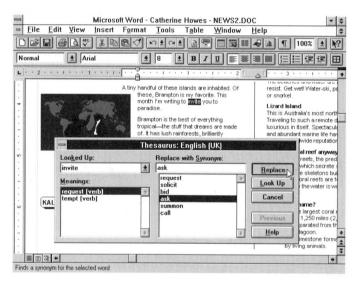

Figure 21. The *Thesaurus* dialog box shows synonyms for the *Looked Up* word in the *Replace with Synonym* list box. Where there are multiple meanings in the *Meanings* list box, you can select a different meaning and a different list of synonyms appears.

Highlight one of the displayed words, and click on *Replace* to replace the selected word.

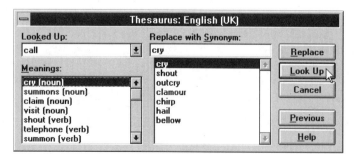

Figure 22. You can also highlight a word from the *Meanings* or *Replace with Synonym* list box, and click on the *Look Up* button to display a list of synonyms for that word.

Figure 23. You may also see *Related Words* in the *Meanings* list box. Click on this to display a list of related words (or antonyms) instead of synonyms.

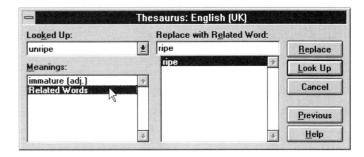

Figure 24. To return back to the word you originally selected, open the *Looked Up* drop-down list box and select the original word. You can also click on the *Previous* button to move back through the list of words.

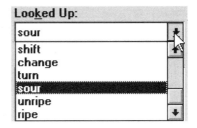

HYPHENATION

In a document you may find a lot of "white" space at the end of lines and between words, especially if you have used multiple columns and full justification. You can use the *Hyphenation* command to help alleviate this problem. It reduces the raggedness of unjustified text so you can fit more text on the page. In justified text, hyphenation can reduce the amount of white space between words.

Figure 25. Word hyphenates your document from where you position the insertion point; if you want to hyphenate only part of the document, select that part of your document. Then, choose *Hyphenation* from the **Tools** menu to open this dialog box.

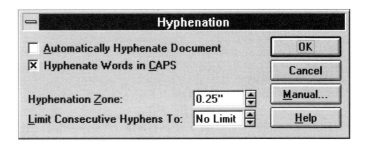

Automatically Hyphenate Document automatically hyphenates text as you type. The *Hyphenate Words in CAPS* check box is selected by default. If you do not want to hyphenate capitalized words, click in the check box to deselect the command.

The *Hyphenation Zone* text box controls whether Word hyphenates a line. If you decrease the *Hyphenation Zone* measurement, Word increases the amount of hyphenation, and this reduces raggedness. If you increase this measurement, Word decreases the amount of hyphenation, so text is more ragged. The default setting is 0.25 inches from the right margin. A word that falls within this zone and is too long for the line is hyphenated.

The *Limit Consecutive Hyphens To* option lets you determine a maximum number of consecutive lines of text that you want to end with hyphens.

Then, start the hyphenation process by clicking on *OK*.

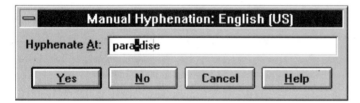

Figure 26. If you click on the *Manual* button in the *Hyphenation* dialog box (Figure 25), Word displays each word to be hyphenated in the *Hyphenate At* text box of the *Manual Hyphenation* dialog box, and suggests where you should hyphenate the word.

Choose:

• *Yes* to hyphenate the word where Word has indicated.

• *No* to leave the word intact.

• *Cancel* to stop hyphenating. (The hyphens that Word has already inserted remain in the document.)

You can also change the hyphen position, and then click on *Yes*.

The dotted vertical line within the word in the *Hyphenate At* text box indicates the margin on your page.

Figure 27. Word indicates that it has completed hyphenation with this dialog box.

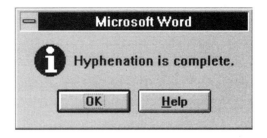

WORD COUNT

Figure 28. When you select *Word Count* from the **Tools** menu, Word opens the *Word Count* dialog box. This gives you statistics about the number of pages, words, characters, paragraphs, and lines in your active document.

Select the check box at the bottom to include footnotes and endnotes in the document statistics.

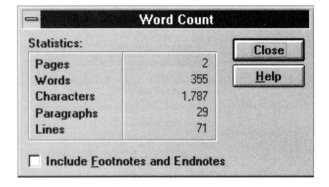

PAGE VIEWS 9

DIFFERENT PAGE VIEWS

Word offers six page views: *Normal, Outline, Page Layout, Master Document, Print Preview,* and *Full Screen.*

NORMAL VIEW

Figure 1. *Normal* view is the default view for Word. You activate *Normal* view with the *Normal* command in the **View** menu, or by clicking on the *Normal View* button at the left of the horizontal scroll bar.

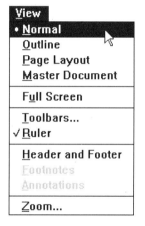

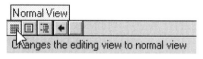

Figure 2. You can perform all editing and formatting in *Normal* view. This view provides WYSIWYG (What You See Is What You Get) text attributes, but displays columns as one long column, and does not show graphics where they print. You cannot see headers and footers directly in *Normal* view.

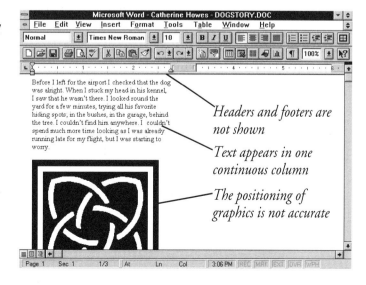

Headers and footers are not shown

Text appears in one continuous column

The positioning of graphics is not accurate

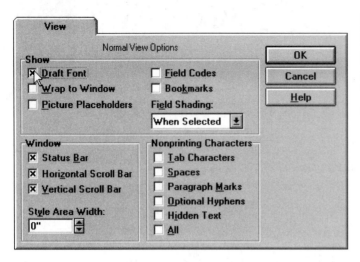

Figure 3. To speed up editing time in *Normal* view, select *Draft Font* in the *View* tab of the *Options* dialog box (activated from the **Tools** menu). This simplifies the editing screen.

OUTLINE VIEW

You use this view for organizing your documents into multiple levels of headings, subheadings, and body text to help structure your ideas and plan your document. *Outline* view shows the relationship between topics. You can collapse and expand text to view and reorganize the main topics.

In *Outline* view, you can type, revise, and apply character formats to text. However, if you want to format paragraphs, you need to do so in *Normal* or *Page Layout* view.

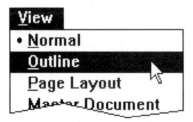

Figure 4. Activate *Outline* view by selecting *Outline* from the **View** menu, or with the *Outline View* button on the horizontal scroll bar.

THE OUTLINE TOOLBAR

Figure 5. In *Outline* view, Word displays the *Outline* toolbar in place of the ruler, and markers appear down the left side of the document.

The following figures summarize the *Outline* toolbar buttons and their functions.

Figure 6. The left-pointing *Promote* button promotes selected text to a higher level heading.

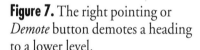

Figure 7. The right pointing or *Demote* button demotes a heading to a lower level.

Figure 8. Click on this button to demote a heading to body text, which is the lowest heading level.

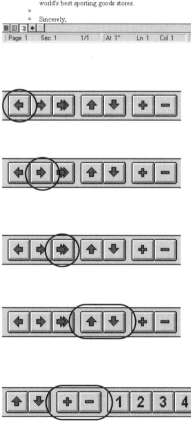

Figure 9. The up and down buttons move the selected heading above or below its preceding heading.

Figure 10. The plus (*Expand*) and minus (*Contract*) buttons expand or contract the text beneath a heading one level at a time. Word refers to the text beneath a heading as subtext.

Figure 11. You use buttons 1 through 8 to expand or contract the outline to a specified level of headings. For example, if you have five different levels of headings, and you only want to see the first three, click on the "3" button to remove levels four and five from the screen. Word does not display them until you expand them again, or you change the view.

Figure 12. The *All* button expands or collapses the whole outline.

Figure 13. Click on this button if you want to show just the first line of body text (or deactivate it to show all the text again).

Figure 14. Use the *Show Formatting* button to show or hide the character formatting of the heading levels.

Figure 15. Click on the *Master Document View* button to switch to this view. See **Master Document** later in this chapter.

CREATING AN OUTLINE

Figure 16. When you assign a level heading to text, Word formats it with a built-in style and indents each level to the default tab settings. If you don't like the appearance of a heading style, you can change it. See **Chapter 6** for more information.

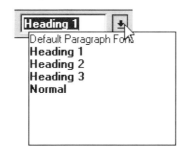

Figure 17. To change the heading level of a paragraph, select the paragraph and click on the *Promote* or *Demote* button. Alternatively, type a new heading or paragraph and apply a built-in style. If you are starting a new document, Word automatically formats the text as a level one heading. When you press Enter, the next paragraph is the same level as the previous heading.

Figure 18. Word displays the heading level of any selected paragraph in the *Styles* window on the *Formatting* toolbar.

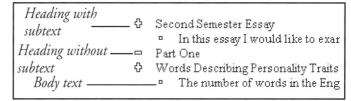

Figure 19. Word displays symbols beside each paragraph to identify the text.

⬦ Second Semester Essay

Figure 20. Word indicates collapsed text by displaying a dotted line under the heading.

PROMOTING AND DEMOTING HEADING LEVELS WITH THE MOUSE

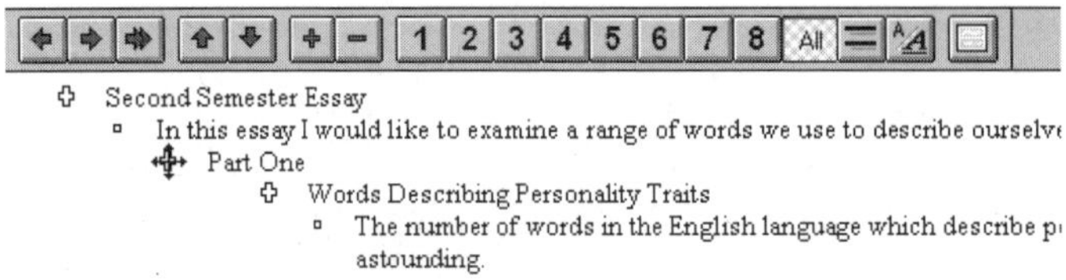

⬦ Second Semester Essay
  ▫ In this essay I would like to examine a range of words we use to describe ourselve
  ✥ Part One
      ⬦ Words Describing Personality Traits
          ▫ The number of words in the English language which describe p
             astounding.

Figure 21. To promote or demote the heading and all text under it, place the mouse pointer over the plus symbol—the pointer becomes a four-headed arrow. Click and drag to the left or right. To promote or demote just the subheading or body text, drag their minus symbols.

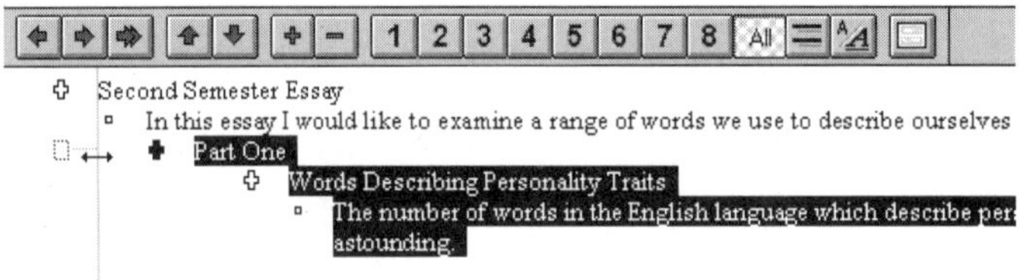

⬦ Second Semester Essay
  ▫ In this essay I would like to examine a range of words we use to describe ourselves
  ✚ Part One
      ⬦ Words Describing Personality Traits
          ▫ The number of words in the English language which describe per
             astounding.

Figure 22. As you drag the symbol, the mouse pointer changes to a two-headed arrow and Word displays a vertical line at each heading level.

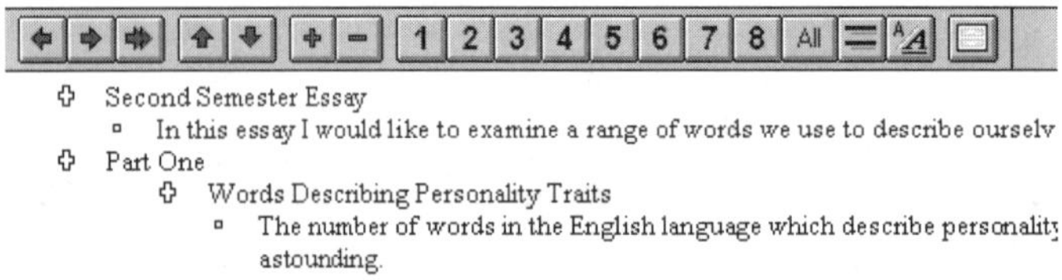

⬦ Second Semester Essay
  ▫ In this essay I would like to examine a range of words we use to describe ourselv
⬦ Part One
      ⬦ Words Describing Personality Traits
          ▫ The number of words in the English language which describe personality
             astounding.

Figure 23. When you release the mouse button, the text changes to the new level.

MOVING TEXT WITH THE MOUSE

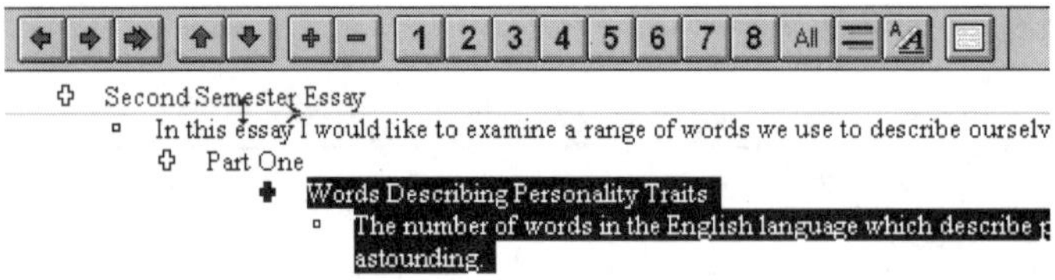

⬦ Second Semester Essay
  ▫ In this essay I would like to examine a range of words we use to describe ourselv
      ⬦ Part One
          ✚ Words Describing Personality Traits
              ▫ The number of words in the English language which describe p
                 astounding.

Figure 24. To move a heading and all the text under it, drag the plus symbol up or down. To move just the subheading or body text, drag its minus symbol. As you drag the symbol, the mouse pointer changes from a four-headed to a two-headed arrow and Word displays a horizontal line.

Figure 25. When you release the mouse button, the text moves to the new location.

NUMBERING HEADINGS

It doesn't matter when you add numbering to your outline; Word updates the numbers whenever you restructure the outline.

Figure 26. Choose *Heading Numbering* from the **Format** menu.

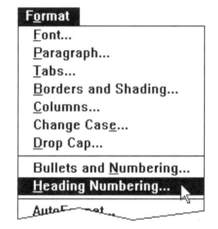

Figure 27. In the *Heading Numbering* dialog box, select a style and click on *OK*.

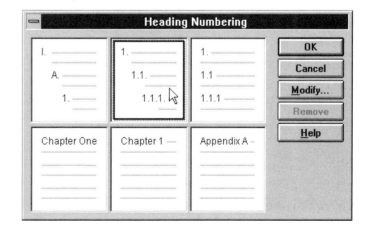

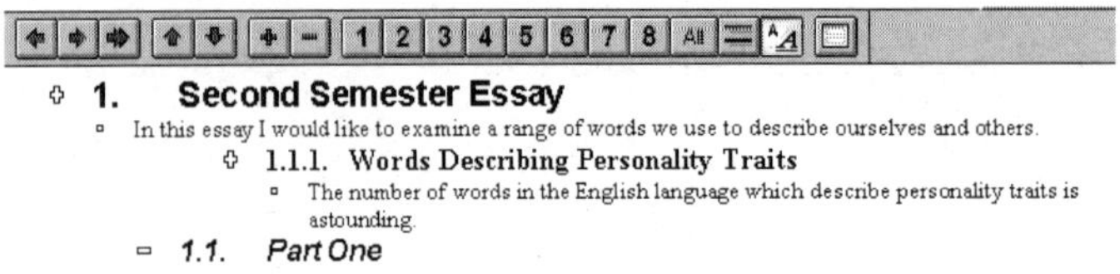

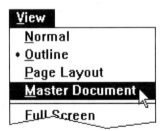

1. Second Semester Essay

In this essay I would like to examine a range of words we use to describe ourselves and others.

1.1.1. Words Describing Personality Traits

The number of words in the English language which describe personality traits is astounding.

1.1. Part One

Figure 28. Word numbers each paragraph in the document that is formatted with a heading style.

If you want to remove the numbering, choose the *Remove* button after re-opening the *Heading Numbering* dialog box (Figure 27).

PRINTING IN OUTLINE VIEW

When printing from *Outline* view, Word prints only the heading levels visible on screen. You can control the text that is printed by expanding or collapsing the outline. The heading symbols do not print.

When you have chosen what levels you want to print, click on the *Print* button on the *Formatting* toolbar. For more information about printing documents, see **Chapter 10**.

MASTER DOCUMENT VIEW

View

N̲ormal

• **O̲utline**

P̲age Layout

Master Document

Fu̲ll Screen

Figure 29. Using a master document helps you organize long documents by dividing them into subdocuments. You use *Master Document* view to create subdocuments and organize the long document as you do in *Outline* view (see the previous section). For more information about using *Master Document* view, see **Chapter 13**.

PAGE LAYOUT VIEW

Figure 30. You activate *Page Layout* view through the *Page Layout* command in the **View** menu, or click on the *Page Layout View* button on the horizontal scroll bar.

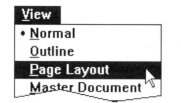

Page Layout view displays how the page will print. In this view, you see page boundaries, frames, columns, headers, footers, and footnotes in their correct positions.

Figure 31. In this view, you can edit and format the document as you normally would. In addition, you can use the mouse to reposition and size framed objects on the page, as well as edit headers and footers directly on the screen.

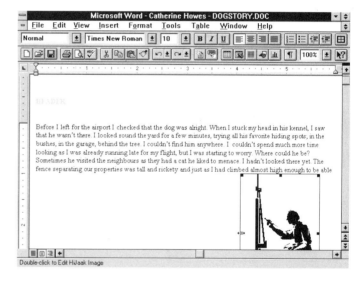

Figure 32. In the *Options* dialog box (choose *Options* from **Tools** menu), in the *Show* section of the *View* tab, you can select the *Text Boundaries* option to display boundaries around items on the page. The *Picture Placeholders* option replaces any graphics with a non-printing border, to speed up the screen redraw time.

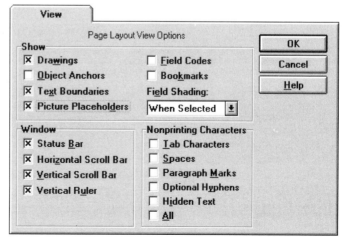

CHANGING PAGES IN PAGE LAYOUT VIEW

Figure 33. To move quickly through a document in *Page Layout* view, click on the Page Back or Page Forward buttons at the bottom right of the screen.

VIEWING A DOCUMENT AT DIFFERENT MAGNIFICATIONS

THE ZOOM CONTROL BOX

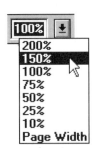

Figure 34. To see different views of your document click on the *Zoom Control* drop-down list on the *Standard* toolbar and select a magnification percentage from the list. You can also type a percentage into the text box.

THE ZOOM COMMAND

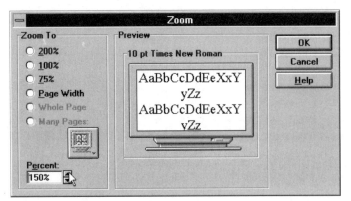

Figure 35. Another way to change views is to choose the *Zoom* command in the **View** menu and choose a preset option in the *Zoom To* section of the *Zoom* dialog box, or define a percentage in the *Percent* text box between 10% and 200%.

Figure 36. The *Page Width* option in the *Zoom To* section reduces or enlarges the display of a document so that the width of the page is visible.

Figure 37. *Whole Page* reduces the display so that the page margins fit within the document window. This is useful if you want to see all the text on pages with landscape orientation.

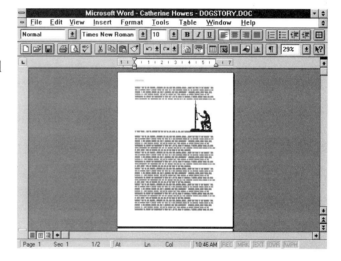

Figure 38. *Many Pages* lets you view more than one page.

You need to be in *Page Layout* view to be able to select the *Whole Page* and *Many Pages* options.

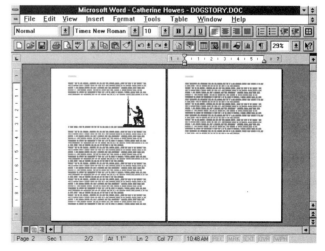

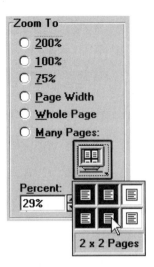

Figure 39. To see more than two pages, click on the monitor in the *Zoom* dialog box. Then click and drag to select the number of pages you want.

Figure 40. The *Preview* box displays how pages and text will look with the options you have selected.

FULL SCREEN VIEW

Figure 41. To view your document on screen without any screen elements and features, choose *Full Screen* from the **View** menu. In this view, you can still choose commands with shortcut keys and display shortcut menus while you work.

To return to your previous view, click on the *Full Screen* button or press Esc.

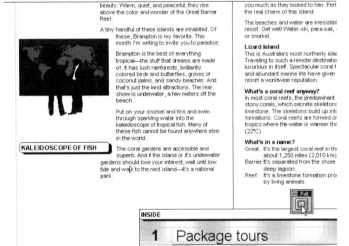

PRINT PREVIEW

Print Preview gives an accurate representation of how the printed page will look. You can change margins, move and resize graphics, and edit your text in *Print Preview*.

Figure 42. You activate it with the *Print Preview* command in the File menu.

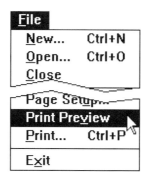

Figure 43. Alternatively, click on the *Print Preview* button on the *Standard* toolbar, or press Ctrl+F2 on the keyboard.

THE PRINT PREVIEW TOOLBAR

Figure 44. The *Print* button prints the document using the current default settings.

VIEWING PAGES

Figure 45. Click on the *One Page* button to display one page at a time.

Figure 46. To display more than one page, click on the *Multiple Pages* button. Then click and drag the mouse over the grid to select the number of pages you want to view.

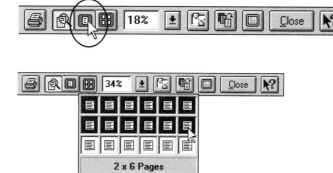

2 x 6 Pages

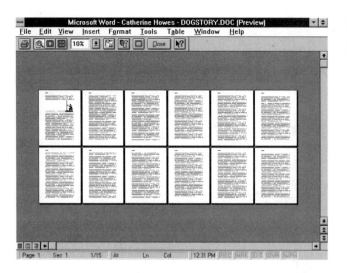

Figure 47. Word displays the pages.

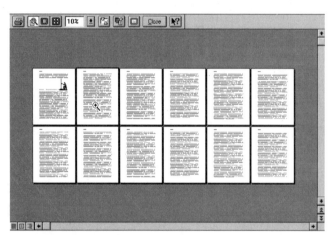

Figure 48. To view a magnified area of a page, first make sure the *Magnifier* button is activated. When you move the mouse on a page the mouse pointer becomes a magnifying glass. Move it to the part of the page you want to view and click the mouse button.

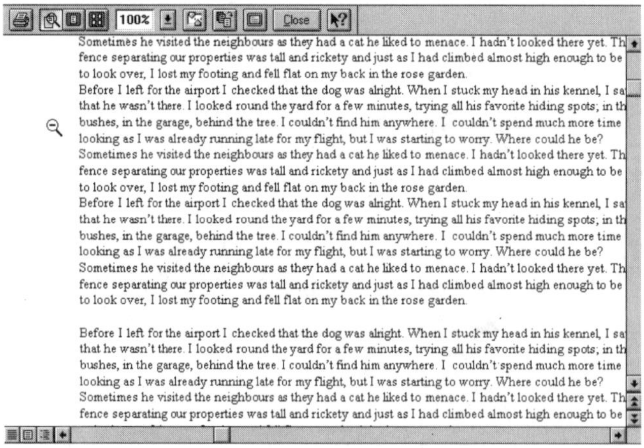

Figure 49. This enlarges your view to 100%. Click the mouse button again to restore the original view.

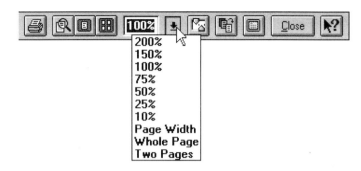

Figure 50. You can also choose magnification options from the *Zoom Control* drop-down list box to change the view of your document or type in your own zoom value in the text box.

You click on the scroll bars to move between pages in the *Print Preview* screen. Use the top or bottom arrow or the Page Back and Page Forward buttons to move one page at a time or drag the scroll box to move a number of pages. The Page Up and Page Down keys on your keyboard also move you one page at a time.

Figure 51. Click on the *Full Screen* button to view document pages without the title bar, menu bar, status bar, and scroll bars.

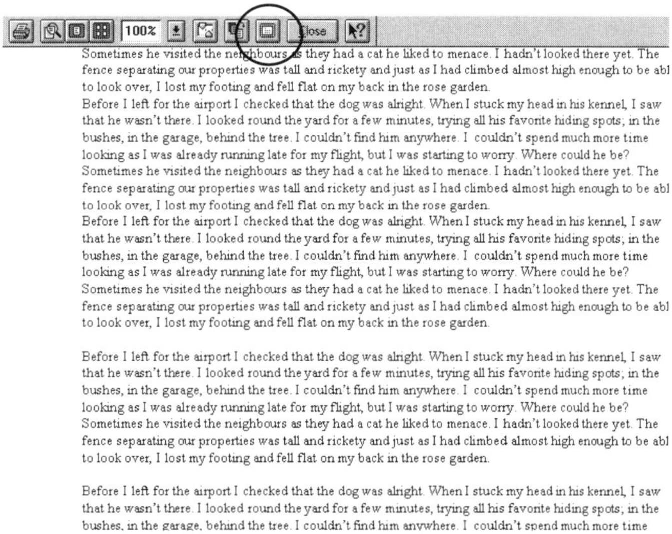

TO MOVE MARGINS

Figure 52. If the rulers are not visible, click on the *View Ruler* button on the toolbar.

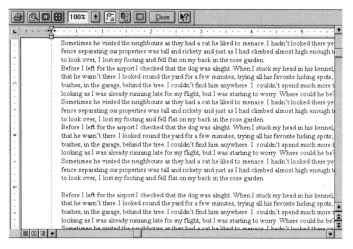

Figure 53. You can alter margins in *Print Preview* the way you do in *Page Layout* view (see **Chapter 5**). Place the mouse pointer on the margin boundary of the horizontal or vertical ruler until it becomes a two-headed arrow. Then click and drag to change the margins. You can also adjust the margins in the *Page Setup* dialog box (see **Chapter 5**).

EDITING TEXT

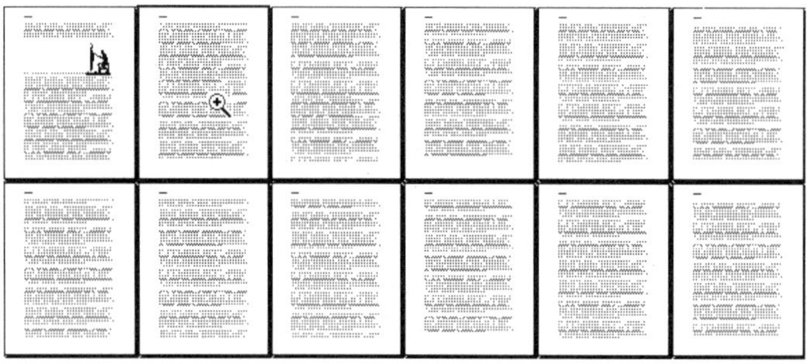

Figure 54. To edit text, you have to magnify the section of the document you want to edit by clicking the area when the mouse pointer is a magnifying glass.

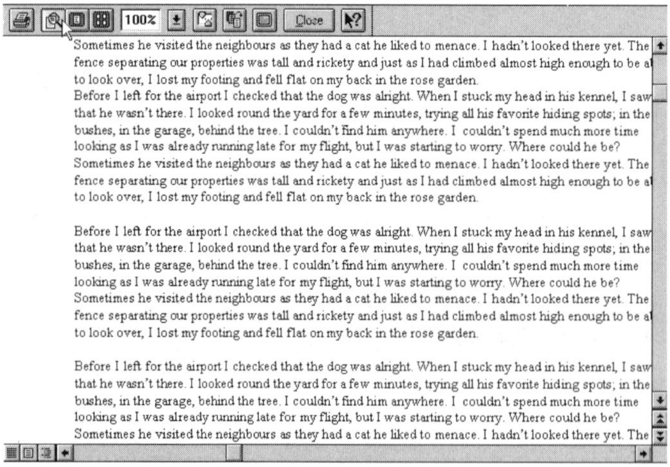

Figure 55. Then deselect the *Magnifier* button to display the I-beam mouse pointer and the insertion point. Now you can edit your document.

SHRINK TO FIT BUTTON

Figure 56. If you have a small amount of text on the last page of your document, choose the *Shrink to Fit* button on the *Print Preview* toolbar to try and reduce the number of pages.

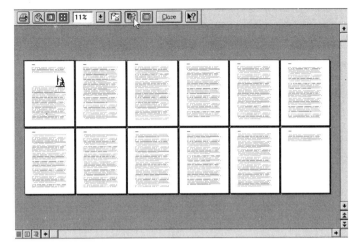

Figure 57. Word displays this dialog box if it can't shrink your document.

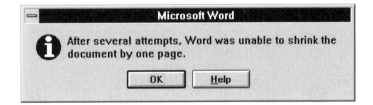

PRINTING YOUR DOCUMENT

You can print from your Word document at any time, during any stage of your document.

   You can also print multiple documents from the *Find File* dialog box. See the **Find File** section in **Chapter 3** for information on how to do this.

Figure 1. You should select a printer before formatting your document, because your choice of fonts in Word depends on the printer you have selected. If you select a printer after you have created your document, it can cause formatting problems throughout your document. To make sure you have the correct printer selected, choose *Print* from the **File** menu.

Figure 2. Then in the *Print* dialog box, click on the *Printer* button.

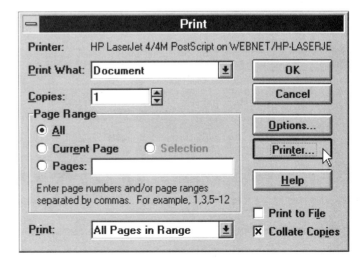

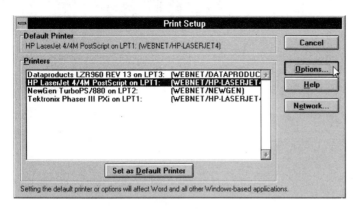

Figure 3. This activates the *Print Setup* dialog box. Select the printer you want from the *Printers* list box. To view the printer setup options, click on the *Options* button.

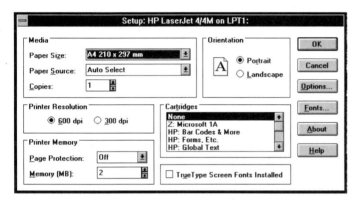

Figure 4. This activates the printer's setup dialog box. From here you can select the paper source from the *Paper Source* drop-down list box; paper size from its drop-down list box; and the paper orientation.

Once you have made your selections, click on the *OK* button to exit the printer's setup dialog box. Click on *Close* in the *Print Setup* dialog box to return to the *Print* dialog box.

PRINT PREVIEW

Figure 5. You can see what your document will look like before you print. To do this, choose *Print Preview* from the **File** menu.

Figure 6. This activates the *Print Preview* screen. In this screen, you can view multiple pages of your document and alter the layout (see **Chapter 9** for more about *Print Preview*).

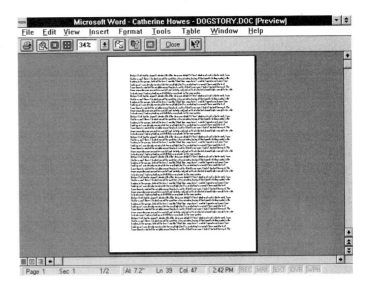

THE PRINT COMMAND

Figure 7. To print one copy of your document with the default settings, click on the *Print* button on the *Standard* toolbar.

Figure 8. To open the *Print* dialog box, select the *Print* command from the **File** menu.

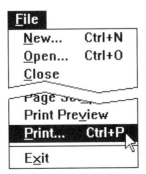

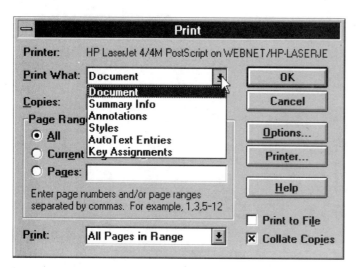

Figure 9. In the *Print What* drop-down list box, the *Document* option is selected by default; this prints the document as you see it in *Print Preview*. The *Print What* drop-down list also shows a list of elements that are related to the document, such as styles, glossary entries, and annotations. You can also print these by selecting them from the list.

Figure 10. In the *Copies* text box, type the number of copies you want to print. You can also click on the up and down arrows to change the value.

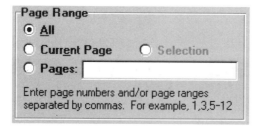

Figure 11. In the *Page Range* section of this dialog box, choose the *All* radio button to print the entire document. If you click on the *Current Page* radio button, Word prints the page containing the insertion point. If you have any text or graphics selected on the page, the *Current Page* option changes to the *Selection* option. This means that Word will only print the highlighted items in the document.

Figure 12. To print only certain pages of your document select the *Pages* radio button. In the text box, specify the pages you want to print. For example to print consecutive pages 23 through 26 (type 23-26); nonconsecutive pages 23 and 26 (type 23,26); section two (type s2).

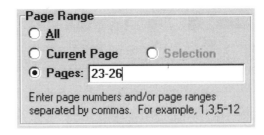

Figure 13. The *Print* drop-down list box lets you choose to print odd or even pages.

Figure 14. If you want to print your Word document to a disk, rather than to a printer, click on the *Print to File* check box at the bottom of the *Print* dialog box. You would do this if you use a service bureau for printing, or you aren't directly connected to the printer.

Figure 15. Selecting the *Print to File* check box displays the *Print to File* dialog box when you click on *OK* in the *Print* dialog box. You need to type in the output path and filename. You can include the drive and directory in the name or use the *Directories* and *Drives* lists to name and direct your file. You must also put a *.prn* extension after the document name.

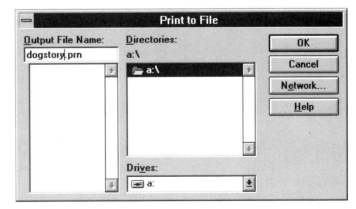

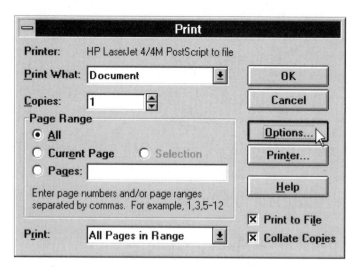

Figure 16. Click on the *Options* button in the *Print* dialog box to activate the *Options* dialog box.

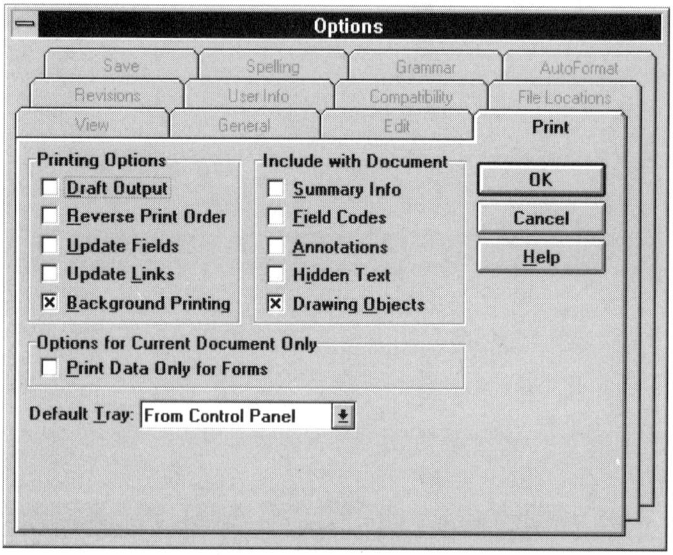

Figure 17. This dialog box contains further options for the printing of a document. Once you have selected an option from this dialog box, it remains in effect until you deselect it.

In the *Printing Options* section of the dialog box, the *Draft Output* option lets you print the document in draft mode. The *Reverse Print Order* option prints the document from the last page to the first page. You can also update fields and links before printing. Click in corresponding check boxes to select these options.

In the *Include with Document* section of the *Options* dialog box, you can choose what else you want to print. The *Summary Info* option prints the document's summary information after it has printed the document. If you select the *Field Codes* option, Word prints the field codes instead of the field results. The *Field Codes* option is available only if you have selected *Document, Annotations,* or *Glossary* from the *Print* drop-down list in the *Print* dialog box.

If you select the *Annotations* option, Word prints all annotations at the end of the document. Annotations are formatted as hidden text, therefore the *Hidden Text* option is automatically selected when you choose the *Annotations* option. The *Hidden Text* option prints all text associated with the document that you have formatted as hidden text.

PRINTING ENVELOPES AND LABELS

You can print envelopes and labels straight away or save them to print later. Word finds the address you've included in your document for the delivery address. For the return address, Word uses the address specified in the *Mailing Address* box on the *User Info* category tab in the *Options* dialog box (see **Chapter 3**).

CREATING AND PRINTING ENVELOPES

Figure 18. To create an address, choose *Envelopes and Labels* from the **Tools** menu. If your document contains more than one address, select the address you want as the delivery address.

Figure 19. This opens the *Envelopes and Labels* dialog box. You need to have the *Envelopes* tab active. Accept the delivery address in the *Delivery Address* box or type another address.

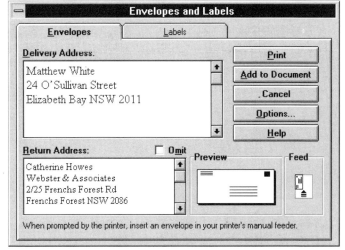

Figure 20. To print a return address, accept the inserted address in the *Return Address* box or type a new return address. If you do not want a return address on your envelope, click in the *Omit* check box.

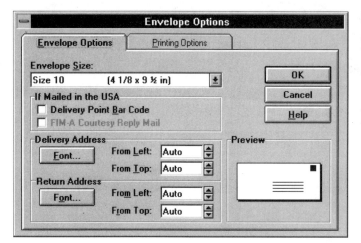

Figure 21. To customize your envelope, choose the *Options* button in the *Envelopes and Labels* dialog box. Then in the *Envelope Options* dialog box, select the *Envelope Options* tab and change the envelope size and formatting.

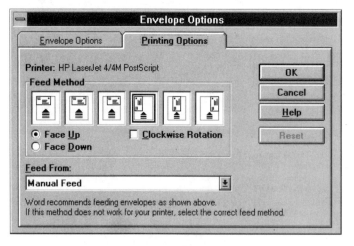

Figure 22. To specify the way you feed envelopes into the printer, select the *Printing Options* tab and choose from the options. Then click on *OK*.

Figure 23. Back in the *Envelopes and Labels* dialog box, you can click on the *Print* button to print the envelope immediately. Alternatively, click on the *Add to Document* button to insert the envelope in a new section at the beginning of the document. Then, choose *Print* from the **File** menu to print the document and the attached envelope. If you want to change an existing envelope that is already attached to your document, choose the *Change Document* button (which replaces the *Add to Document* button).

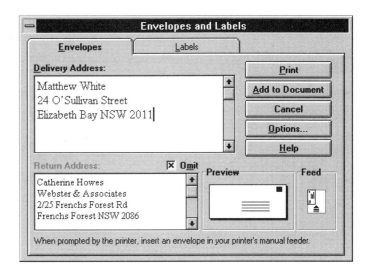

You can print the envelope by itself, even after you have added it to the document. Word inserts the envelope in your document on a page numbered "0." In the *Print* dialog box, type "0" in both the *From* and *To* boxes.

Figure 24. If you have typed in a return address in the *Envelopes and Labels* dialog box for the first time or replaced an existing return address, Word asks you whether you want to save the return address as the default return address for future documents.

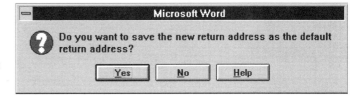

CREATING AND PRINTING LABELS

You can print an address on a single mailing label or it can print the same address on a whole sheet of labels.

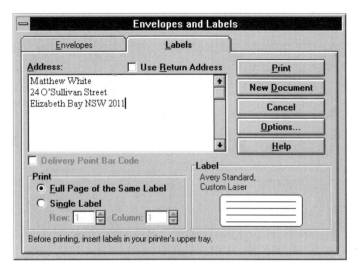

Figure 25. Choose *Envelopes and Labels* from the **Tools** menu to open the *Envelopes and Labels* dialog box. Then select the *Labels* tab. Accept the inserted delivery address or type a new one in the *Address* box.

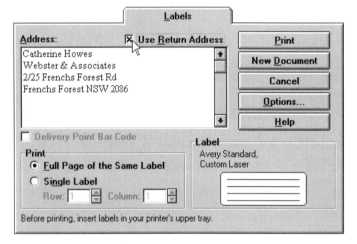

Figure 26. To print a return address, select the *Use Return Address* check box and accept this or type a new address.

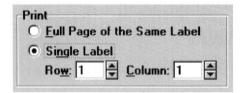

Figure 27. In the *Print* section, select the *Full Page of the Same Label* option to print a whole sheet of labels. To print a single mailing label, choose the *Single Label* option. Then in the *Row* and *Column* boxes, select the label you want to print.

Figure 28. Choose the *Options* button so you can customize the label in the *Label Options* dialog box, and click on *OK*.

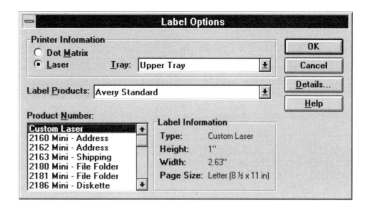

Figure 29. Back in the *Envelopes and Labels* dialog box, choose *Print* to print labels, or *New Document* to save the labels as a table in your document to use later.

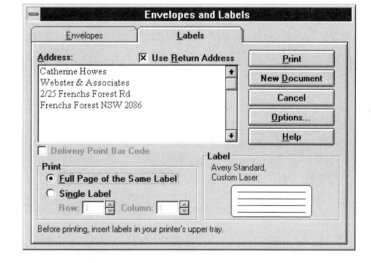

INTRODUCTION

A frame is like a container; you can insert frames around items such as text, graphics, and tables to put them anywhere in your document. You can use your mouse or the *Frame* dialog box to position a frame. When you move a frame, all the contents of the frame move with it.

WORKING WITH FRAMES

Figure 1. You should work with frames in *Page Layout* view because it displays the frame's actual size and position on the page. *Normal* or *Outline* views do not show the frame's location or size, and you cannot alter frames with the mouse in these views.

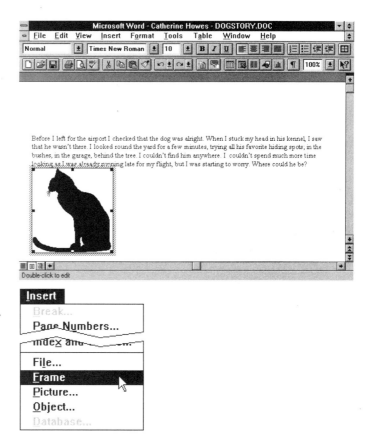

INSERTING FRAMES

AROUND SELECTED ITEMS

Figure 2. In *Page Layout* view, select the item you want to frame. Then choose *Frame* from the Insert menu.

Figure 3. Word inserts a frame around the item. Word shows the frame is selected by eight sizing handles and a border.

AN EMPTY FRAME

When you have to leave space for an element that you don't yet have, such as an illustration or some pending text, you can insert an empty frame as a placeholder, which lets you set up your final page layout without having all the elements.

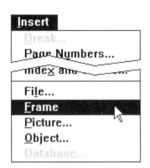

Figure 4. Make sure nothing is selected in your document, and choose the *Frame* command from the **Insert** menu.

Figure 5. The pointer changes to a crosshair; this is the frame-drawing pointer. To draw a frame, position the pointer where you want the top left corner of the frame to be and click and hold down the mouse button. Then drag the pointer diagonally to the size you want. As you draw the frame, a gray dotted line appears, which indicates the dimensions of the frame.

Figure 6. Release the mouse button to display the frame on the screen, and Word puts the insertion point in the frame ready for you to type text.

When you insert a frame around text or insert an empty frame, Word places a line border around the contents of the frame. No border is added when you frame imported graphics or tables.

Figure 7. If you are not in *Page Layout* view when you choose *Frame* from the **Insert** menu, Word prompts you to change views.

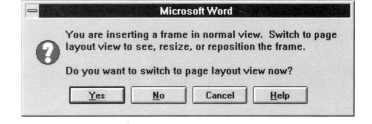

SELECTING A FRAME

Figure 8. You need to select a frame before you can alter it in any way. When the mouse pointer is over the border of the frame, the pointer changes to the positioning pointer. You use the positioning pointer to select and drag a frame. Click the mouse to select the frame. A selected frame has a border and eight sizing handles.

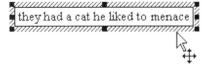

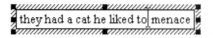

Figure 9. When you position the pointer over the contents of a frame, the pointer becomes an I-beam. Use the I-beam to select the text contents of a frame.

RESIZING FRAMES

If the frame contains an imported graphic, the graphic and the frame is resized when you resize the frame. If the frame contains text, the text wraps to adjust to the new size of the frame. If you specify dimensions in the *Frame* dialog box, the frame does not expand to contain additional text. So if you add too much text it won't be visible until you change the size of the frame.

WITH THE MOUSE

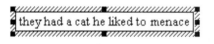

Figure 10. To resize a frame with the mouse, first select the frame you want to resize.

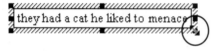

Figure 11. Put the mouse pointer over a corner handle to change the pointer to a diagonal arrow. This allows you to simultaneously change both the width and height of the frame by dragging in the direction of the arrow heads.

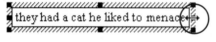

Figure 12. Placing the mouse over a left or right side handle, changes the cursor to a horizontal two-headed arrow. This allows you to change the width of a frame by dragging to the left or right.

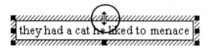

Figure 13. Placing the mouse over the top or bottom handles changes the pointer to a vertical arrow. This allows you to change the frame height by dragging up or down.

As you drag and resize, Word replaces the handles and the border with a dotted outline.

Figure 14. You can resize a framed graphic the same way you resize frames containing text (using the arrows over the handles), but this may distort the graphic.

Figure 15. You can avoid distorting graphics if you drag with the diagonal arrows on the corners of the frame, rather than with the arrows on the side handles. The diagonal arrows increase both width and height, and so keep the graphic in proportion.

Figure 16. You can also hold down the Shift key, while dragging the handles of the frame, to increase the frame size without increasing the size of, or distorting, the graphic. The mouse pointer changes shape to a cropping tool.

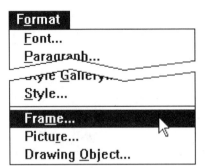

WITH THE FRAME DIALOG BOX

Figure 17. To size a selected frame exactly, first select *Frame* from the **Format** menu, or double-click on the frame's border.

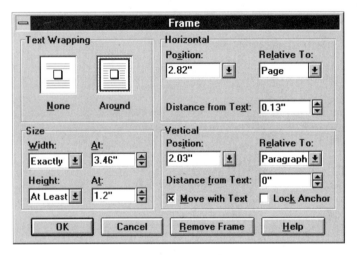

Figure 18. This activates the *Frame* dialog box containing the specifications for the selected frame.

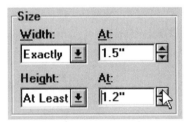

Figure 19. In the *Size* section of the dialog box, you can set the options for *Width* and *Height*. Do this by typing in the required measurement, or by clicking on the up and down arrows of the *At* text boxes.

Figure 20. In the *Width* drop-down list box, you can select either *Auto* or *Exactly*.

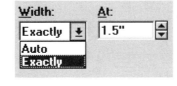

Auto adjusts for the largest width of an item in the frame. *Exactly* allows you to type, or select in the *At* box, the exact width you want for your frame.

Figure 21. In the *Height* drop-down list you can select *Auto, At Least,* or *Exactly*.

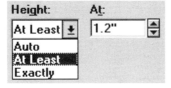

Auto adjusts for the tallest height in the frame. *At Least* allows you to specify a minimum height in the *At* box, and also adjusts for the tallest height.

Figure 22. *Exactly* allows you to specify a fixed height in the *At* box. This may hide parts of the item if the item is too big for the frame.

WITH THE RULER

Figure 23. Select the frame and drag the boundaries on the ruler to alter the frame's size.

POSITIONING FRAMES

WITH THE MOUSE

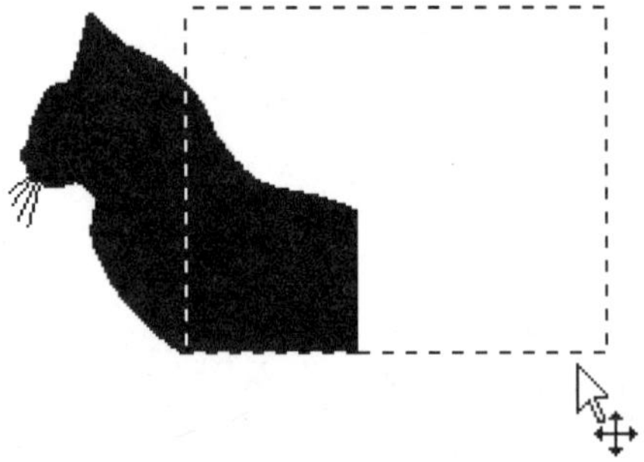

Figure 24. Place the mouse pointer on the frame border so it becomes the positioning pointer. Then click, and drag the frame to a new position. A dotted border shows the position of the frame as you drag it.

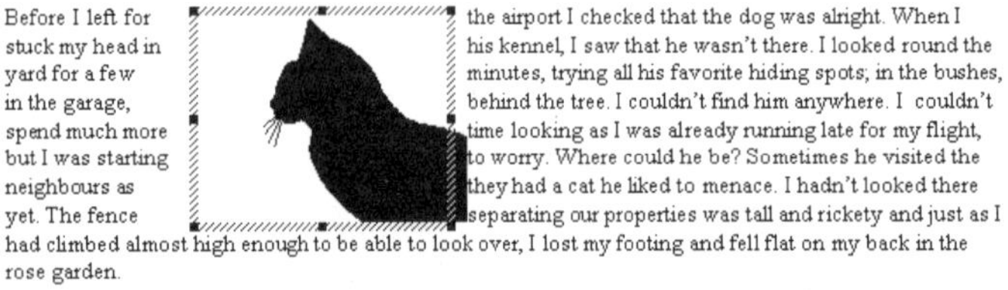

Before I left for stuck my head in yard for a few in the garage, spend much more but I was starting neighbours as yet. The fence had climbed almost high enough to be able to look over, I lost my footing and fell flat on my back in the rose garden.

the airport I checked that the dog was alright. When I his kennel, I saw that he wasn't there. I looked round the minutes, trying all his favorite hiding spots; in the bushes, behind the tree. I couldn't find him anywhere. I couldn't time looking as I was already running late for my flight, to worry. Where could he be? Sometimes he visited the they had a cat he liked to menace. I hadn't looked there separating our properties was tall and rickety and just as I

Figure 25. Word places the frame at the new location when you release the mouse button.

WITH THE FRAME DIALOG BOX

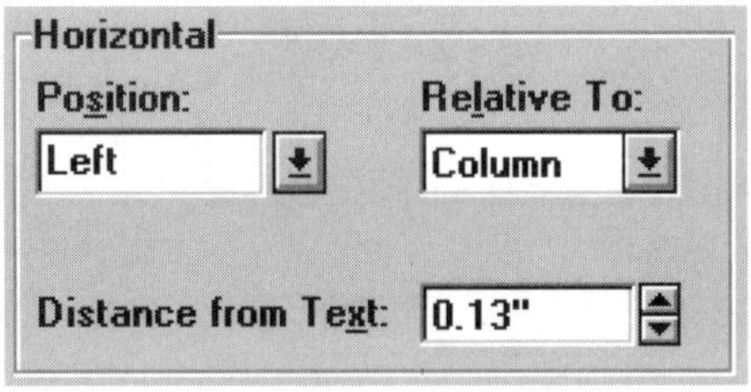

Figure 26. To position a frame exactly, select *Frame* from the **Format** menu to activate the *Frame* dialog box. The *Horizontal* section of the dialog box is where you set the horizontal position of the selected frame.

Horizontal

Position: Left

Relative To: Column

Distance from Text: 0.13"

Type a measurement directly into the *Position* text box to place the frame at a set distance from the page, margin, or column.

To align a frame horizontally either flush left, right, or centered, see the details following.

Figure 27. In the *Horizontal* section's *Position* box you can either type in your own setting, or choose from the following settings in the drop-down list box:

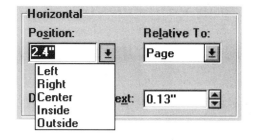

- *Left* – this places the frame at the left edge of the page, left margin, or column.

- *Right* – this places the frame at the right edge of the page, right margin, or column.

- *Center* – this centers the frame horizontally in the page, within the margins, or in a column.

- *Inside* – this places the frame at the inside edge of the page, the inside margin, or the inside edge of a column.

- *Outside* – this places the frame at the outside edge of the page, the outside margin, or the outside edge of a column.

Figure 28. The *Relative To* drop-down list in the *Horizontal* section lets you choose whether you position the frame with respect to the page, the margins, or a column.

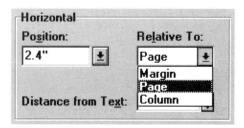

Figure 29. The *Vertical* section of the *Frame* dialog box is where you set the vertical position of the selected frame.

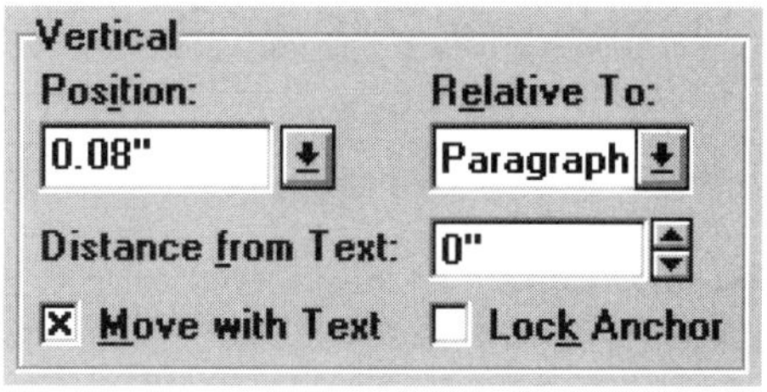

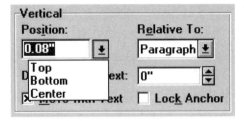

Figure 30. In the *Position* box in the *Vertical* section, you can type in your own setting to specify a vertical distance for the frame relative to the page, margins, or paragraph. Alternatively, you can choose from the following:

• *Top* – places the selected frame at the top of the page or the top margin.
• *Center* – centers the frame between the top and bottom edges of the page, or between the top and bottom margins.
• *Bottom* – places the frame at the bottom of the page or on the bottom margin.

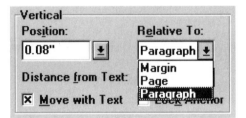

Figure 31. The *Relative To* drop-down list in the *Vertical* section lets you choose whether you position the frame vertically with respect to the page, the margins, or a paragraph.

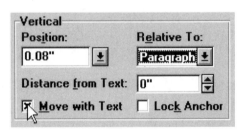

Figure 32. Select the *Move with Text* check box in the *Frame* dialog box if you want the frame to move up and down with the paragraph that you originally inserted the frame into. Word automatically adjusts the frame's vertical position, moving it with the related text. If you do not select this check box, the frame remains in a fixed position on the page.

Figure 33. By default, frames are anchored to the closest paragraph. To see what paragraph a frame is currently anchored to, select the frame and click on the *Show/Hide* button on the *Standard* toolbar.

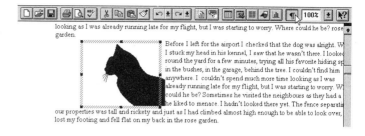

Figure 34. Word shows an anchor to indicate which paragraph the frame is connected to.

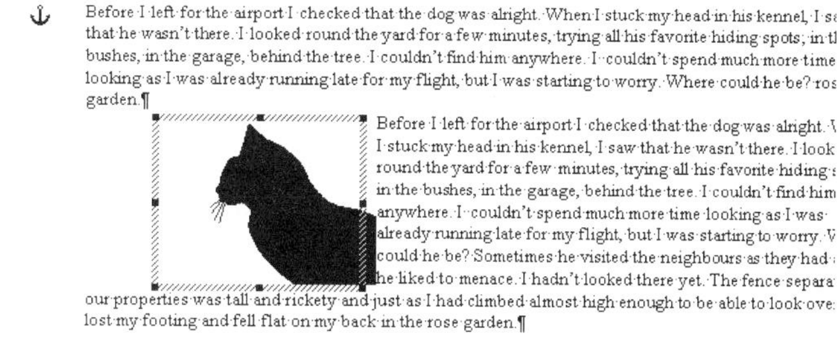

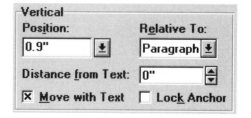

Figure 35. To specify a distance from the frame and the anchored paragraph, select *Paragraph* from the *Relative To* drop-down list in the *Vertical* section of the *Frame* dialog box. Then insert a value into the *Position* text box. If you type a positive number, the frame will move that distance below the paragraph; type a negative number to move the frame above the paragraph.

Even if you add text above the paragraph, Word moves the frame with the paragraph and maintains its set distance. This set distance is not maintained if you move the frame to a new position—it may then anchor to another paragraph.

If you want to lock a frame to its anchor paragraph, select the *Lock Anchor* check box in the *Frame* dialog box.

Figure 36. The *Distance from Text* options in the *Horizontal* and *Vertical* sections allow you to set the amount of white space between the frame and the surrounding text.

Distance from text 0"

Horizontal distance from text 1", Vertical distance from text 0.5"

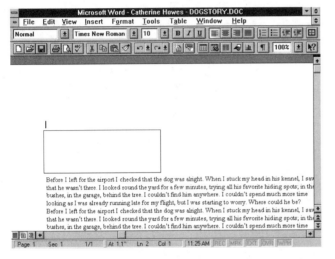

Figure 37. If you insert a frame at the beginning of your document, and later want to add text above the frame, put the insertion point in the frame, and then press Ctrl+Shift+Enter. Word adds the insertion point above the frame for you to begin typing in the *Normal* style.

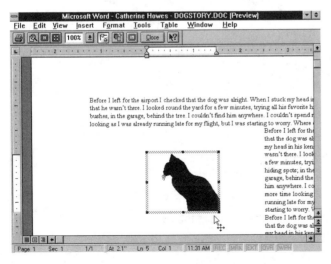

Figure 38. In *Print Preview*, you can also resize a frame and drag it to a new page or position as you do in *Page Layout* view (see earlier in this chapter).

TYPING AND FORMATTING TEXT IN A FRAME

You type, edit, and format text in a frame the same way you edit and format normal text in your document; you can use all the editing and formatting features. To change the formatting of all the paragraphs in a frame, select the frame and then apply formatting.

If you want to apply styles to the text, you should apply them before you insert the frame. If you insert the frame first, and then apply the style to the framed item, the style may remove the frame or change the frame's position according to the style definition (unless you create a style that includes a frame and its position). For more information, see **Chapter 6.**

REMOVING FRAMES

Figure 39. To remove a frame without removing the contents of the frame, select the frame and choose *Frame* from the **Format** menu. Click on the *Remove Frame* button in the *Frame* dialog box.

To remove the contents of the frame as well as the frame, select the frame, then press the Delete key.

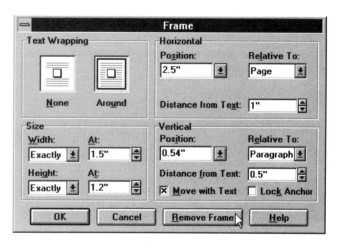

ADDING CAPTIONS

You can add a caption to a frame containing a picture, graphic, table, or other item. The caption becomes part of the frame and moves with the frame if you reposition the frame.

Figure 40. Select the item you want to add a caption to (don't select the frame). Then choose *Caption* from the **Insert** menu.

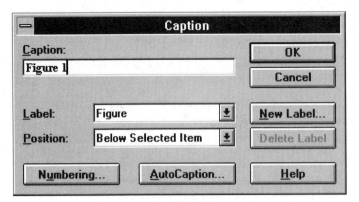

Figure 41. This opens the *Caption* dialog box. From here you can add text in the *Caption* text box.

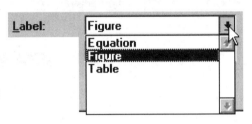

Figure 42. Choose a different label from the *Label* drop-down list box.

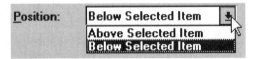

Figure 43. You also need to select a position for the caption from the *Position* drop-down list box.

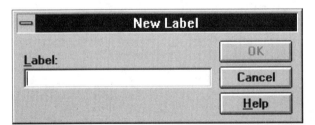

Figure 44. Click on the *New Label* button in the *Caption* dialog box to open the *New Label* dialog box and type a new label name.

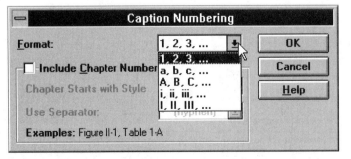

Figure 45. If you want to change the number format of the caption, click on the *Numbering* button. Then in the *Caption Numbering* dialog box, choose from the options in the *Format* drop-down list box.

Figure 46. To automatically add captions to items, click on the *AutoCaption* button in the *Caption* dialog box.

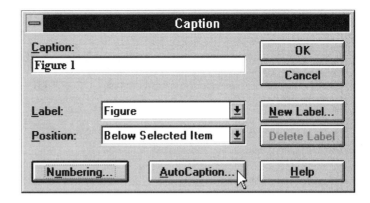

Figure 47. In the *AutoCaption* dialog box, select the check box for the type of item you want Word to add captions to from the *Add Caption When Inserting* list box.

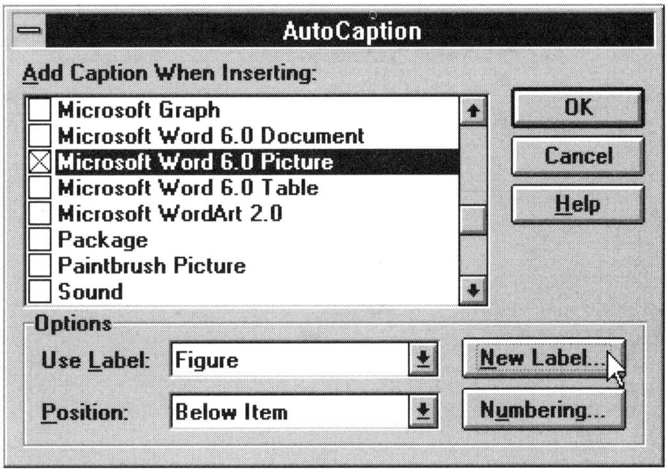

Select the label you want from the *Use Label* drop-down list box. (Click on the *New Label* button if you want to customize your own label.) Select a location for the label from the *Position* drop-down list box. If you want to change the number format, click on *Numbering.*

Repeat this process for all items you want Word to automatically add a caption to when you insert the type of item into your document.

WRAPPING TEXT AROUND A FRAME

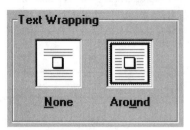

Figure 48. To wrap text around a frame, select the frame and choose *Frame* from the **Format** menu. In the *Frame* dialog box, there are two options for text wrapping: *None* or *Around*. *Around* is the default mode.

Word wraps text around a frame if there is at least 1 inch between the frame and either a column, margin, or another frame. If you do not want text to wrap around the frame, click on *None*.

Figure 49. When you select the *None* option, Word displays text above and below the frame, but not to the left and right of the frame.

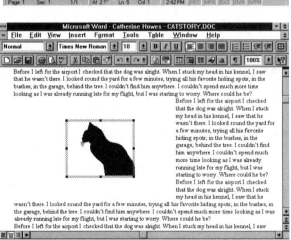

Figure 50. When you select the *Around* option, Word wraps text around the frame.

Figure 51. If you are wrapping text around a frame, you can set the distance between the text and the frame with the *Distance from Text* text boxes in the *Horizontal* and *Vertical* sections of the *Frame* dialog box. This is explained earlier in this chapter under **Positioning Frames with the Frame Dialog Box**.

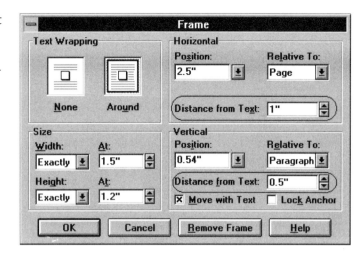

ADDING BORDERS

Figure 52. When you insert a frame in your document, Word automatically puts a simple border around the frame. If you do not want the border, you can remove or change it without affecting the frame.

You can add shading to a frame's contents. But graphics inserted using the *Picture* command cannot be shaded.

You can also apply borders to individual paragraphs and graphics that are inside a frame.

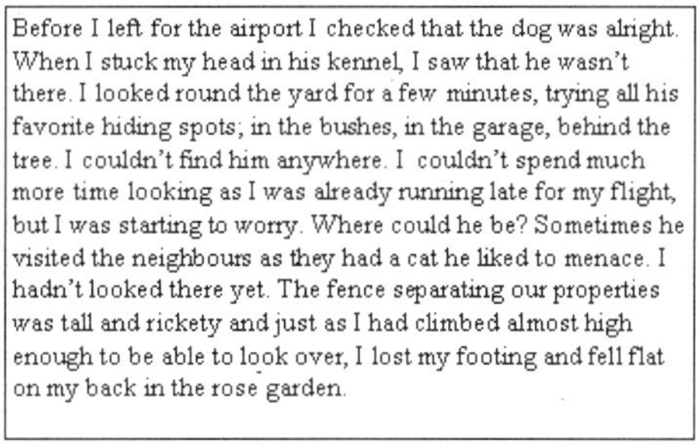

Before I left for the airport I checked that the dog was alright. When I stuck my head in his kennel, I saw that he wasn't there. I looked round the yard for a few minutes, trying all his favorite hiding spots; in the bushes, in the garage, behind the tree. I couldn't find him anywhere. I couldn't spend much more time looking as I was already running late for my flight, but I was starting to worry. Where could he be? Sometimes he visited the neighbours as they had a cat he liked to menace. I hadn't looked there yet. The fence separating our properties was tall and rickety and just as I had climbed almost high enough to be able to look over, I lost my footing and fell flat on my back in the rose garden.

Figure 53. To apply borders, click on the *Borders* button on the *Formatting* toolbar.

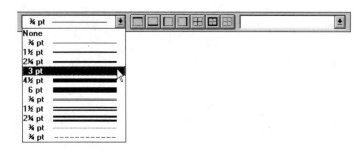

Figure 54. This displays the *Borders* toolbar. Select the frame, or an item in the frame. Then choose a line from the *Line Style* drop-down list box.

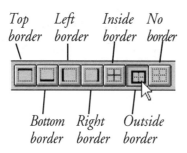

Top border   Left border   Inside border   No border

Bottom border   Right border   Outside border

Figure 55. Now click on the button that corresponds to the area of the frame you want to apply that line style to.

Figure 56. You can apply shading using the options from the *Shading* drop-down list box.

Figure 57. Click on the *No Border* button to remove the border for the selected frame or item.

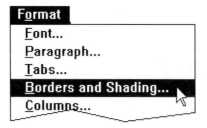

Figure 58. Alternatively, choose *Borders and Shading* from the **Format** menu.

Figure 59. Word opens the *Paragraph Borders and Shading* dialog box where you can apply the same (and more) options from the *Borders* and *Shading* tabs as on the *Borders* toolbar.

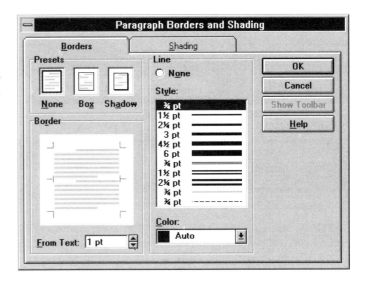

GRAPHICS 12

INTRODUCTION

You can add all sorts of graphics to your Word documents, including:

- graphics you create yourself using the drawing application that comes with Word;
- clip art (pre-drawn images), some samples of which come with Word; and
- any other graphics in one of the many formats that Word accepts.

When you have imported a graphic into your Word document, you can move it, resize it, and crop it. You can also edit graphics using the *Drawing* command.

ADDING GRAPHICS TO YOUR WORD DOCUMENT

Figure 1. Word accepts graphics saved in a variety of formats.

There are two ways to import externally created graphics into your Word document: using the *Picture* command from the **Insert** menu, and using the clipboard. To import an entire graphics file, you need the appropriate graphics filter installed on your computer.

USING THE PICTURE COMMAND

Figure 2. To import a graphic, position the insertion point in your document where you want to place the graphic.

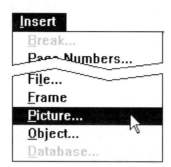

Figure 3. Choose the *Picture* command from the **Insert** menu, to import the graphic saved in a Word-compatible format.

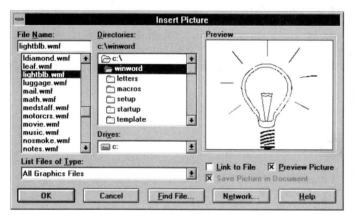

Figure 4. In the *Insert Picture* dialog box, type the path and name of the graphic file you want to import in the *File Name* text box, or select the filename from the list box.

If the *Preview Picture* check box is selected, Word displays the selected graphic in the *Preview* box.

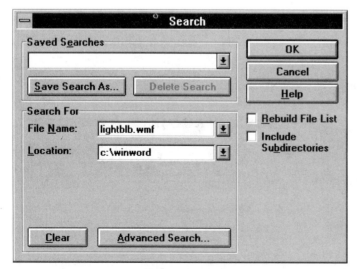

Figure 5. If you don't know, or can't remember, the name of the file, and it is not shown in the list box, select a different drive or directory. You can also search for the file using the *Find File* option. Click on the *Find File* button in the *Insert Picture* dialog box to open the *Search* dialog box.

The clip art files that are installed with Word are located in the *clipart* subdirectory of the *winword* directory.

Figure 6. If you want to create a link with a graphics file and reduce the size of your Word file, you can specify that the document stores only the link and not the representation of the graphic. Do this by selecting the *Link to File* check box in the *Insert Picture* dialog box.

Click on *OK* when you have found your graphic file.

Figure 7. The selected graphic now appears within your document.

USING THE CLIPBOARD

Figure 8. To copy a graphic into your document from another application, select the graphic in the other Windows application, and then *Copy* it to the clipboard.

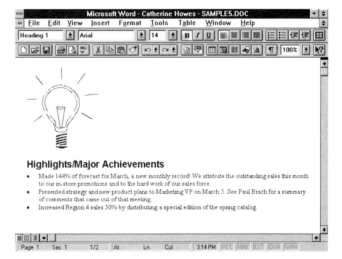

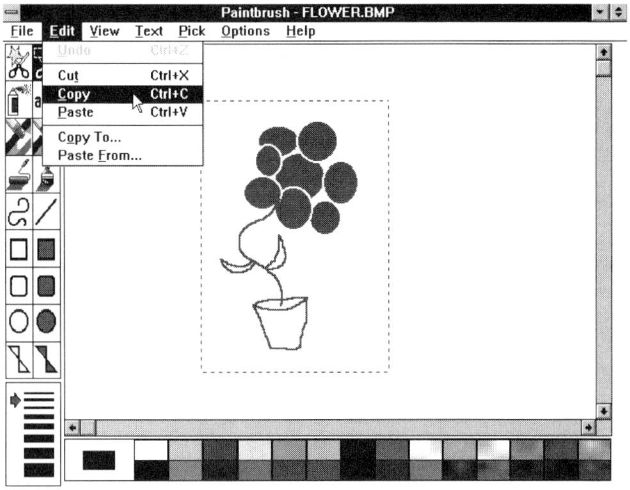

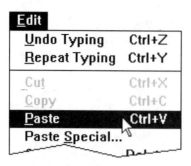

Figure 9. Then in your Word document, click where you want to place the graphic and choose *Paste* from the **Edit** menu or the *Paste* button from the *Standard* toolbar.

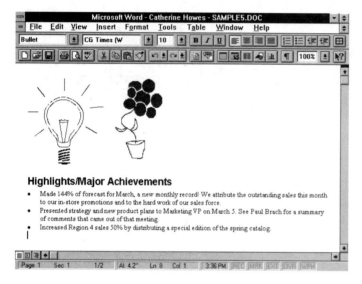

Figure 10. The graphic is pasted as a Windows metafile (*.WMF*) and appears as part of your Word document.

MODIFYING GRAPHICS

Once you have imported a graphic, you can size, crop, and scale it using the mouse or a dialog box. You can also edit the graphic in a separate window or add a border to it.

RESIZING GRAPHICS

Figure 11. Before you can resize a graphic, you need to select it— eight sizing handles appear around the edges of the graphic.

Figure 12. To resize a selected graphic and keep it in proportion, with the mouse pointer on one of the corner handles, click and hold the mouse button down. The mouse pointer changes to a two-headed arrow. Then simply drag to decrease or increase the size of the graphic as required.

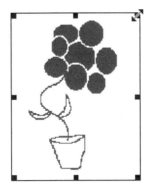

Figure 13. Resizing with the middle handles stretches the graphic out of proportion.

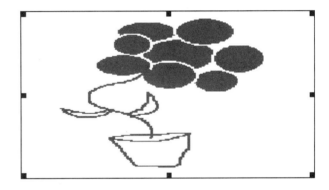

Figure 14. As you drag to resize the graphic, Word displays the percentage of the graphic's original size in the status bar.

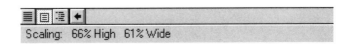

Figure 15. Release the mouse button once the graphic is the size you want.

CROPPING GRAPHICS

By cropping, you can hide the parts of the image you don't want to display or print, or create more white space around the graphic.

Figure 16. Click on the graphic to select it, then hold down the Shift key while dragging the handles inwards. The mouse pointer changes to the cropping tool.

Figure 17. To add white space around the graphic you do the same as in Figure 16, except that you drag the handle outwards.

USING THE PICTURE DIALOG BOX

Figure 18. To specify exact measurements for sizing, cropping and scaling graphics, first select the graphic. Then, choose *Picture* from the **Format** menu.

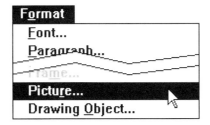

Figure 19. This opens the *Picture* dialog box.

Click on the up and down arrows of the text boxes or type in measurements in the *Crop From*, *Scaling*, or *Size* sections of the dialog box to modify the graphic.

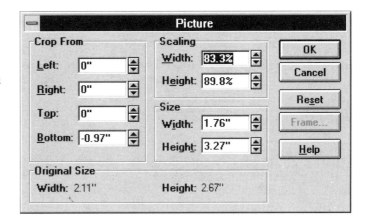

Figure 20. Word remembers the way the graphic looked when you first imported it into your document. So after you have cropped or resized it, you can restore the graphic to its original size by clicking on the *Reset* button in the *Picture* dialog box.

Alternatively, you can hold down the Ctrl key on the keyboard and double-click on the graphic to restore it to its original size.

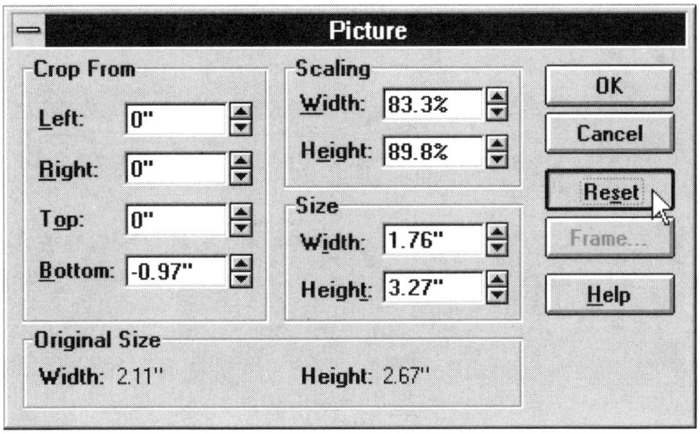

MOVING GRAPHICS

Figure 21. To move an imported graphic from one part of your document to another, you need to put the graphic in a frame. (See **Chapter 11** for information on how to do this.) Select the frame, then drag it to a new position.

ADDING BORDERS

Borders button

Borders toolbar

Figure 22. To apply a border to your graphic, select it then choose the *Borders* button on the *Formatting* toolbar to display the *Borders* toolbar.

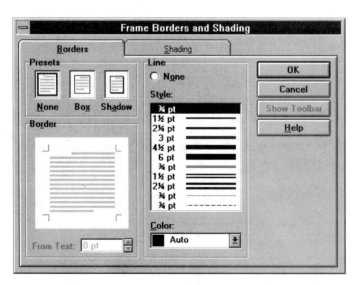

Figure 23. Alternatively, you can apply borders to graphics with or without a frame by selecting *Borders and Shading* from the **Format** menu. If the graphic is framed, the *Frame Borders and Shading* dialog box appears; if not, Word opens the *Picture Borders* dialog box.

See **Chapter 11** for more information about how to add borders.

EDITING IMPORTED GRAPHICS

Figure 24. To edit an imported graphic, double-click on it to open the graphic in a separate picture editing window. If the graphic is a draw-type (vector) graphic, you can edit it as if it had been drawn with the Word drawing tools.

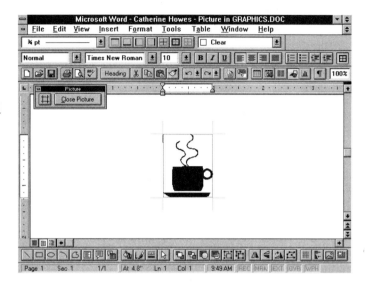

Figure 25. You can select, separate, and manipulate the components of the graphic.

You can use the *Drawing* toolbar to modify the graphic. (For information on how to use the tools on the *Drawing* toolbar, see **The Drawing Toolbar** section later in this chapter.)

The changes you make to the graphic in the Word document don't affect the original graphics file.

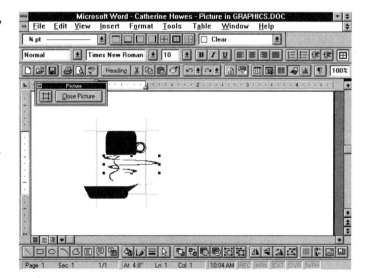

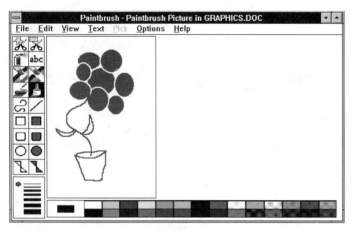

Figure 26. If the graphic is a bitmap, such as one created in Paintbrush, when you double-click on it, the graphic is opened in its source application (Paintbrush) for you to edit. If you want these changes to be reflected in your Word document you need to update the graphic. (See **Object Linking and Embedding** later in this chapter.)

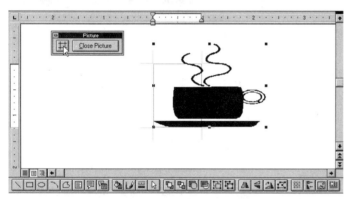

Figure 27. The boundaries that surround the graphic show its size. Anything that extends outside these boundaries is cropped off when you return to the Word document. If you've made the graphic larger or smaller, you can reset the graphic boundary by clicking on the *Reset Picture Boundary* button on the *Picture* toolbar in the picture editing window.

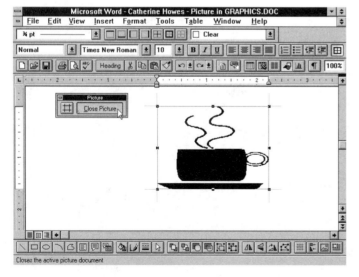

Figure 28. Close the picture editing window by clicking on the *Close Picture* button.

Figure 29. Any changes you made and everything inside the boundaries is transferred to your Word document.

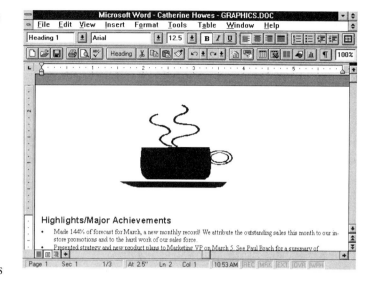

THE DRAWING TOOLBAR

To draw and edit drawing objects you need to be in *Page Layout* view—drawing objects are not visible in *Normal, Outline,* or *Master Document* views.

Figure 30. To display the *Drawing* toolbar between the status bar and the horizontal scroll bar, click on the *Drawing* button on the *Standard* toolbar. Reselecting this button hides the toolbar.

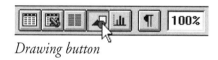

Drawing button

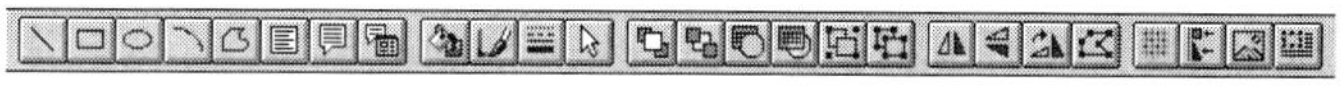

Drawing toolbar

CREATING OBJECTS

Figure 31. To draw an object, click on one of the drawing tool buttons. If you want to draw several objects with the same tool, double-click on the button; the tool remains active until you click on another toolbar button or do anything other than dragging the mouse and drawing objects.

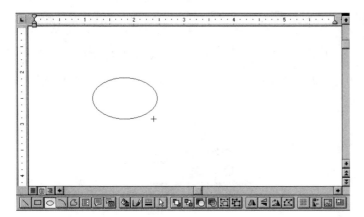

Figure 32. To draw an object, click, hold and drag.

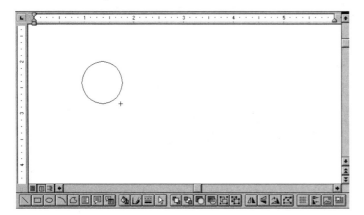

Figure 33. If you want to draw a square or circle using the rectangle or ellipse tool, hold down the Shift key as you drag.

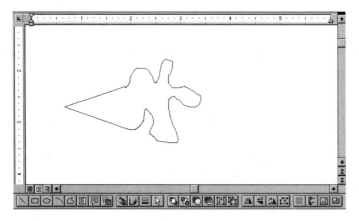

Figure 34. To create a shape with the *Freeform* tool, click the mouse button, then move the mouse and click again to create straight line segments. Click, hold and drag, then release the mouse button to draw freeform lines and shapes. Then double-click the mouse to finish the object and join the two ends.

Figure 35. To draw shapes from their center outwards, hold down the Ctrl key as you drag the mouse.

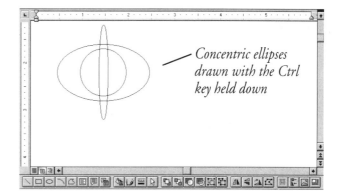

Concentric ellipses drawn with the Ctrl key held down

SELECTING OBJECTS

Figure 36. You need to select a drawing object before you can affect it in any way. Objects are selected when the black handles are visible.

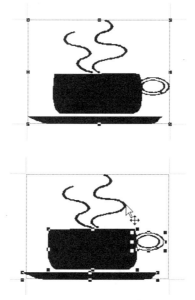

Figure 37. To select a drawing object, position the mouse pointer on the object and click. To select more than one object, hold down the Shift key while you click on each of the drawing objects.

Figure 38. You can also select more than one object by clicking on the *Select Drawing Objects* button and dragging around all of the objects you want to select.

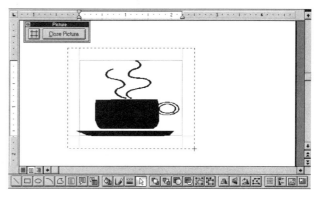

Figure 39. To select the line segments of a freeform object, select it, then click on the *Reshape* button.

RESIZING AND MOVING OBJECTS

RESIZING AND MOVING WITH THE MOUSE

Figure 40. Drag any handle of a selected object to resize it.

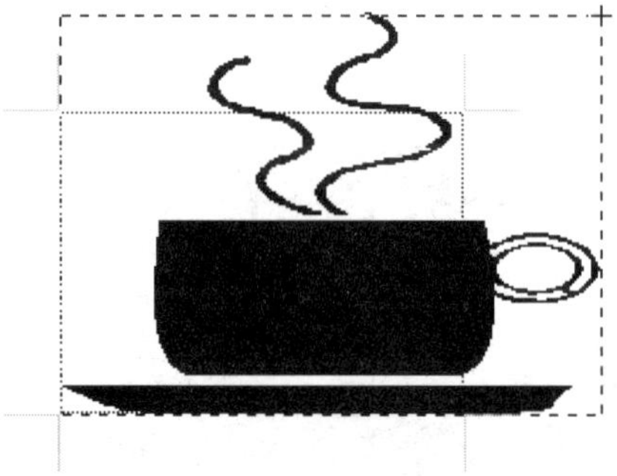

Figure 41. To resize the drawing object and keep it in proportion, hold down the Shift key and drag a corner handle.

Figure 42. Hold down the Ctrl key and drag a handle to resize the shape from its center.

Figure 43. To move an object, put the mouse pointer on the object (but not on a handle) so the mouse pointer changes shape; then drag the object to its new location. If the object is filled, you can put the mouse pointer in the middle of the object.

Figure 44. If you hold down the Ctrl key and drag, the mouse pointer changes. When you release the mouse, Word produces a copy of the object.

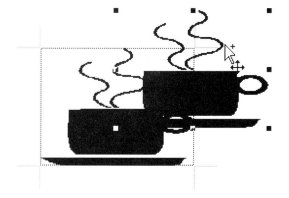

RESIZING AND MOVING WITH THE DRAWING OBJECT DIALOG BOX

Figure 45. With an object selected, choose *Drawing Object* from the **Format** menu to open the *Drawing Object* dialog box.

The options on the *Size and Position* tab let you precisely alter the object's size and location on the page by changing the values in the text boxes.

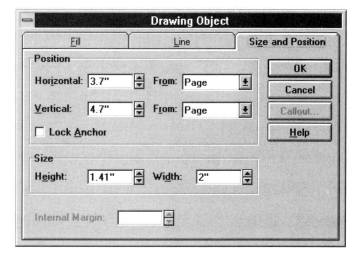

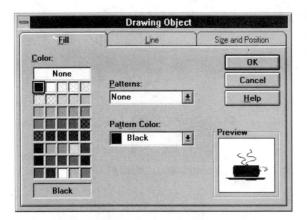

Figure 46. The *Fill* and *Line* tabs contain options that let you change such things as line color and fill pattern.

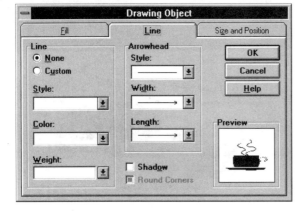

Figure 47. If you didn't have an object selected, Word displays the *Drawing Defaults* dialog box after you choose *Drawing Object* from the **Format** menu. This lets you change the default settings for the line and fill styles that Word uses automatically when you draw an object using the *Drawing* toolbar.

Selecting new options using the *Fill Color, Line Color*, and *Line Style* buttons (see Figures 52 through 54) also changes the default settings.

THE TOOLS

The following figures briefly describe and give examples of what the
Drawing tools (shown in Figure 30) can do after you have clicked on
their button to activate them.

Figure 48. Text Box: Drag the
mouse to specify the size of the
text box. You use a text box
instead of a frame if you want to
position text or an imported
graphic behind or in front of the
main text layer in your document.

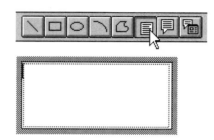

Figure 49. Type text or import a
graphic into the text box. Edit
and format text as usual (see
Chapter 2). Unlike frames, text
boxes do not expand as you add
text. You need to make the box
larger to be able to see the
additional text.

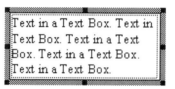

Figure 50. Callout: You use
callouts to highlight items in an
illustration. Drag the mouse to
the size you want the callout to be
and then type the text.

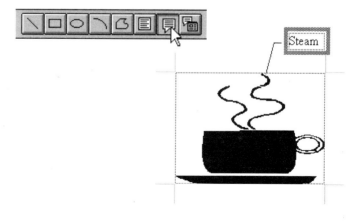

Figure 51. **Format Callout:** Opens the *Format Callout* dialog box where you can customize the callout.

Figure 52. Fill Color: Lets you fill an object with a pattern.

Figure 53. Line Color: Lets you change the color of your drawing line.

Figure 54. Line Style: Lets you change the style of the lines you draw.

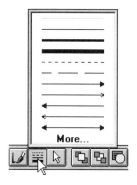

Figure 55. Bring to Front: Brings the selected object to the front.

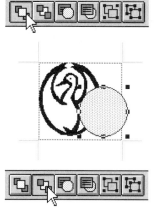

Figure 56. Bring to Back: Sends the selected object to the back.

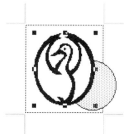

Figure 57. Bring in Front of Text: Brings the object in front of the text layer.

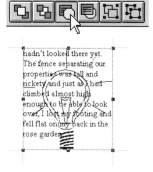

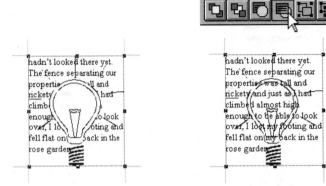

Figure 58. Send Behind Text: Sends the object behind the text layer.

Grouped

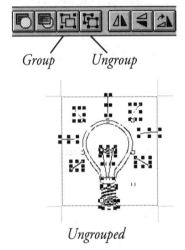

Group   *Ungroup*

Ungrouped

Figure 59. Group: You can group two or more objects so they act as a single unit, making it easier to apply commands to all of the objects. Click on the *Select Drawing Objects* button and drag to select a number of drawing objects. You then click on the *Group* button to group them.

Use the *Ungroup* button to ungroup the objects again.

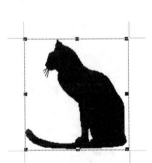

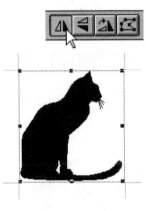

Figure 60. Flip Horizontal: Flips the selected object horizontally.

Figure 61. **Flip Vertical**: Flips the selected objected vertically.

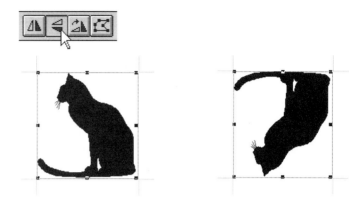

Figure 62. **Rotate Right**: Rotates objects in 90 degree increments to the right. If you want to rotate text, use WordArt.

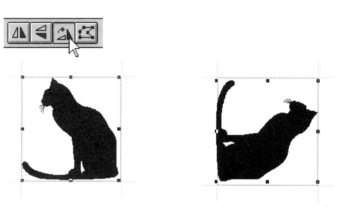

Figure 63. **Reshape**: To reshape a freeform object, select it and click on the *Reshape* button to select all the individual segments. You can then drag the handles to reshape the object.

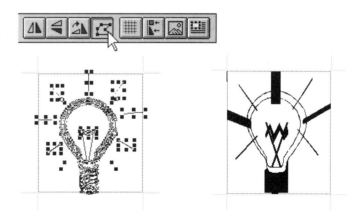

Figure 64. If you want to add a handle to the shape, hold down Ctrl and click on the line where you want the handle.

To delete a handle, press Ctrl and click on the handle.

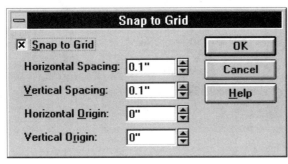

Figure 65. Snap to Grid: An invisible grid of lines covers the drawing area and, by default, pulls objects into alignment by snapping to the grid. The *Snap to Grid* button opens this dialog box where you can change the spacing between the gridlines or disable the snap to grid affect.

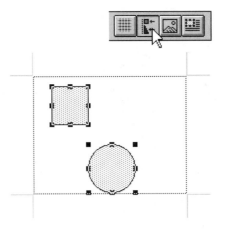

Figure 66. Align Drawing Objects: Select objects you want to align, then click on this button.

Figure 67. The *Align Drawing Objects* button opens the *Align* dialog box. Choose from the options and click on *OK*.

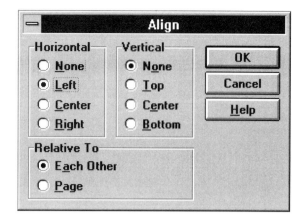

Figure 68. Word aligns the objects.

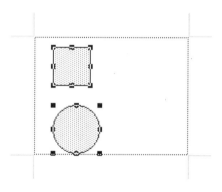

Figure 69. Create Picture: Opens the picture editing window or inserts the selected objects into a picture.

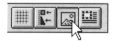

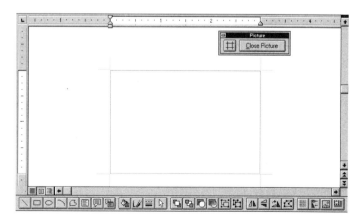

Figure 70. Insert Frame: Lets you draw an empty frame or place a frame around selected items.

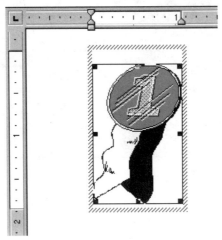

OBJECT LINKING AND EMBEDDING (OLE)

You can link or embed information or items from other applications in your Word document. Embedded objects become part of the Word document; whereas linked documents are stored in the source file and a representation is displayed in the Word document.

EMBEDDING

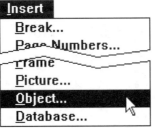

Figure 71. To embed an object, put the insertion point where you want the object in your document. Then choose *Object* from the **Insert** menu.

Figure 72. Word opens the *Object* dialog box. To create and embed a new object, select the *Create New* tab and select an application from the *Object Type* list box. (The available options depend on which applications installed on your computer support embedding and linking.) Choose *OK*.

The application opens, so you can create a new file.

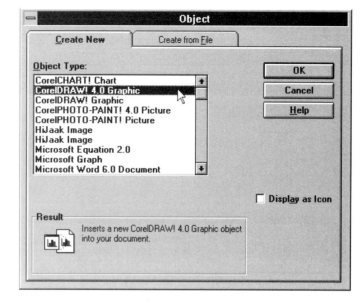

Figure 73. If the application is in a separate window to Word, choose *Exit* from the **File** menu to return to your Word document.

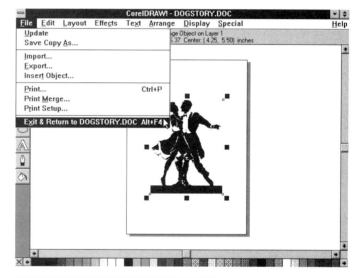

Figure 74. A prompt box appears asking if you want to update the file into your Word document. Choose *Yes* to insert it.

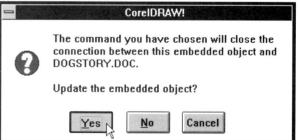

Figure 75. If the application is active within Word (such as WordArt), click anywhere in the Word document to return to it and insert the object.

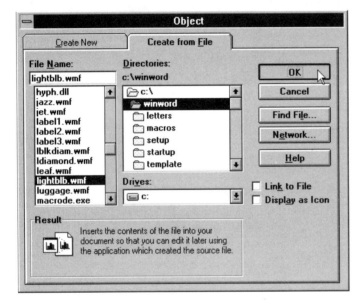

Figure 76. If you want to embed an existing object, select the *Create from File* tab in the *Object* dialog box. In the *File Name* text box, type the name of the file you want to embed, or select it from the list box and choose *OK*.

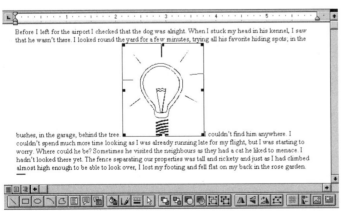

Figure 77. The file is then inserted in your Word document.

Figure 78. If you want to embed only part of a file, place the insertion point in your Word document then switch to the source application. Open the file and select the information you want to embed. Choose *Copy* from the application's **Edit** menu to place a copy of it in the clipboard.

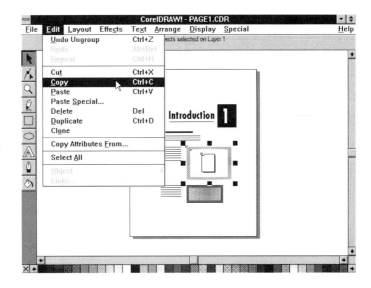

Figure 79. Switch to your Word document and choose *Paste Special* from the **Edit** menu.

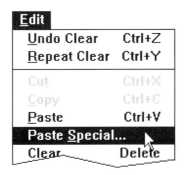

Figure 80. In the *Paste Special* dialog box, choose the *Paste* radio button. Select the first item in the *As* list box with the word "object" in its name. Click on the *Display as Icon* check box if you want the embedded information to appear as an icon. Choose *OK*.

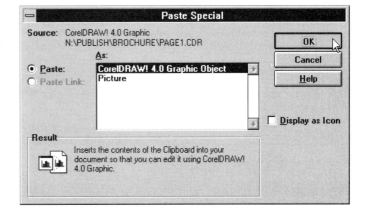

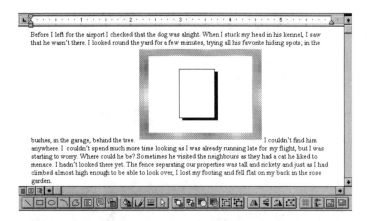

Figure 81. The object appears in the Word document.

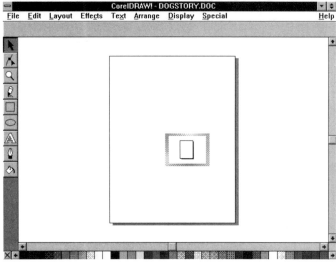

Figure 82. To edit an embedded object, double-click on it. This opens the application it was created in so you can change it.

LINKING

You can create a link between your Word document and another application that supports dynamic data exchange (DDE) or object linking and embedding (OLE).

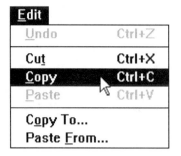

Figure 83. You need to save the source file before you link. Then select the information in the source file, and choose *Copy* from the Edit menu.

Figure 84. Switch to the Word document and put the insertion point where you want the information. Choose *Paste Special* from the **Edit** menu.

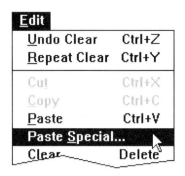

Figure 85. In the *Paste Special* dialog box, select the *Paste Link* radio button. Choose the format you want from the *As* list box. Click on *OK*.

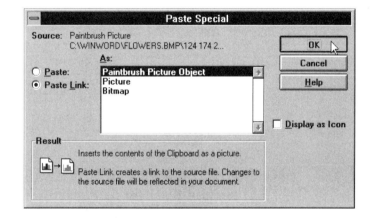

Figure 86. You can also create a link by choosing *Object* from the **Insert** menu.

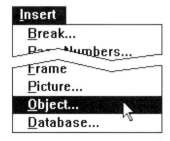

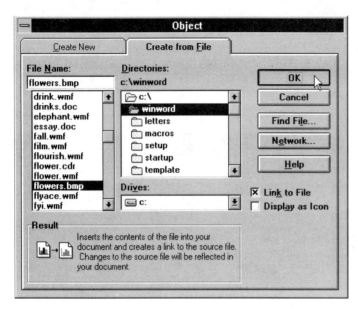

Figure 87. On the *Create from File* tab of the *Object* dialog box, select the name of the file you want to link so it appears in the *File Name* text box. Click in the *Link to File* check box and click on *OK*. Using this method, you can link an entire file only.

UPDATING AND EDITING LINKS

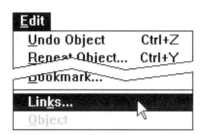

Figure 88. You can control how Word updates links. Choose *Links* from the **Edit** menu to open the *Links* dialog box.

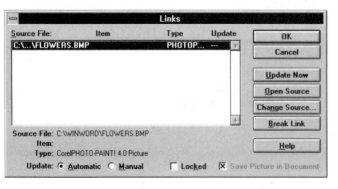

Figure 89. Select the information you want to update from the list box. To update every time the source file changes, choose the *Automatic* radio button. Choose the *Manual* radio button to update links only when you choose.

Figure 90. To update a link manually, click on the *Update Now* button in the *Links* dialog box.

To lock a link and prevent it from being updated, select the *Locked* check box.

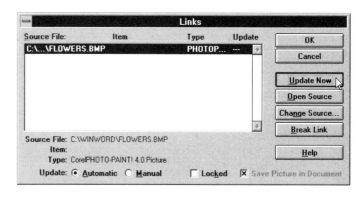

Figure 91. Choose the *Break Link* button to break a link. The information stays in your document, but you can't update it and you can't reconnect the link.

Then reconfirm your decision in the prompt box that appears.

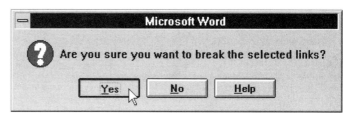

Figure 92. To edit a linked object, select it. Then choose the link type at the end of the **Edit** menu and select *Edit* from the submenu.

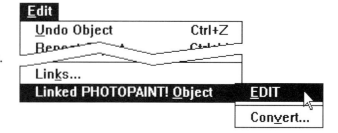

Figure 93. Alternatively, click on the *Open Source* button in the *Links* dialog box.

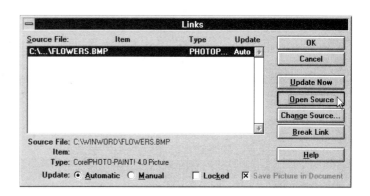

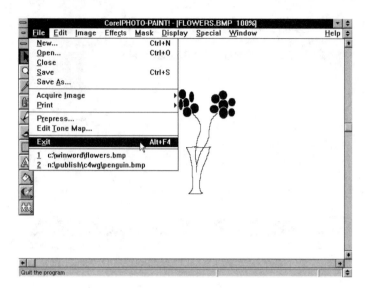

Figure 94. The source application opens. Make your changes then choose *Exit* from the **File** menu, or *Close* if the source file is a Word document.

LONG DOCUMENT CAPABILITIES 13

WORKING WITH LONG DOCUMENTS

Word has functions which are useful in long documents. These include: creating headers, footers, page numbering, footnotes, endnotes, cross-references and bookmarks, indexes and table of contents.

CREATING HEADERS AND FOOTERS

Figure 1. A header is text or graphics in the margin at the top of the page, and a footer is located in the margin at the bottom of the page.

The headers and footers option allows you to have as many different headers and footers as you like throughout a document. You can have different text on the first, even, and odd pages, as well as for each section. You can also include the date, time, and page numbers in headers and footers.

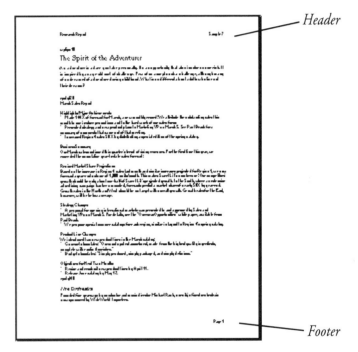

Header

Footer

Figure 2. Choose *Header and Footer* from the **View** menu.

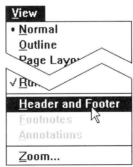

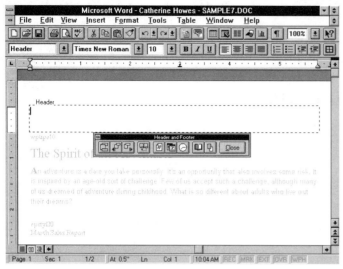

Figure 3. Word displays your document and the *Header and Footer* toolbar in *Page Layout* view. The header (or footer) area is defined by a nonprinting dashed box and your document text is dimmed.

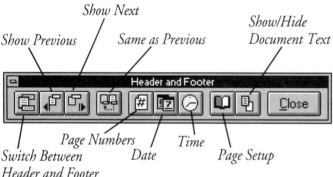

Figure 4. The *Header and Footer* toolbar contains buttons that let you control your headers and footers.

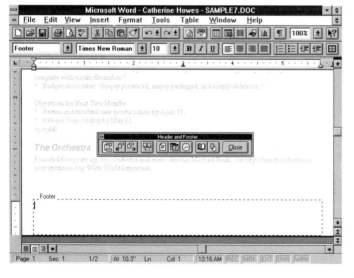

Figure 5. Click on the *Switch Between Header and Footer* button on the *Header and Footer* toolbar to move to the footer area. You can also use the scroll bars.

Figure 6. To display or hide the dimmed document text, click on the *Show\Hide Document Text* button.

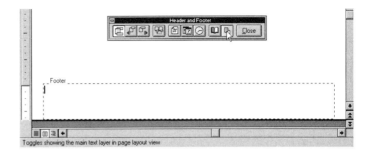

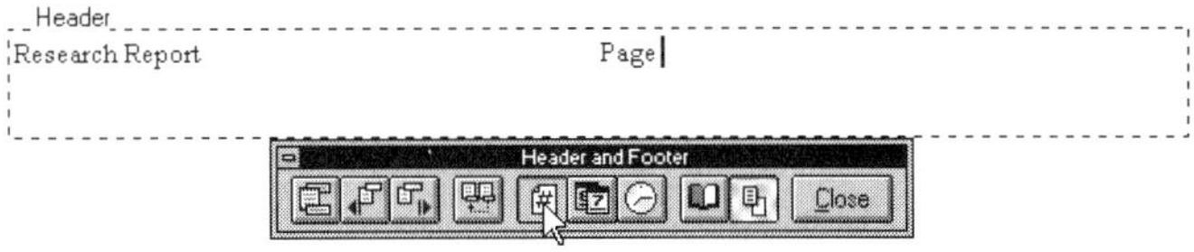

Figure 7. Type any header or footer text, using the Tab key to move to the center and the right of the box. You can format text as you would with any other text (see **Chapter 2**).

To insert the page number, click on the *Page Numbers* button.

Figure 8. Insert the current date and time by clicking on the *Date* and *Time* buttons on the *Header and Footer* toolbar.

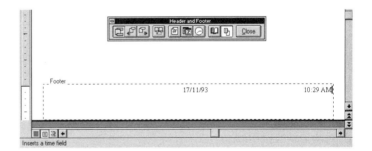

The *Show Previous* and *Show Next* buttons let you move between headers and footers of different sections in your document (see **Chapter 5**). If you want different headers or footers in each section, you need to apply new header and footer text for each section.

The *Same as Previous* button connects any headers and footers of the current document section with the previous section. If you want to create different headers and footers in different sections, deselect this button then create a new header or footer for that document section.

POSITIONING HEADERS AND FOOTERS

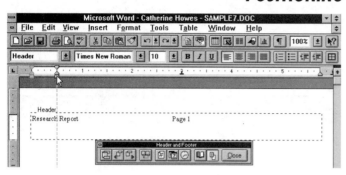

Figure 9. You can align the header or footer text to the left or right margin, to the center of the page, or indent it. To do this, press the Tab key on the keyboard to move to the two preset tab stops; use the alignment buttons on the *Formatting* toolbar; or drag the indent markers on the ruler.

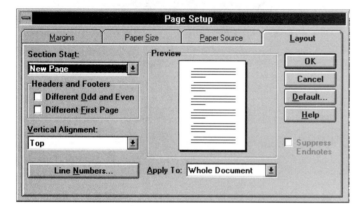

Figure 10. Click on the *Page Setup* button on the *Header and Footer* toolbar (Figure 4) to open this dialog box. On the *Layout* tab, the *Different First Page,* and *Different Odd and Even* check boxes allow you to have various header and footer combinations.

Select *Different First Page* if you want to create a different header or footer on the first page, or if you do not want a header or footer on the first page of your document (by leaving the header or footer area blank).

Different Odd and Even allows you to have different headers and footers on odd and even pages. Click in the check box to select this command. (Make sure you have also selected *Mirror Margins* on the *Margins* tab in the *Page Setup* dialog box.)

Figure 11. If you select the *Different First Page* or the *Different Odd and Even* check boxes, Word labels the header and footer editing box to show what sort of header or footer it is.

Click on the *Show Previous* and *Show Next* buttons on the *Header and Footer* toolbar to move between the different header and footer types so you can create them.

Figure 12. On the *Margin* tab of the *Page Setup* dialog box, the *From Edge* section allows you to control the distance the header or footer prints from the top or bottom edge of the paper. The default setting for headers and footers is 0.5 inches from the top and bottom of the page. You can type or select your own measurements in the text boxes.

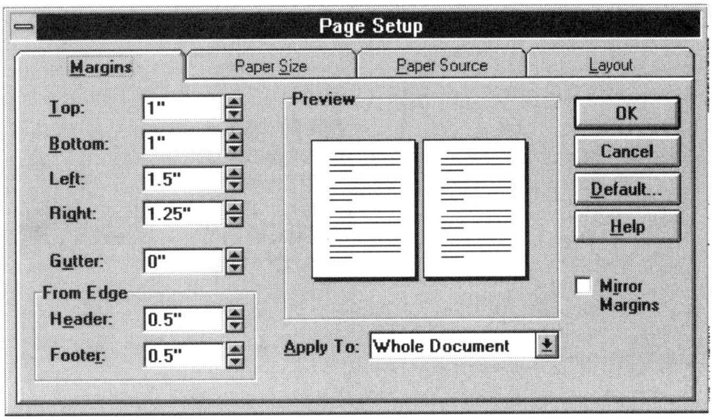

Click on *Close*, or double-click in the main document area to return to the document editing window.

Figure 13. To change the distance between document text and a header or footer, move the margin boundaries on the vertical ruler.

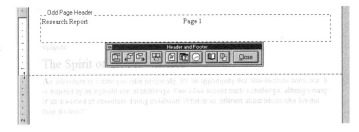

DELETING AND EDITING HEADERS AND FOOTERS

Place the insertion point in the document section with the header or footer you want to edit or delete. Then choose *Header and Footer* from the **View** menu (Figure 2) to open the header and footer editing window (Figure 3) where you can delete or edit your headers and footers.

PAGE NUMBERING

You can set up page numbers in headers and footers (see the **Creating a Header or Footer** section earlier in this chapter) or using the *Page Numbers* command in the **Insert** menu. Using the latter method, you can move the page number anywhere on the page.

INSERTING PAGE NUMBERING

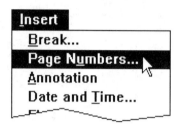

Figure 14. Add the insertion point to the section of your document you want to number, or in the first section to number all sections. Then choose the *Page Numbers* command from the **Insert** menu.

Note: Headers and footers start out connected to the ones in previous document sections and so numbering affects connected sections. To change page numbers in one section only, you need to click on the Same as Previous button on the Header and Footer toolbar to disconnect the header or footer.

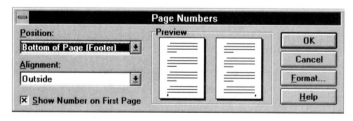

Figure 15. This opens the *Page Numbers* dialog box.

Deselect the *Show Number on First Page* check box if you don't want page numbers on the first page of your document or, if your document has sections, the first page of the current section.

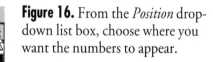

Figure 16. From the *Position* drop-down list box, choose where you want the numbers to appear.

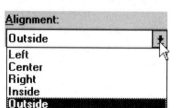

Figure 17. Choose an option from the *Alignment* drop-down list box.

Figure 18. To change the numbering style, click on the *Format* button of the *Page Numbers* dialog box. This opens the *Page Number Format* dialog box. Select a style from the *Number Format* drop-down list box.

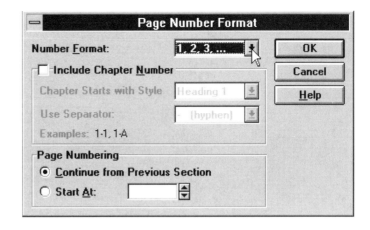

Figure 19. If you want to start the page numbering at a different number, click in the *Start At* radio button, and change the number in the text box.

Figure 20. Click in the *Include Chapter Number* check box and choose from these options, if you want to include the chapter number with the page number. (Make sure you have formatted chapter headings with the built-in heading styles, and that you've numbered them using the *Heading Numbering* command from the **Format** menu.)

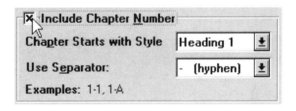

Figure 21. When you open the header or footer editing window, the page number is added to the header or footer. (If the page code is showing, you have *Field Codes* selected on the *View* tab of the *Options* dialog box. See **Chapter 15** for information about codes.)

Figure 22. The page number is actually in its own frame that you can select and move around the page when the mouse pointer has a four-headed arrow attached to it. However it is still part of the header or footer.

You can also insert page numbers using the *Page Numbers* button on the *Header and Footer* toolbar (see **Creating Headers and Footers** earlier in this chapter). The page number is inserted as part of the text, not in a frame, and can't be dragged to a new position.

REMOVING PAGE NUMBERING

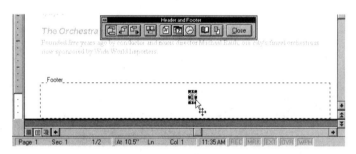

Figure 23. Position the insertion point in the section from where you want to remove page numbers, then choose *Headers and Footers* from the **View** menu.

Select the page number and press Delete or the Backspace key to remove it. Click on *Close* on the *Header and Footer* toolbar to return to the document.

FOOTNOTES AND ENDNOTES

Footnotes and endnotes provide extra information for text in a document.

Footnotes usually appear at the bottom of the same page as the text they explain, with a reference mark in the document text.

Endnotes appear at the end of the document, or section, with a reference mark in the document text.

Word automatically numbers and places the notes for you. You can customize reference marks, but Word can't update custom reference marks.

INSERTING FOOTNOTES AND ENDNOTES

Figure 24. To insert footnotes and endnotes in your document, the insertion point has to be to the right of the text you want to reference (this is where Word inserts the reference mark). Then choose *Footnote* from the **Insert** menu.

Figure 25. This activates the *Footnote and Endnote* dialog box. In the *Insert* section, select the *Footnote* or *Endnote* radio button. Then under *Numbering*, choose *AutoNumber* if you want Word to number notes automatically. Word also renumbers reference marks whenever you add, delete, or move notes.

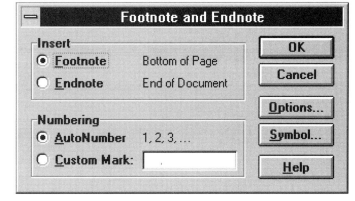

Figure 26. If you want to create your own reference mark, choose the *Custom Mark* radio button and type up to 10 characters in the text box.

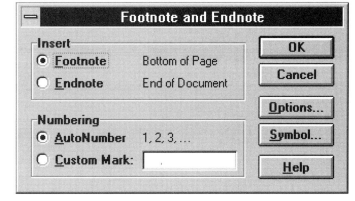

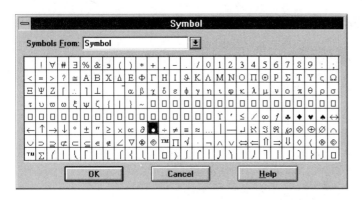

Figure 27. You can click on the *Symbol* button, which brings up the *Symbol* dialog box, where you can select a character to use.

Remember, Word does not renumber and update custom reference marks.

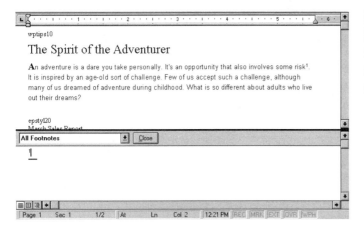

Figure 28. Click on *OK*. Word inserts the reference mark in the text and opens the note pane ready for you to type the footnote or endnote.

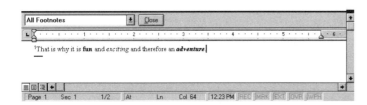

Figure 29. You can format note text in the window pane as you do with normal document text. You can also display the ruler in the note pane to change text alignment by choosing *Ruler* from the **View** menu.

If you want to change the format of all footnotes and endnotes, change the built-in styles (see **Chapter 6** for more information).

To close the note window and return to your document, click on the *Close* button. To return to the document and keep the note pane open, click the mouse in the document window.

VIEWING FOOTNOTES AND ENDNOTES

Figure 30. To view footnotes and endnotes, double-click on a reference mark. In *Normal* view, Word opens the note pane and puts the insertion point in the corresponding note text.

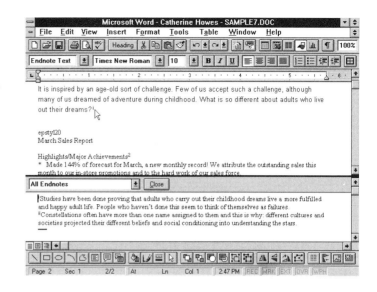

Figure 31. You can switch between viewing footnotes and endnotes by choosing *All Footnotes* or *All Endnotes* from the *Notes* drop-down list box.

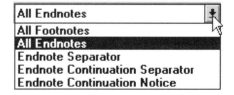

Figure 32. If you are in *Page Layout* view when you double-click on a reference mark, the insertion point moves to the corresponding note text at the position it will be printed on the page.

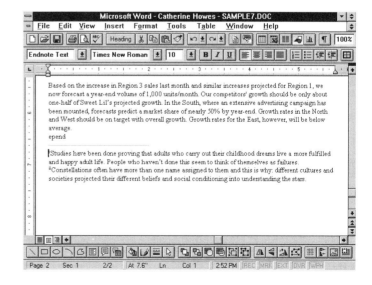

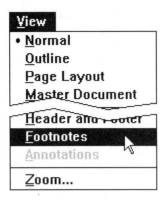

Figure 33. You can also choose *Footnotes* in the **View** menu to view notes. In *Normal* view, this opens the notes window pane.

To see where a note is in the document, click in the note text in the footnote or endnote editing window; the document window then shows the note reference mark in the document text.

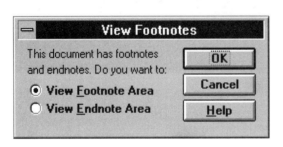

Figure 34. If you are in *Page Layout* view when you choose *Footnotes* from the **View** menu, Word opens the *View Footnotes* dialog box so you can choose if you want to view footnotes or endnotes.

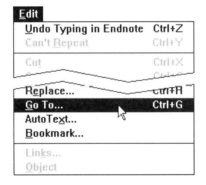

Figure 35. Alternatively, choose *Go To* from the **Edit** menu.

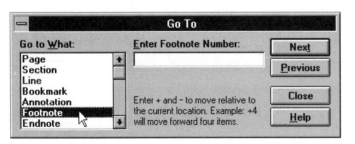

Figure 36. This brings up the *Go To* dialog box. In the *Go to What* list box, select *Footnote* or *Endnote*. To go to the next or previous note, click on the *Next* or *Previous* button.

Figure 37. Type the number (or custom mark) in the text box and choose the *Go To* button.

When you have found the note you are looking for, click on *Close.*

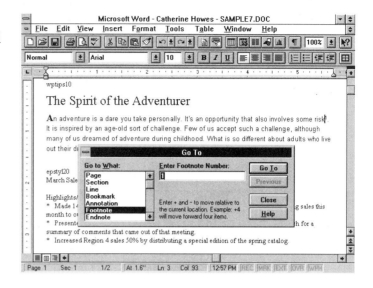

Figure 38. Also, in *Normal* view you can hold down the Shift key and drag the split box (at the top of the vertical scroll bar) down the screen to open the footnote pane.

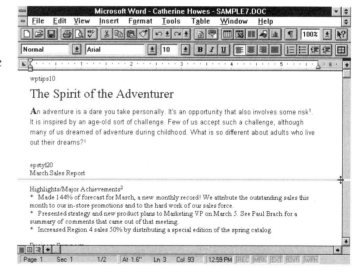

Figure 39. You can resize the pane by dragging the top of the window when the mouse pointer changes its shape to that shown here.

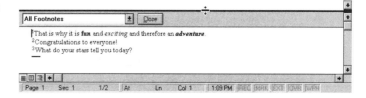

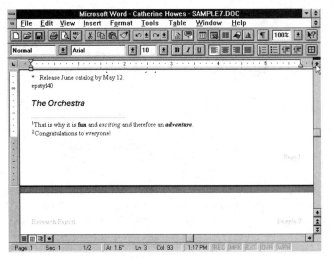

Figure 40. In *Page Layout* view, use the scroll bars to move your page and view your note text. You can also edit note text in this view.

DELETING, MOVING, AND COPYING FOOTNOTES AND ENDNOTES

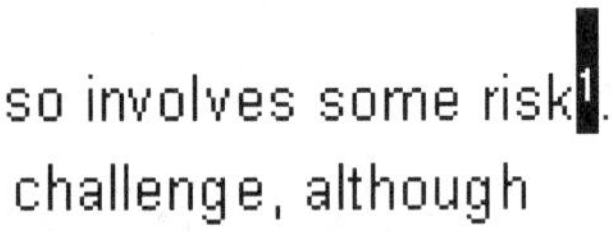

so involves some risk[1].

challenge, although

Figure 41. In the document window, highlight the reference mark you want to delete, move or copy. To delete a note and its reference, press Delete or Backspace on the keyboard.

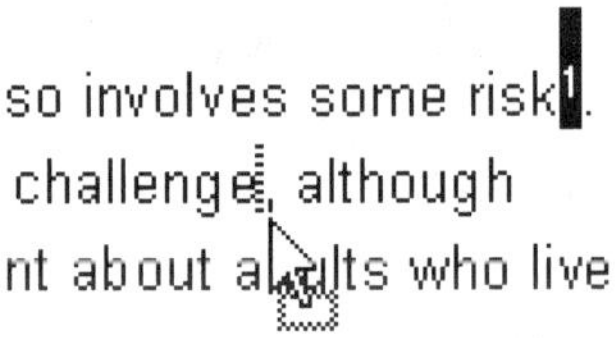

so involves some risk[1].

challenge, although

nt about aults who live

Figure 42. To move the reference mark, drag it to a new location in the document and release the mouse button.

Figure 43. To copy the reference mark to a new location, hold down the Ctrl key as you drag the mouse. The mouse pointer changes to look like this.

Figure 44. You can also use the *Cut, Copy,* and *Paste* commands on the *Standard* toolbar or in the Edit menu to reposition notes.

Word renumbers automatically numbered notes and adjusts any moved or copied note text in the note pane.

CUSTOMIZING FOOTNOTES AND ENDNOTES

Figure 45. Choose *Footnote* from the **Insert** menu, and in the *Footnote and Endnote* dialog box, click on the *Options* button.

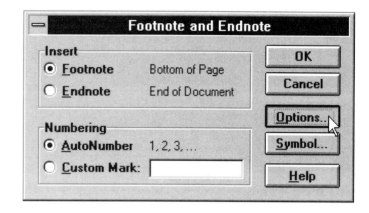

Figure 46. Use the options on the *All Footnotes* and *All Endnotes* tabs to change the position of the notes in the document, change the numbering format, change the starting number, and change where the numbering restarts through the document.

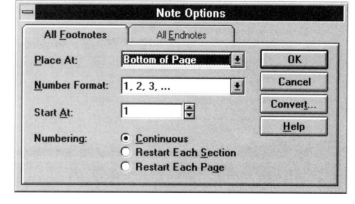

Figure 47. You can delete or change the default note separators that Word inserts between footnote and endnote text and the document text. Choose from the options in the *Notes* drop-down list box in the footnote or endnote window pane.

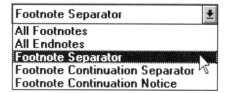

BOOKMARKS AND CROSS-REFERENCES

You can insert a bookmark into a Word document to name and mark a particular location, selection of text, or other items. You can jump to these locations quickly, refer to them in a cross-reference, or use them in creating an index.

You can create cross-references to refer the reader to further information in another part of the document.

INSERTING BOOKMARKS

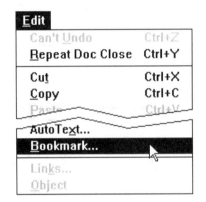

Figure 48. To place a bookmark in a document, select the text or item you want to mark or position the cursor at the desired location. Then choose *Bookmark* from the **Edit** menu.

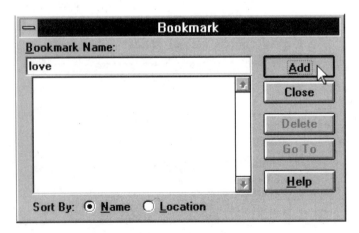

Figure 49. This activates the *Bookmark* dialog box. In the *Bookmark Name* text box, type in a name for the position or text you want to mark. The name must be 40 characters or less, begin with a letter, and cannot contain spaces.

Click on *Add* to return to the document editing window.

Figure 50. To view bookmarks in the document, choose *Options* from the **Tools** menu to open the *Options* dialog box. In the *Show* section of the *View* tab, select the *Bookmarks* check box. Then click on *OK*.

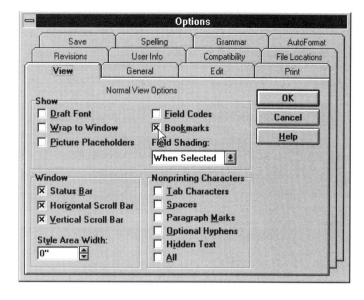

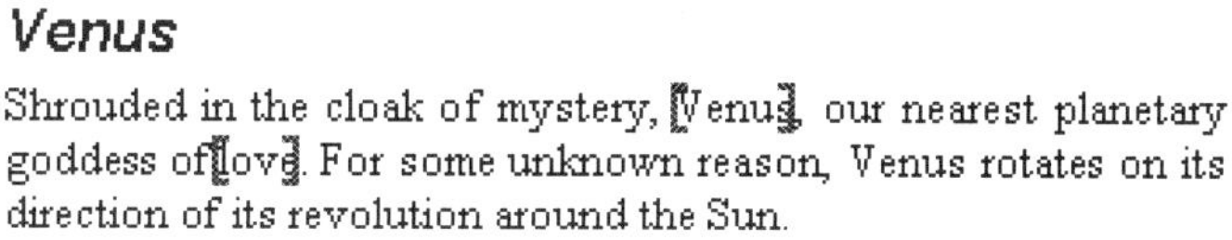

Figure 51. Word indicates a bookmark by placing square brackets around the item.

Venus

Shrouded in the cloak of mystery, [Venus], our nearest planetary goddess of [love]. For some unknown reason, Venus rotates on its direction of its revolution around the Sun.

GOING TO A BOOKMARK

Figure 52. To find a bookmark, choose *Bookmark* from the **Edit** menu. In the *Bookmark* dialog box, the list box contains any bookmark names in the document. The *Sort By* options arrange the list alphabetically or in order of location in the document.

Select the name of the bookmark you want to find, and click on the *Go To* button.

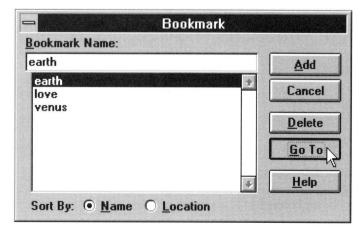

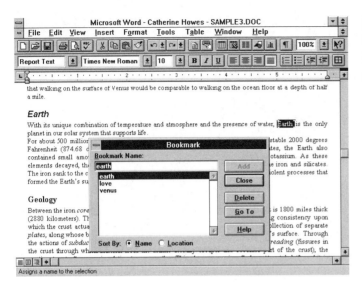

Figure 53. Word finds the bookmark and highlights the item. The dialog box stays open so you can find other bookmarks.

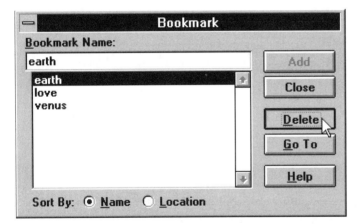

DELETING BOOKMARKS

Figure 54. To delete a bookmark, select the bookmark name from the *Bookmark* dialog box and click on the *Delete* button.

Also, if you insert a new bookmark location and call it by the same name as another bookmark, Word deletes the bookmark from the first location and uses the name to mark the new item.

CREATING CROSS-REFERENCES

You can create cross-references to headings formatted with built-in styles (see **Chapter 6**), footnotes and endnotes (see section earlier in this chapter), captions (see **Chapter 11**), and bookmarks (see section earlier in this chapter).

Figure 55. Type any introductory text in your document, then choose *Cross-reference* from the **Insert** menu.

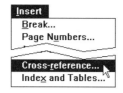

Figure 56. Word displays the *Cross-reference* dialog box. In the *Reference Type* list box, select the item you want to refer to.

From the *Insert Reference To* list box, choose the type of information you want Word to insert.Then from the *For Which Bookmark* list box, select the specific item. Now click on the *Insert* button.

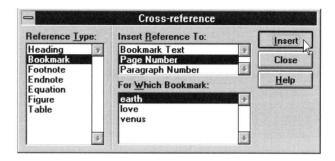

Figure 57. Word inserts the information into your document. The *Cross-reference* dialog box stays open. You can put the insertion point in the document and type additional text (click on the dialog box to make it active again).

Repeat these steps to add new cross-references. When you have finished, click on *Close*.

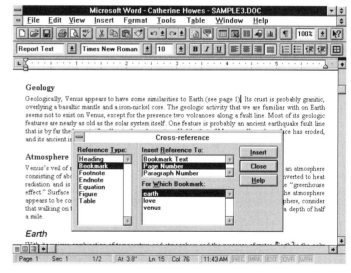

UPDATING

If you change the referenced text at all, you can update your cross-references by placing the insertion point in them and pressing F9 (the Update key). To update all cross-references in a document, choose *Select All* from the **Edit** menu and then press F9. Whenever you print the document, Word automatically updates all cross-references.

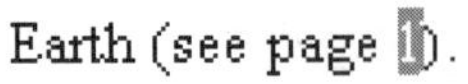

Earth (see page 1).

DELETING

Figure 58. To delete cross-reference information inserted by Word, select the information and press the Backspace or Delete key. (You need to select the information because it is a field result.)

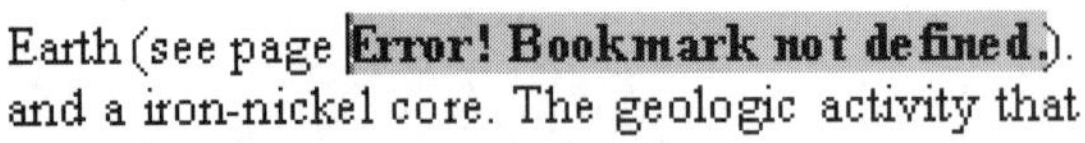

Earth (see page Error! Bookmark not defined.).
and a iron-nickel core. The geologic activity that

Figure 59. If you delete an item that you use in a cross-reference, Word displays an error message when you update.

INDEXES AND TABLES OF CONTENTS

You can create an index and a table of contents in Word to help your readers find information in your document. You can create an index which consists of single-level or multiple-level entries.

CREATING AN INDEX

You create an index for a document by inserting index entries into the document and then compiling the entries into an index. Word updates page numbers in the index when you print or repaginate the document.

Insert
Break...
Page Numbers...
Index and Tables...
File...
Frame
Picture...
Object...
Database...

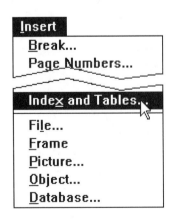

INSERTING AN INDEX ENTRY

Figure 60. To insert an index entry, either select the text you want indexed, or put the insertion point where you want to insert the index entry. Then, select *Index and Tables* from the **Insert** menu.

Figure 61. On the *Index* tab of the *Index and Tables* dialog box, click on the *Mark Entry* button.

Alternatively, press Alt+Shift+X.

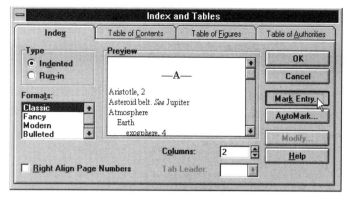

Figure 62. This opens the *Mark Index Entry* dialog box. Type the *Main Entry* name in the text box if you did not select text in the document, or you can edit the text if necessary.

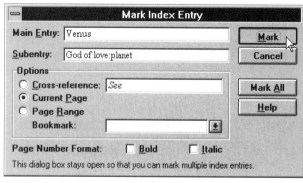

To create a subentry, type text in the *Subentry* text box. To have multiple subentries, you need to separate each subentry with a colon.

If you want the page number to be bold, italic, or both, click in the corresponding check box. Then click on the *Mark* button.

Figure 63. To create an index cross-reference, select the *Cross-reference* radio button and type text in the text box.

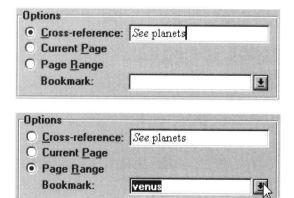

Figure 64. If you want to include an index entry which is a number of pages long, you need to mark it with a bookmark (see **Bookmarks and Cross-references** earlier in this chapter).

Click in the *Page Range* radio button in the *Option* section. Then you can select the bookmark name from the *Bookmark* drop-down list box, and click on the *Mark* button.

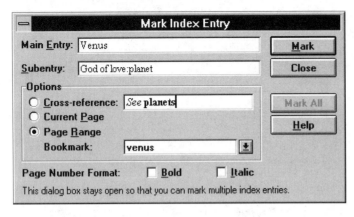

Figure 65. You can format text in the *Main Entry*, *Subentry*, and *Cross-reference* text boxes by selecting the text and pressing shortcut keys, such as Ctrl+B and Ctrl+I.

The *Mark Index Entry* dialog box stays open. You can move through your document, selecting text you want as an entry. Then click on the dialog box to make it active again and create the entry. When you have finished marking index entries, close the *Mark Index Entry* dialog box.

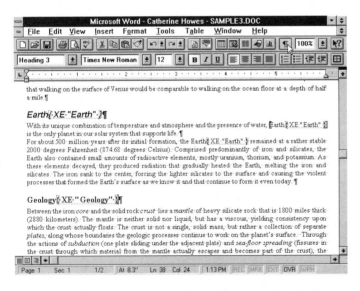

Figure 66. Word inserts an *Index Entry* field as hidden text after each entry. To see the hidden text, click on the *Show/Hide* (¶) icon on the *Standard* toolbar.

COMPILING AN INDEX

Add the insertion point where you want your index. To ensure accurate page numbering in the index, clear hidden text and field codes from the screen. Do this by clicking on the *Show/Hide* (¶) button, and deselecting *Field Codes* from the *Options* dialog box (**Tools** menu).

Figure 67. Then select *Index and Tables* from the **Insert** menu.

Figure 68. On the *Index* tab of the *Index and Tables* dialog box, select an index type. (The *Preview* list box displays examples of these when you select their radio buttons.)

Select an index format you want from the *Formats* list box.

The *Right Align Page Numbers* check box aligns page numbers with the right margin (for an indented index).

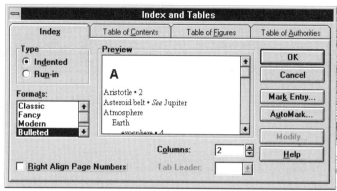

Figure 69. The *Tab Leader* drop-down list box lets you choose a leader character between entries and page numbers (if you selected the *Right Align Page Numbers* check box).

Figure 70. The *Columns* option formats the index with the number of columns in the text box (from 1 to 4). The *Auto* option keeps the existing number of columns in the document.

All choices are reflected in the example in the *Preview* list box. Click on *OK* in the *Index and Tables* dialog box to compile your index.

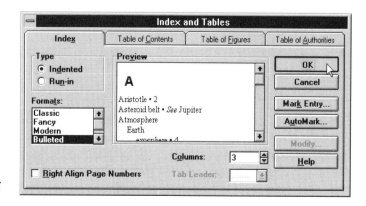

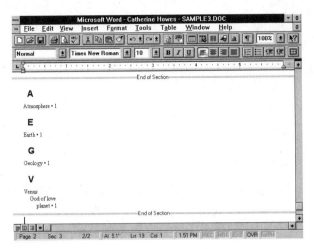

Figure 71. Word inserts the index into your document.

{INDEX \e " • " \h "A" \c "3" }

Figure 72. If it appears as an INDEX field code, press Shift+F9. (See **Chapter 15** for information about viewing codes.)

CREATING A TABLE OF CONTENTS

The easiest way to compile a table of contents is to use the built-in heading styles. Word uses the headings as the entries in a table of contents. (See **Chapter 6** for more information about applying style to your document.)

You can also create a table of contents if you have styles other than built-in heading styles applied to headings in your document.

USING BUILT-IN HEADING STYLES

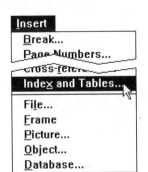

Figure 73. Place the insertion point where you want to insert the table of contents (type a table of contents title if you want a heading). Select the *Index and Tables* command from the **Insert** menu.

Figure 74. This brings up the *Index and Tables* dialog box. Select the *Table of Contents* tab. Select the format you want from the *Formats* list box. You can specify the number of heading levels you want in the table of contents in the *Show Level* text box.

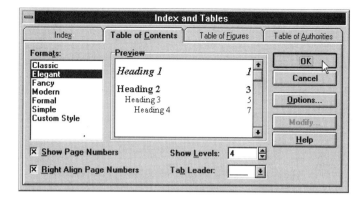

The *Preview* list box shows an example of your choices. Click on *OK* to compile the table of contents.

Figure 75. Word inserts the table of contents into your document.

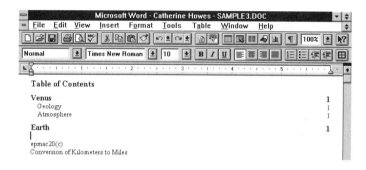

Figure 76. If it appears as an TOC field code, press Shift+F9. (See **Chapter 15** for information about codes and how to view them.)

{ TOC \o "1-4" }

USING OTHER STYLES

Figure 77. Place the insertion point where you want to insert the table of contents (type a table of contents title if you want a heading). Select *Index and Tables* from the **Insert** menu.

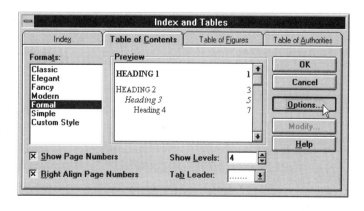

This opens the *Index and Tables* dialog box. Select the *Table of Contents* tab. Choose the format you want from the *Formats* list box. Then click on the *Options* button.

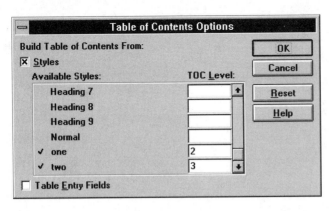

Figure 78. Word opens the *Table of Contents Options* dialog box. In the *Available Styles* list box, find which styles you applied to your text and want in the table of contents. In the *TOC Level* text box to the right of the style name, type a number from 1 to 9 to indicate what level you want formatted with what style to the table of contents.

Do this for all styles you want Word to include in the table of contents. A check mark appears beside the style name. You also need to delete the level numbers for the styles you don't want in the table of contents.

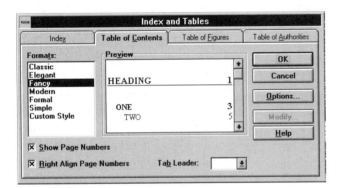

Figure 79. The *Preview* list box in the *Index and Tables* dialog box displays an example. Click on *OK*.

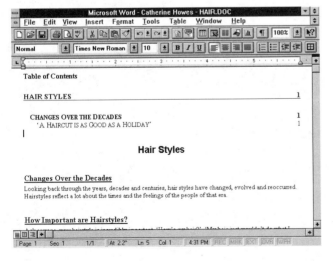

Figure 80. Word inserts the table of contents into your document.

Figure 81. If it appears as a TOC field code, press Shift+F9. (See **Chapter 15** for information about codes and how to view them.)

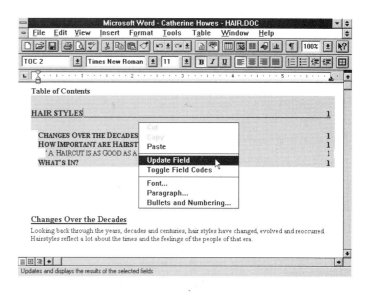

{ TOC \t "HEADING,1,TWO,3,ONE,2"}

UPDATING THE TABLE OF CONTENTS

Figure 82. You can update the table of contents to include any changes you make to the document, such as changing headings or page breaks. (To ensure the accuracy of page numbers in the table of contents, clear the hidden text and field codes from the screen before updating.)

To update, position the insertion point in the table of contents. You can then activate the shortcut menu by clicking the right mouse button and selecting *Update Field* (or press F9).

Figure 83. Then in the *Update Table of Contents* dialog box, choose an option.

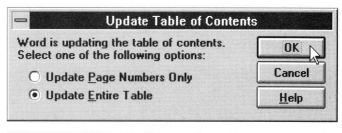

Figure 84. Alternatively, you can open the *Index and Tables* dialog box again to change formatting and update the table of contents. Word asks you if you want to replace the selected table of contents. Select *OK* to generate the new contents.

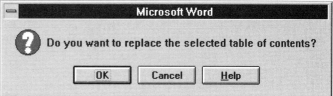

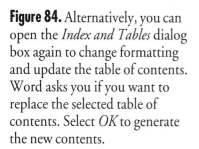

MASTER DOCUMENTS

Master documents are a good way of organizing and controlling long documents by dividing the document into smaller, linked subdocuments. You can create cross-references between subdocuments and produce an index and table of contents. Master documents also make printing easier.

You use *Master Document* view to create and open subdocuments, and to reorganize the long document. Whereas you can view and edit the whole document as if it were a single document in *Normal* view.

Any Word document can be a master or subdocument. A master document can contain up to 80 subdocuments and its total size cannot exceed 32 Mb, excluding graphics.

CREATING MASTER DOCUMENTS

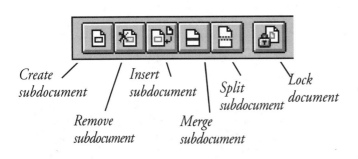

Create subdocument / Remove subdocument / Insert subdocument \ Merge subdocument \ Split subdocument \ Lock document

Figure 85. You create master documents in *Master Document* view using the *Outline* and *Master Document* toolbars. (See **Chapter 9** for information about using the *Outline* toolbar.)

CREATING A NEW MASTER DOCUMENT

Figure 86. In a new document window, choose *Master Document* from the **View** menu.

Figure 87. Word displays the *Outline* and *Master Document* toolbars (see Figure 85). Type an outline for the master document and apply the built-in heading styles to format the text. You use these headings to indicate where you want Word to break the master document into subdocuments. (If you promote and demote text using the *Outline* toolbar, Word automatically applies level headings. See **Chapter 9** for more information.)

For example, you could use *Heading 1* to represent the master document and *Heading 2* to indicate the beginning of the subdocuments.

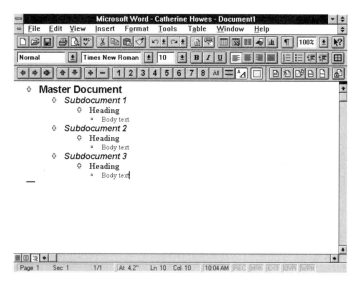

Figure 88. Select the text you want to divide into subdocuments. The first heading in the selection should be the level of heading you want Word to use to separate the master document into subdocuments. So, if you use *Heading 2* to indicate subdocuments, Word divides the master document into subdocuments whenever it comes across a level *Heading 2* style.

Click on the *Create Subdocument* button on the *Master Document* toolbar.

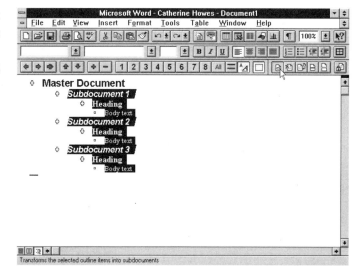

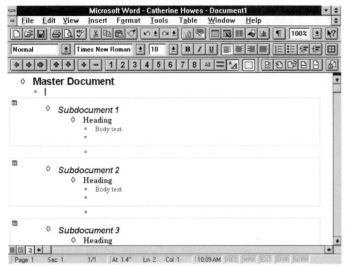

Figure 89. Word puts each subdocument in a box and displays a subdocument icon in the upper-left corner. Subdocuments are also separated by section breaks (click on the *Show/Hide* button on the *Standard* toolbar to see the section breaks, or view the document in *Normal* view). Sections affect the formatting of the long documents, just like any document with sections (see **Chapter 4** for information).

Name and save the master document (see **Chapter 3** for information about saving).

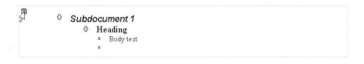

Figure 90. When you save a master document, Word automatically assigns a filename to each subdocument using the first characters of the heading that begins each subdocument. This lets you open and edit subdocuments separately if you want to. To see what a subdocument is called, double-click on the subdocument icon.

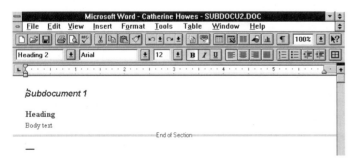

Figure 91. This opens the subdocument and you can see its name in the title bar.

CONVERTING AN EXISTING DOCUMENT TO A MASTER DOCUMENT

You can also convert an existing document to a master document by opening it in *Master Document* view, and following the same process outlined above starting from Figure 87.

INSERTING A DOCUMENT INTO AN EXISTING MASTER DOCUMENT

Figure 92. With the master document open in *Master Document* view, place the insertion point where you want to add the document. Now click on the *Insert Subdocument* button (see Figure 85).

In the *Insert Subdocument* dialog box (which is the same as the *Open* dialog box), select the document you want to insert and click on *OK*.

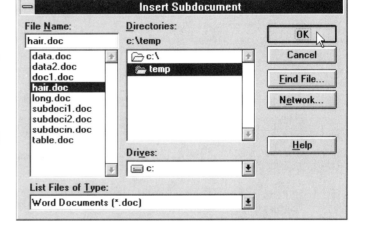

Figure 93. Word adds the document to the master document as a subdocument, and its filename stays the same.

If the templates are different between the two documents, the master document template overrides the subdocument's template, however the section formatting of the subdocument remains. If you open the existing document outside the master document, Word uses its original template.

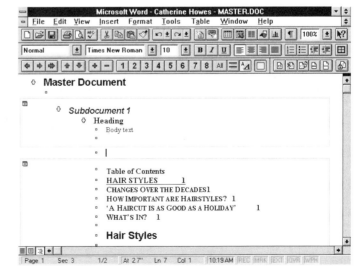

EDITING MASTER DOCUMENTS

Apply formats and choose settings for the entire long document in the master document, not a subdocument.

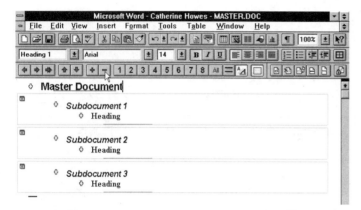

Figure 94. You can condense and expand the contents of subdocuments by clicking on the *Collapse* and *Expand* buttons on the *Outline* toolbar, but only when the insertion point is in the master document section.

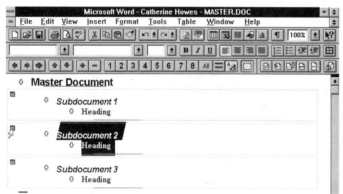

Figure 95. Use *Master Document* view to change the structure of the long document by dragging heading levels. You can also use this view to open the subdocuments. (See **Chapter 9** for more information about using the commands on the *Outline* toolbar, as well as editing and moving level headings.)

To select an entire subdocument, click on the subdocument icon.

Figure 96. To split a subdocument into two, place the insertion point where you want to separate the subdocument and click on the *Split Subdocument* button on the *Master Document* toolbar.

Figure 97. If you want to merge subdocuments, move the subdocuments next to each other. Click on the subdocument icon of the first subdocument to select it. Then, hold down the Shift key and click on the icon of the next subdocument.

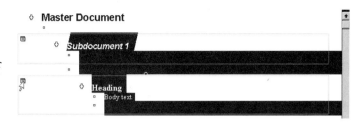

Figure 98. Now click on the *Merge Subdocument* button on the *Master Document* toolbar to merge the subdocuments.

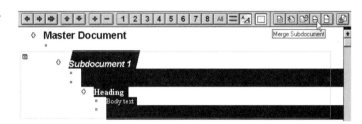

To remove a subdocument and its contents from the master document, select it by clicking on the subdocument icon and then press Backspace or Delete.

Don't just delete the subdocument from disk; if you do, you'll get an error message when you open the master document.

If you want to rename or move a subdocument, make sure you do this through the master document.

Figure 99. To remove a subdocument from the master document but keep the subdocument text as part of the master document, select the subdocument and click on the *Remove Subdocument* button on the *Master Document* toolbar.

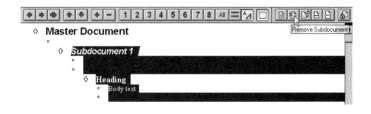

CROSS-REFERENCES, INDEXES, AND TABLES OF CONTENTS

You create and update cross-references, indexes and table of contents in master documents the same way you do for a normal document (see sections earlier in this chapter). Make sure you create and update them in your master document.

You insert cross-references with your master document displayed in *Normal* view and follow the same procedures as described earlier in this chapter.

PRINTING MASTER DOCUMENTS

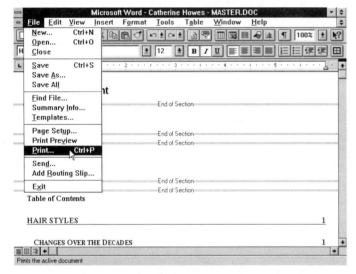

Figure 100. To print the entire document, display the master document in *Normal* view. If you want to print an outline of the document, display it in *Master Document* view, and collapse and expand the headings to show what you want to print.

Then choose *Print* from the **File** menu.

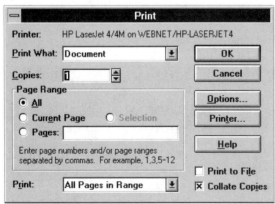

Figure 101. Select printing options from the *Print* dialog box. (See **Chapter 10** for more information.)

MACROS AND AUTOTEXT

14

INTRODUCTION

AutoText can contain formatted text or graphics. Retrieving
AutoText is a quick way to put this information into your
document. Macros are similar, but far more complex and powerful,
as you can use them to record keystrokes, as well as previously
created AutoText entries.

CREATING SIMPLE MACROS

The main difference between AutoText and a macro is the way you
create them. You create AutoText from a finished product, while a
macro records a series of actions and keystrokes as you perform
them, then groups them as a single command. Macros can contain
AutoText entries.

   While recording macros, you cannot select text with the mouse;
you must use keystrokes instead (see **Chapter 2**). However, you can
still use the mouse to choose menus and options in dialog boxes.

Figure 1. To record a macro, you
can double-click on REC on the
status bar.

| At 2.1" | Ln 8 | Col 77 | 11:02 AM | REC | MRK | EXT | OVR | WPH |

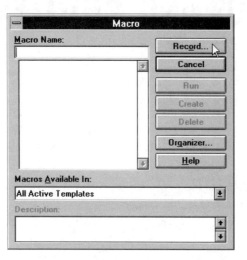

Figure 2. Alternatively, choose *Macro* from the **Tools** menu and click on the *Record* button in the *Macro* dialog box.

Figure 3. In the *Record Macro* dialog box, type a name for the macro in the *Record Macro Name* text box, or use the macro name that Word suggests. You can type a description of your macro in the *Description* text box.

If you want to assign the macro to a toolbar, menu, or shortcut key, choose a button from the *Assign Macro To* section.

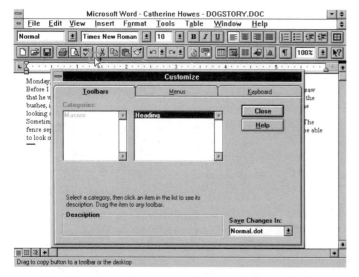

Figure 4. These buttons open the *Customize* dialog box.

To assign a macro to a toolbar, click and drag the macro name from the list box to a toolbar. The mouse pointer changes shape.

Figure 5. Release the mouse button to display a button outline on the toolbar, and Word opens the *Custom Button* dialog box. Choose a button or keep *Text Button* selected and click on *Assign*.

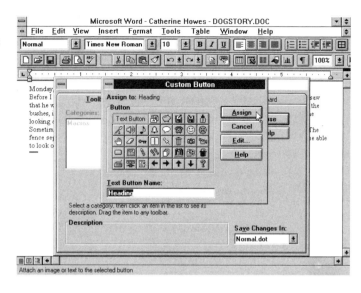

Figure 6. Word adds the macro name to the button. Now close the *Customize* dialog box.

Figure 7. If you choose to assign a macro to a menu, Word opens the *Customize* dialog box with the *Menus* tab active.

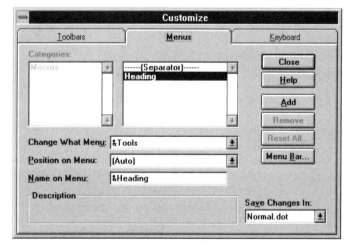

Figure 8. Choose a menu from the *Change What Menu* drop-down list box.

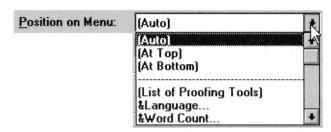

Figure 9. Choose a position from the *Position on Menu* drop-down list box.

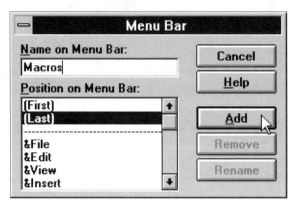

Figure 10. To create your own menu to contain macros, click on the *Menu Bar* button. In the *Menu Bar* dialog box, type a name for the menu in the *Name on Menu Bar* text box and select a position for the macro from the list box. Then click on the *Add* button, and close the dialog box.

When you return to the *Customize* dialog box, close it.

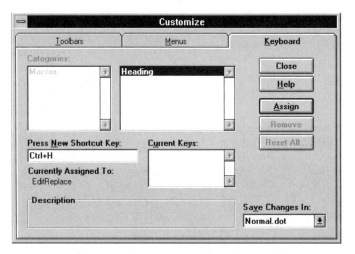

Figure 11. If you chose *Keyboard* from the *Assign Macro To* section of the *Record Macro* dialog box, Word displays the *Keyboard* tab of the *Customize* dialog box. In the *Press New Shortcut Key* text box, press the keys you want to assign to the macro.

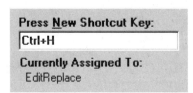

Figure 12. Word indicates if that key combination is currently assigned to another command or not. Click on the *Assign* button.

Figure 13. The key combination appears in the *Current Keys* list box. You can select it from here and click on *Remove* if you want to delete it. Then close the dialog box.

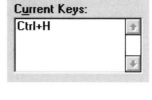

Click on *OK* in the *Record Macro* dialog box if you didn't choose to assign the macro.

Figure 14. When you return to your document, Word highlights REC in the status bar, changes the mouse pointer, and displays the *Macro Record* toolbar to show it is ready to record the macro.

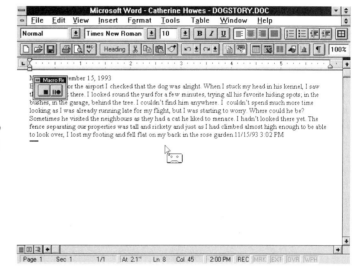

Perform any actions you want to record. REC remains in the status bar until you stop recording the macro.

Figure 15. You can pause the recording by clicking on the *Pause* button on the *Macro Record* toolbar. This is useful if you want to do something that you don't want to record in the macro. Click on this button again to resume the recording.

Figure 16. To finish recording the macro, click on the *Stop* button on the *Macro Record* toolbar, or double-click on REC on the status bar.

PLAYING MACROS

Figure 17. To play a macro, choose *Macro* from the **Tools** menu. In the *Macro* dialog box, select the macro that you want to run from the list box.

In the *Macros Available In* drop-down list box, select the list of macros you want to see.

Click on the *Run* button when you have chosen the macro.

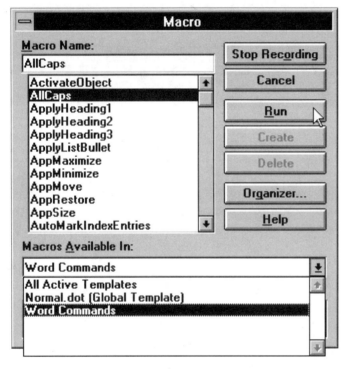

Figure 18. If you've assigned the macro to a toolbar, menu, or shortcut key (see **Creating Simple Macros** earlier in this chapter), click on the macro button on the toolbar, select the macro name from the menu, or press the keyboard combination to run the macro.

Figure 19. Word does all the actions you recorded, operating from the insertion point in your document.

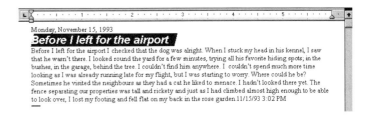

DELETING, RENAMING, COPYING AND MACROS

DELETING A MACRO

Figure 20. To delete a macro, open the *Macro* dialog box by choosing *Macro* from the **Tools** menu. To delete a macro, highlight it in the list, and click on the *Delete* button. You can also delete macros from the *Organizer* dialog box, which appears if you click on the *Organizer* button.

RENAMING A MACRO

Figure 21. If you want to rename a macro, click on the *Organizer* button to open the *Organizer* dialog box. Select the macro you want to rename. Choose the template where the macro you want to rename is stored from the *Macros Available In* drop-down list. If the template you need is not open, click on *Close File*.

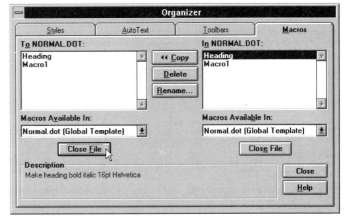

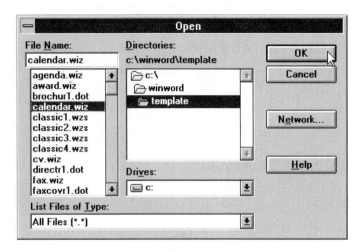

Figure 22. Then click on the *Open File* button that appears and open the template you want from the *Open* dialog box.

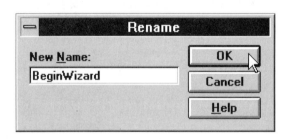

Figure 23. Back in the *Organizer* dialog box, choose the *Rename* button and type a new name in the *Rename* dialog box and choose *OK*.

COPYING A MACRO

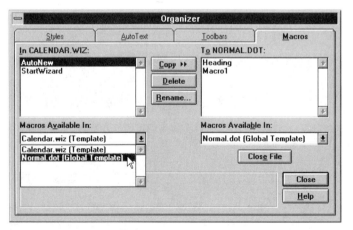

Figure 24. To copy a macro, select the template where the macro is stored from the *Macros Available In* drop-down list box on the left.

Figure 25. If the template is not open, click on *Close File* and then on the *Open File* button to choose a template from the *Open* dialog box.

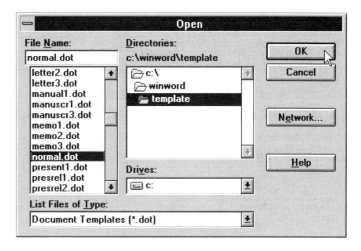

Figure 26. Then on the right-hand side of the dialog box, open the template that you want to copy the macro to.

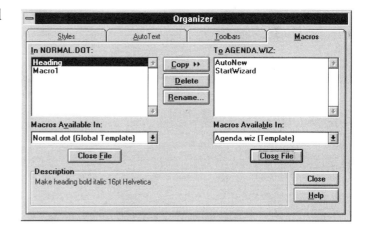

Figure 27. Then with the macro highlighted in the *In* list box, click on the *Copy* button.

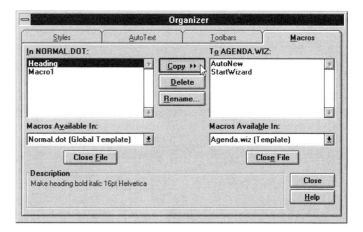

EDITING MACROS

Figure 28. You can edit a macro you have created by choosing it in the *Macro* dialog box and clicking on the *Edit* button.

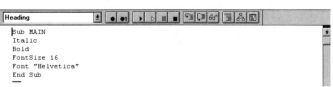

Figure 29. Word opens the macro in its editing window, shows the command in the macro, and displays the *Macro* toolbar.

You can edit a macro using the macro language, WordBasic, and the buttons on the *Macro* toolbar.

STANDARD MACROS

Figure 30. The macros that come with Word are stored in the templates in the *macros* directory of the *winword6* directory. To use them, you need to load these templates as global templates (see **Chapter 7** for information on how to do this). You can then choose the macros you want to use in your document from the *Macro* dialog box.

AutoText

CREATING AUTOTEXT

You can use AutoText to store text, graphics, or anything else you need on a regular basis in your documents.

Figure 31. Select the items you want to store as AutoText; include the paragraph mark if you also want to save the paragraph formatting. Then click on the *Edit AutoText* button on the *Standard* toolbar.

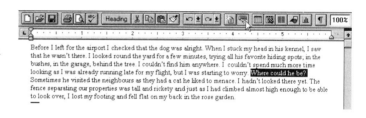

Figure 32. You can also choose *AutoText* from the **Edit** menu.

Figure 33. In the *AutoText* dialog box that appears, type a name for the AutoText entry in the *Name* text box. Word automatically adds the first few words of your selection to the *Name* text box to make it easier to create.

Once you've decided on the name, click on *Add*.

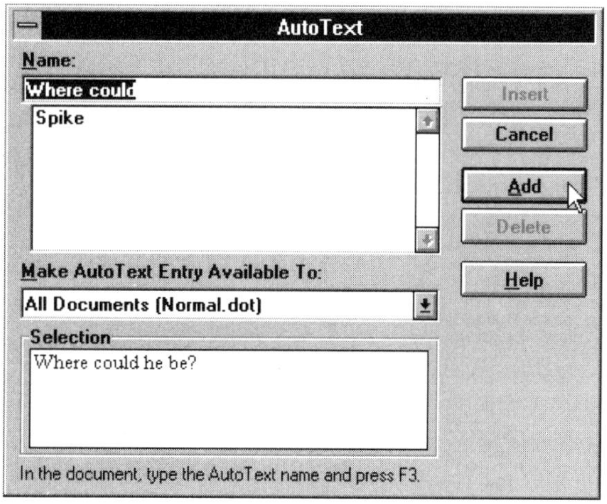

INSERTING AUTOTEXT

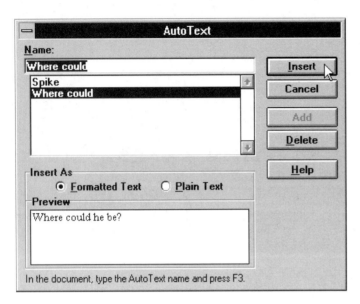

Figure 34. To insert an AutoText entry at the insertion point in your document, choose *AutoText* from the **Edit** menu (Figure 32). Then in the *AutoText* dialog box, select an AutoText name from the list box.

To insert the AutoText without any formatting, select the *Plain Text* radio button; any text in the AutoText entry adopts the format of the text around it. Choose the *Formatted Text* radio button to insert the entry with its original formatting. Then click on *Insert*.

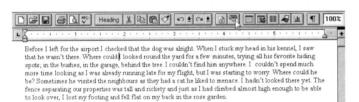

Figure 35. Alternatively, you can insert AutoText by typing the name of the entry and clicking on the *Insert AutoText* button on the *Standard* toolbar. You can also press F3.

EDITING ENTRIES

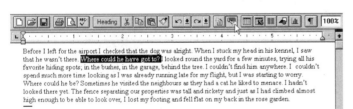

Figure 36. To edit an AutoText entry, insert it in your document and make any changes. Then select the AutoText (including paragraph marks) and click on the *Edit AutoText* button on the *Standard* toolbar.

Figure 37. Select the original name of the entry from the list box in the *AutoText* dialog box, or type it in the *Name* text box. Then click on the *Add* button.

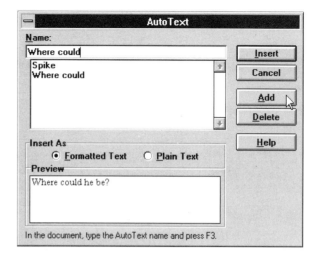

Figure 38. Choose *Yes* when Word displays this prompt box.

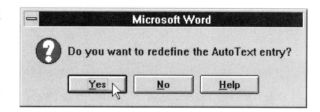

DELETING ENTRIES

To delete saved AutoText, select the *AutoText* command from the **Edit** menu.

Figure 39. In the *AutoText* dialog box, select the entry you want to delete and click on the *Delete* button.

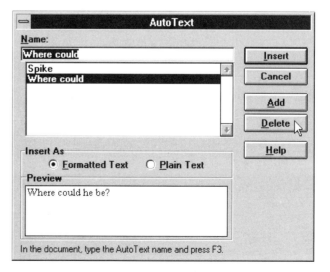

RENAMING ENTRIES

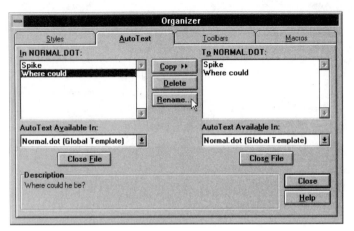

Figure 40. You can rename an AutoText entry through the *Organizer* dialog box. (Activate this dialog box by selecting *Style* from the **Format** menu, and then clicking on the *Organizer* button in the *Style* dialog box). On the *AutoText* tab, select the AutoText entry from the list box on the left and click on the *Rename* button.

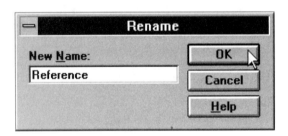

Figure 41. Word opens the *Rename* dialog box where you can type a new name for the AutoText entry. Click on *OK*, then close the *Organizer* dialog box.

FIELD CODES 15

INTRODUCTION

A field code is a set of coded directions that instruct Word to automatically insert information into a document at a position you choose. You can use field codes to add things such as the date, time, author, and page numbers. Fields are useful in documents that contain information that changes regularly.

ELEMENTS OF A FIELD CODE

Each code has three basic parts:

1. The *field characters* ({ })—these characters mark the beginning and the end of a field code. You use the Insert Field key (Ctrl+F9) to insert these characters—not the braces from the keyboard.

2. The *field type*—identifies the data you want Word to insert, such as DATE for the date; TC for a table of contents entry.

3. The *instructions*—the details of how you want the action performed. Instructions can contain "switches" that modify the action.

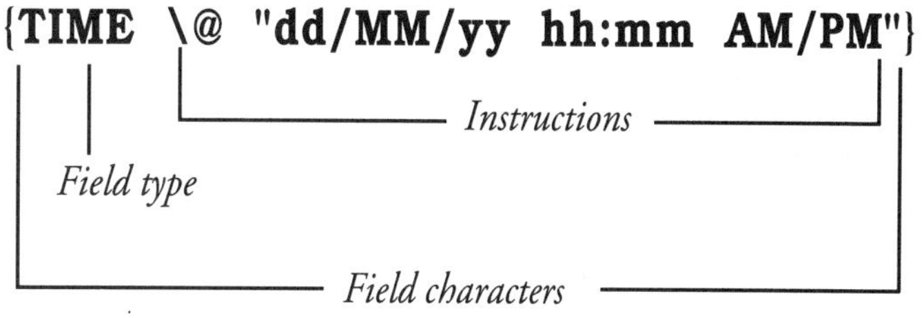

Figure 1. The three basic elements of a field code are shown in this figure.

{TIME \@ "dd/MM/yy hh:mm AM/PM"}

Instructions

Field type

Field characters

INSERTING FIELDS

Figure 2. Put the insertion point in your document where you want to insert the field, and choose *Field* from the **Insert** menu.

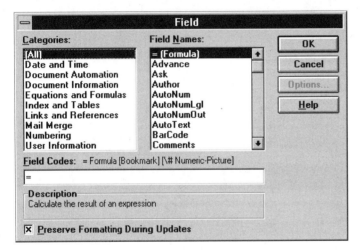

Figure 3. This opens the *Field* dialog box. From the *Categories* list, select a field category. Choose *[All]* to see all the field types.

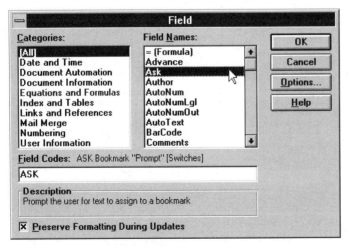

Figure 4. From the *Field Names* list box, select the field type you want. (You can press F1 to get Help and information about the selected field type.) The field type appears in the *Field Codes* text box below.

To add instructions, type these after the field type in the *Field Codes* text box.

Figure 5. Alternatively, choose the *Options* button. Select the options you want in the *Field Options* dialog box for the selected field name, and click on *Add to Field* button. Then choose *OK* to return to the *Field* dialog box.

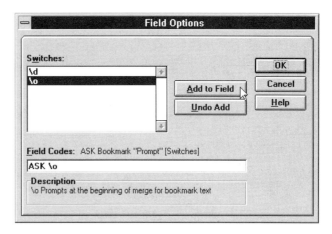

Figure 6. Choose *OK* in the *Field* dialog box to insert the field in your document.

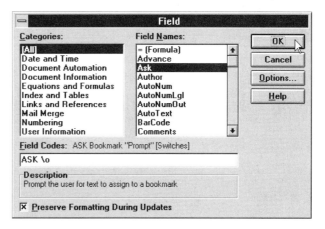

Figure 7. If you make a mistake when typing the instructions, an error message appears instead of the result. See the **Editing Fields** section later in this chapter to see how to edit the field and correct the problem.

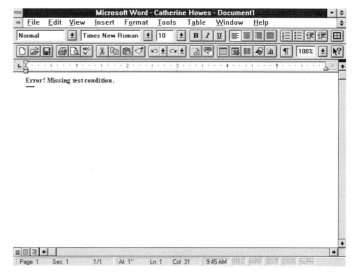

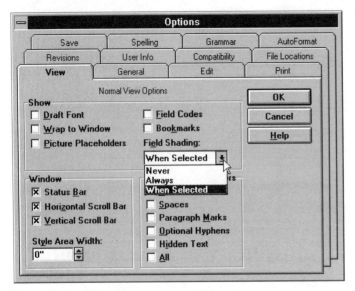

Figure 8. To help identify field results, you can have Word apply shading to highlight them. Choose *Options* from the **Tools** menu and select the *View* tab. From the *Field Shading* drop-down list, select if you want Word to shade field results *Never*, *Always*, or *When Selected* (the default).

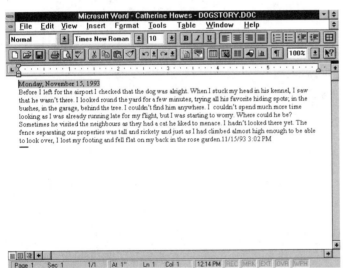

Figure 9. By default, field results look like any other text in your document and Word shades them when you put the insertion point in a field.

VIEWING FIELD CODES OR RESULTS

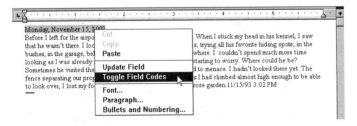

Figure 10. To view the field codes (or the results if the codes are already visible), position the mouse pointer over the field and click the right mouse button. Then from the shortcut menu, choose *Toggle Field Codes*.

Figure 11. When you do this in *Normal* view, Word displays the field code for that selected field only. In *Page Layout* view, field codes appear instead of field results throughout the whole document.

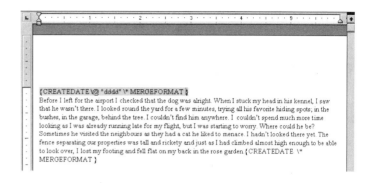

Figure 12. Alternatively, choose *Options* from the **Tools** menu. On the *View* tab in the *Options* dialog box, select the *Field Codes* check box in the *Show* section. Then click on *OK* to display field codes in the document.

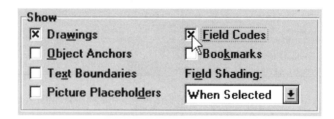

If you don't have *Help for WordPerfect Users* active you can press Alt+F9 as a keyboard shortcut to switch between viewing field codes and field results for the whole document.

EDITING FIELDS

Figure 13. To edit fields, add the insertion point to the field and make sure the field code is showing. You can edit the instructions in the same way you would any normal text. (If you select either the opening or closing field characters, see Figure 1, Word selects the whole field.)

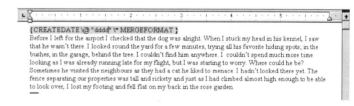

Switch the view back to the field results before you update it.

Note: You cannot overtype a field character ({}). Nor can you delete a single field character; you must select both field characters and delete them together.

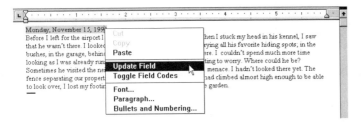

UPDATING FIELDS

Figure 14. To update a field, put the mouse pointer over the field result. Click the right mouse button and select *Update Field* from the shortcut menu. This displays the new field result.

Alternatively, you can press the F9 function key to update the field if *Help for WordPerfect Users* is not active.

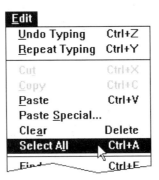

Figure 15. If you want to update all fields in the document, first choose *Select All* from the **Edit** menu, then press F9 to update the fields.

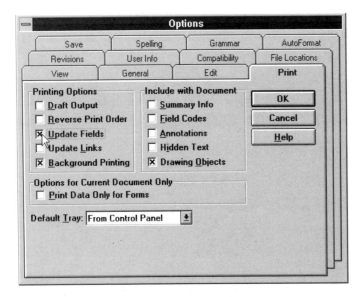

Figure 16. You can also update all fields when you print the document. Open the *Options* dialog box by choosing *Options* from the **Tools** menu. In the *Printing Options* section of the *Print* tab, select the *Update Fields* check box.

PREVENTING FIELDS FROM BEING UPDATED

If you want to prevent a selected field from being updated, you can either "unlink" or "lock" the field. When you unlink a field, its result becomes regular text and Word no longer updates. Locking a field is useful if you want to temporarily block any updating.

To unlink a field, place the insertion point in the field then press Ctrl+Shift+F9 on the keyboard.

To lock a field, select the field and press Ctrl+F11 (if *Help for WordPerfect Users* is not active).

To unlock a selected field, press Ctrl+Shift+F11.

MERGING DOCUMENTS 16

INTRODUCTION

Using the *Mail Merge* command, you can combine a list of variable information with a standard document to create multiple documents, such as personalized letters, legal documents, mailing labels, envelopes, and catalogs.

Merging generally involves two files: a *data document* which contains the variable information, such as names and addresses; and a *main document* which contains the information that stays the same in each version of the finished documents. When you merge the two documents together, Word replaces mail merge fields in the main document with the appropriate information from the data file to produce different versions of the main document.

There are three stages to merging documents: creating the main document; creating the data document; and completing the main document and merging the two files.

CREATING THE MAIN DOCUMENT

Figure 1. Make the document you want to use as the main document active. You can open an existing file or begin a new document. You don't have to complete the document now; you just need to indicate that this is the main document you want to use. You can finish typing, editing, and inserting merge fields in the main document later.

Tools	
Spelling...	F7
Grammar...	
Thesaurus...	Shift+F7
Hyphenation...	
Language...	
Word Count...	
AutoCorrect...	
Mail Merge...	
Envelopes and Labels...	

Choose *Mail Merge* from the **Tools** menu.

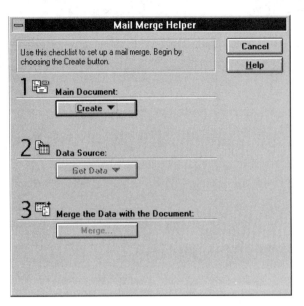

Figure 2. The *Mail Merge Helper* dialog box shows the steps you need to complete the merge.

Figure 3. Click on the *Create* button, and select the type of merge from the drop-down list. (We will use *Form Letters* as an example.)

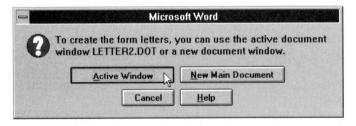

Figure 4. In the Word prompt box, click on the *Active Window* button to make your active document the main document. (The *New Main Document* button creates a new main document based on the *Normal* template.)

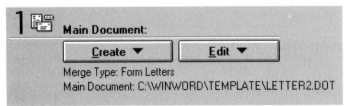

Figure 5. In the *Mail Merge Helper* dialog box, Word indicates the type of merge and the name of the main document under the *Create* button.

CREATING THE DATA DOCUMENT

You need to indicate the data source you want to merge with the main document. You can open an existing data file, or create a new file and fill in the variable information.

The data file contains the variable information for each version of a merged document. You can decide what and how many categories of information, or *data fields*, you want to make up one *data record* in the data file. For example, one record in a customer mailing list contains all the relevant information for one client. Each record is made up of fields of information. Fields are the variable information, such as contact name, phone number, and address. The first record of the data file is called the *header record*. You list the data field categories in the header record, and the data records are listed underneath.

Figure 6. To create a new data source file, choose *Create Data Source* from the *Get Data* drop-down list in the *Mail Merge Helper* dialog box.

Figure 7. Word displays the *Create Data Source* dialog box. You use this dialog box to create the field names that guide you when typing your variable information. In the *Field Names in Header Row* list box, Word provides a list of field names of data categories commonly used in data files. You can use this list as a basis to customize your header row, i.e. decide what data fields you want.

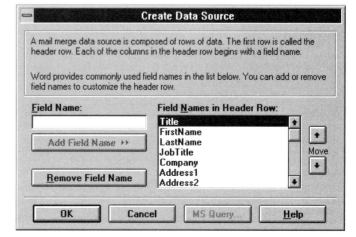

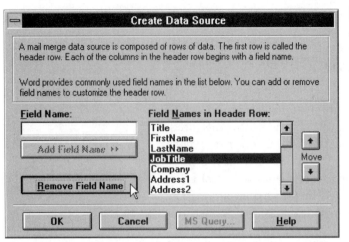

Figure 8. To delete a data field category from the list box, select the field name and click on the *Remove Field Name* button.

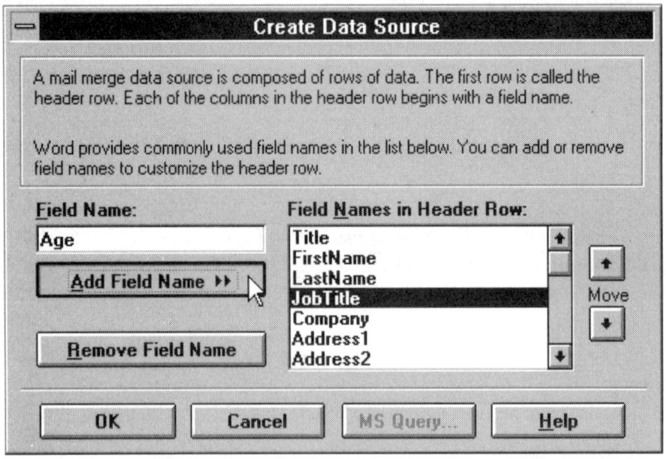

Figure 9. To add a data field to the data source, type a new field name in the *Field Name* text box and click on the *Add Field Name* button.

A field name can have up to 40 characters (you can't use spaces).

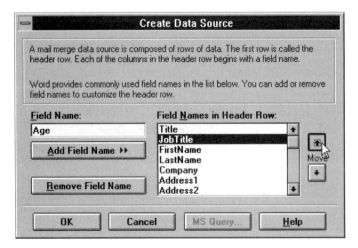

Figure 10. To change the order of field names, select a name from the list box and click on the up and down arrows to move it up and down the list.

Figure 11. Once you have finished entering the field names, click on *OK.* Word opens the *Save Data Source* dialog box so you can name and save the new data source file.

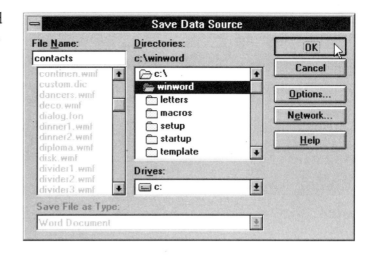

Figure 12. Word displays a prompt box. Choose *Edit Data Source* to insert the data records you want to use in your merge.

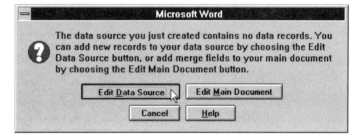

Figure 13. In the *Data Form* dialog box, type information for each data field in its text box then press Enter.

To move to the next and previous field text box, press Tab or Shift+Tab, or click the mouse in the text box to place the insertion point in it.

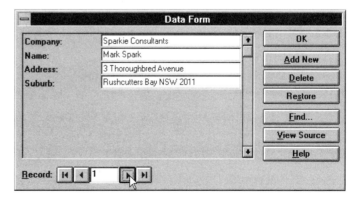

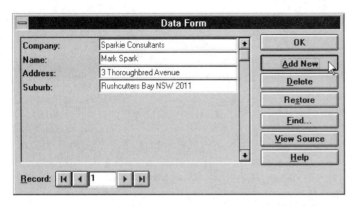

Figure 14. When you have finished typing all the data field information for that record, choose *Add New* to start a new record set on a blank form.

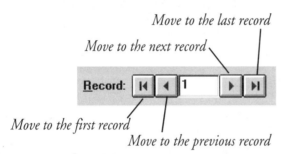

Move to the last record

Move to the next record

Record:

Move to the first record

Move to the previous record

Figure 15. Use the *Record* arrow buttons to move between data records to view and edit them.

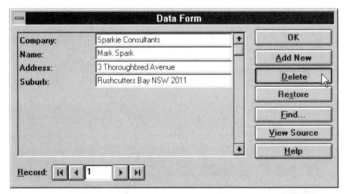

Figure 16. You can click on the *Restore* button to cancel changes made to the current record.

Click on the *Delete* button to remove a data record from the source file.

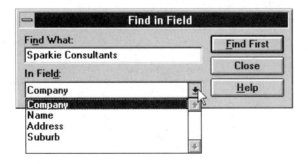

Figure 17. The *Find* button opens the *Find in Field* dialog box, which you can use to find specific records. Type in what you want in the *Find What* text box and select a field from the *In Field* drop-down list box.

Figure 18. If you click on the *View Source* button of the *Data Form* dialog box, Word displays the data records in a table in the data document window. Click on the *Data Form* button on the *Database* toolbar to return to the *Data Form* dialog box.

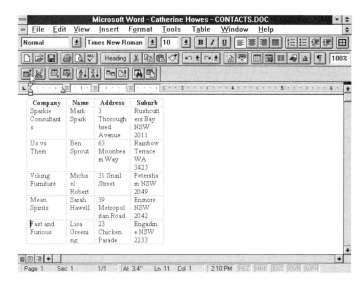

Figure 19. To open an existing data source file, click on the *Get Data* button in the *Mail Merge Helper* dialog box and choose *Open Data Source*.

Figure 20. The *Open Data Source* dialog box appears (this is the same as the *Open* dialog box). Select the data file you want and click on *OK*.

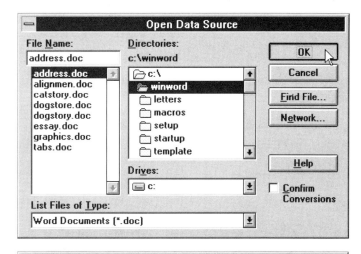

Figure 21. Word displays this prompt box. Click on *Edit Main Document*.

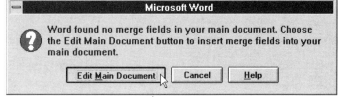

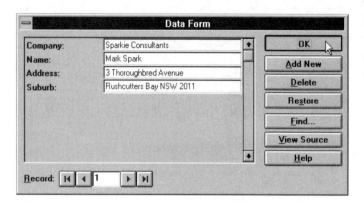

EDITING THE DATA FILE

Figure 22. If you click on *OK* in the *Data Form* dialog box, Word also takes you to the data document window.

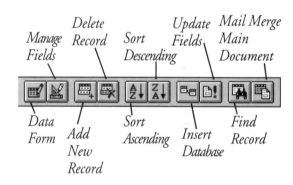

Figure 23. You can use the *Database* toolbar to delete, add and sort records, and add new fields to the data table.

DATA FORM BUTTON

Figure 24. The *Data Form* button opens the *Data Form* dialog box so you can edit the data fields.

MANAGE FIELDS BUTTON

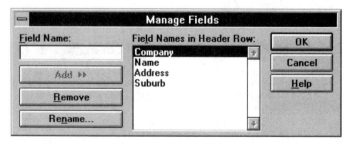

Figure 25. Click on the *Manage Fields* button to open this dialog box so you can add, remove, or rename fields in the data source.

ADD NEW RECORD BUTTON

Figure 26. To add a record to the end of the data source table, click on the *Add New Record* button. Then type in the field data.

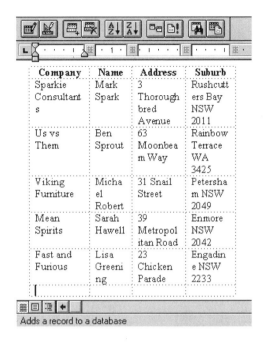

DELETE RECORD BUTTON

Figure 27. Click on the *Delete Record* button to delete the selected record or the record containing the insertion point.

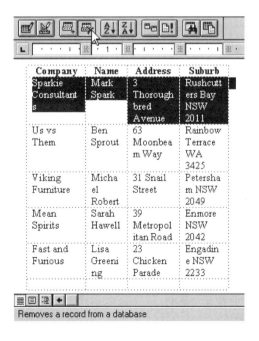

SORT ASCENDING AND SORT DESCENDING BUTTONS

You can sort the data in the table alphabetically or numerically, and in ascending or descending order. To sort by up to three data fields, do so from the *Query Options* dialog box (see Figure 46 under **Selecting Data Records to Merge** later in this chapter).

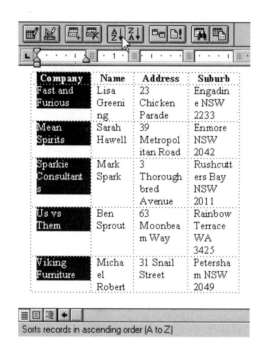

Figure 28. To sort records by a single field, place the insertion point in the column of the data field you want to sort by. Then click on the *Sort Ascending* or *Sort Descending* button.

INSERT DATABASE BUTTON

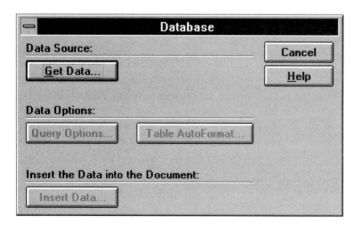

Figure 29. Click on the *Insert Database* button if you want to select data records from another data source and add them to an existing data file in Word.

UPDATE FIELDS BUTTON

This button updates and displays the results of the selected fields.

FIND RECORD BUTTON

Figure 30. Click on the *Find Record* button to find data records through the *Find In Field* dialog box (see Figure 17 in the **Creating the Data Document** section previously in this chapter for more information).

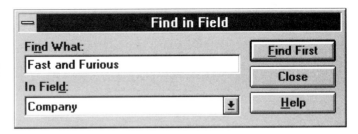

MAIL MERGE MAIN DOCUMENT BUTTON

Click on the *Mail Merge Main Document* button to make the main document active.

COMPLETING THE MAIN DOCUMENT AND MERGING THE FILES

INSERTING MERGE FIELDS IN MAIN DOCUMENT

To tell Word where you want to print the variable information in the main document, you insert the field names you defined in the *Data Form* dialog box. When you merge the two files, Word replaces the field names in the main document with the corresponding field information in the data source file.

Figure 31. To return to your main document, you can either click on the *Mail Merge Main Document* button on the *Database* toolbar in the data file window (Figure 18), or choose the main document name from the **Window** menu.

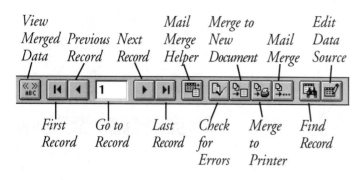

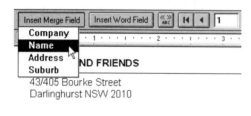

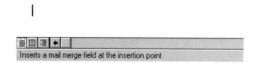

Figure 32. The main document window now appears, showing the *Mail Merge* toolbar you use to control the setup and printing of your merge documents.

Type and edit the text and graphics you want to appear in each version of the merged documents.

Figure 33. When you reach the place or have positioned the cursor where you want to insert data field information in the main document, click on the *Insert Merge Field* button on the *Mail Merge* toolbar. Select a merge field from the drop-down list box.

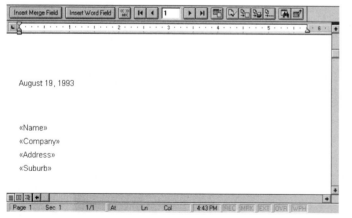

Figure 34. Word then inserts the merge field into your main document. Make sure to type spaces and punctuation between and after merge fields.

By default, merge fields appear as in this figure (with *Field Codes* deselected in the *Options* dialog box).

Figure 35. If you select the *Field Codes* check box in the *Options* dialog box (from the **Tools** menu), merge fields display as in this figure. (See **Chapter 15** for more information about field codes and viewing them.)

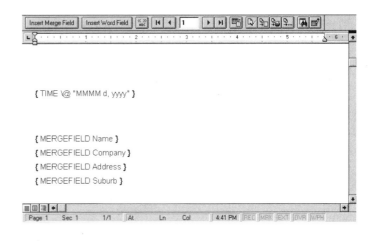

Repeat this procedure to insert other merge fields from the data file into your main document. You can insert the field names in any order, and as many times as you need if you want the corresponding data information in more than one place in your document.

Figure 36. Choose *Save* from the File menu or *Standard* toolbar to save the main document.

MERGING THE DOCUMENTS

Figure 37. Click on the *View Merged Data* button on the *Mail Merge* toolbar to display merge field information instead of the field codes in the main document window.

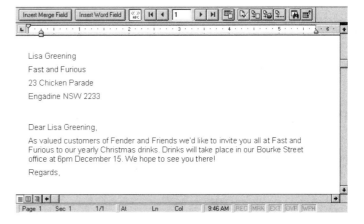

The record number that appears in the *Go to Record* text box is the data information Word uses. Click on the arrows to view the information of other data records in the data source file.

Figure 38. You can also preview a data record by clicking on the *Find Record* button. Then in the *Find in Field* dialog box, specify a field and information you want to find (see Figure 17 for more information about this dialog box).

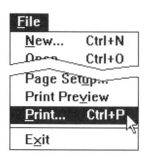

Figure 39. You can print just the active, previewed document by choosing *Print* from the **File** menu. (See **Chapter 10** for information about using the *Print* dialog box.)

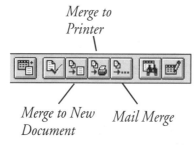

Merge to Printer

Merge to New Document *Mail Merge*

Figure 40. To merge the main document with the data document, click on one of these buttons on the *Mail Merge* toolbar. (If you want to merge only certain data records, see the **Selecting Data Records to Merge** section later in this chapter.)

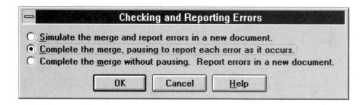

Figure 41. *Check for Errors* button checks the main document and data file for any field naming errors. In this dialog box, indicate how you want Word to check for errors.

Figure 42. The *Merge to New Document* button merges to another document and stores the results. This is convenient if you want to review the documents before you print them, and add any extra information to further personalize them.

Each document is in a separate section, shown by double dotted lines. Word names this temporary document "Form Letters 1." You can save this document if you want to print it later.

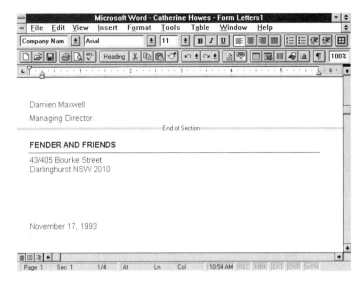

Figure 43. *Merge to Printer* opens the *Print* dialog box so you can send the merge results directly to the printer.

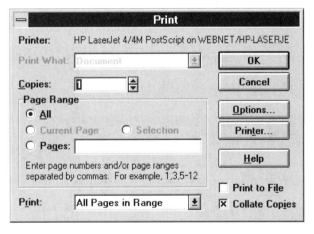

Figure 44. The *Mail Merge* button opens the *Merge* dialog box. From here you can choose which data records you want to merge, using the *Query Options* button (Figure 46), and the *Records to Be Merged* section. You can also specify if you want to print blank lines for empty fields, and if you want to merge to electronic mail (choose from the *Merge To* drop-down list box).

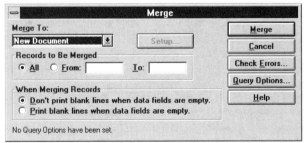

SELECTING DATA RECORDS TO MERGE

You can specify criteria to select the data records you want to merge; the merge process then skips all data records that do not meet the rules. Once you have set queries to select records, only those records can be merged with the main document until you change or clear the query rules.

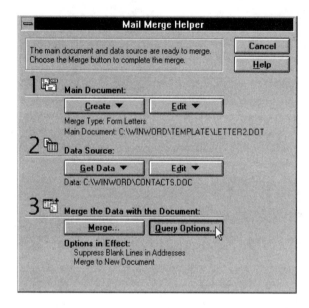

Figure 45. Choose *Mail Merge* from the **Tools** menu. Then, click on the *Query Options* button in the *Mail Merge Helper* dialog box, under step 3.

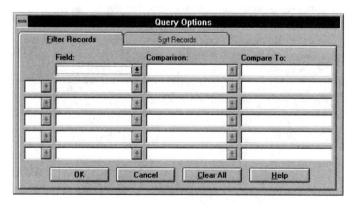

Figure 46. This opens the *Query Options* dialog box. On the *Filter Records* tab, you can specify record selection rules.

Figure 47. Select a field type from the *Field* drop-down list box.

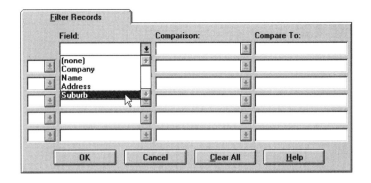

Figure 48. Then select a comparison phrase from its drop-down list box.

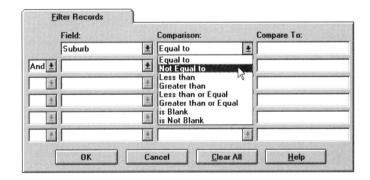

Figure 49. In the *Compare To* text box, type what you want Word to compare with the data field. The data records that meet this comparison are included in the merge.

When comparing text, letters are less than letters that come after them in the alphabet. For example, "apple" is less than "banana." (The case doesn't matter.)

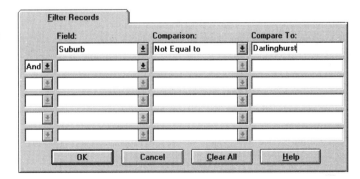

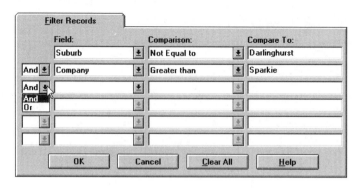

Figure 50. You can specify up to six rules to narrow the range of data records to merge. Select *And* or *Or* from the drop-down list box next to each query rule.

Choose *And* to merge only those records that satisfy both (or all) rules. If you select *Or,* Word selects the records that satisfy at least one of the connected rules. You can choose *And* or *Or* for each selection rule you specify. The way you connect the rules with *And* or *Or* affects which data records you merge. Word finds the records that meet the rules connected with *And* and then applies the rules connected with *Or* to these data records.

Repeat these steps for each rule you want to create. Click on the *Clear All* button to delete all the selection rules.

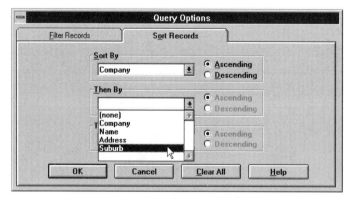

Figure 51. On the *Sort Records* tab, you can sort the data records and arrange them in alphabetic or numeric order based on the information in the data fields you select from the drop-down list boxes.

Choose a field name from the *Sort By* drop-down list box. Then choose the *Ascending* or *Descending* radio button.

To sort by additional fields, do the same in the *Then By* sections.

USING FIELDS IN MERGED DOCUMENTS

In your main document, you can insert field codes that get Word to insert information into a document to further personalize it.

Figure 52. Put the insertion point in your main document where you want to insert the Word field. Click on the *Word Field* button on the *Mail Merge* toolbar and select a field command from the drop-down list box.

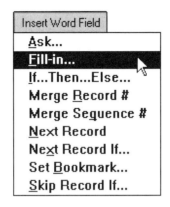

If...Then...Else lets you print information in a merged document only if the data record meets the conditions you specify. *Set Bookmark*, *Ask* and *Fill-in* let you insert comments that aren't in your data source. (Refer to Help for information about what each field does.)

Figure 53. You can type in the relevant information for the selected field in its dialog box.

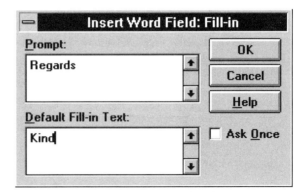

See **Chapter 15** for more information about fields and how to view codes or their results.

ENVELOPES AND MAILING LABELS

If you have performed a print merge of letters, then you probably need to create envelopes or labels to go with these letters.

ENVELOPES

Figure 54. In a new document window, choose *Mail Merge* from the **Tools** menu to open the *Mail Merge Helper* dialog box. Click on the *Create* button and choose *Envelopes* from the drop-down list.

Figure 55. When Word displays this prompt box, click on *Active Window*.

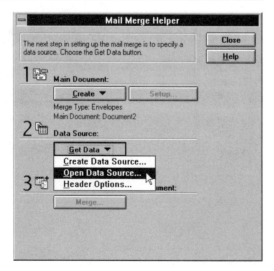

Figure 56. Then in the *Mail Merger Helper* dialog box under step 2 (*Data Source*), click on *Get Data*.

If you want to use the same data file you created for your form letters, or have already saved a data file, choose *Open Data Source*.

Figure 57. Select the data source file.

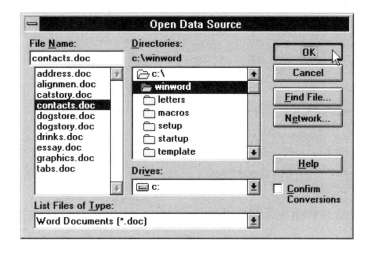

Figure 58. Word displays this dialog box; click on *Set Up Main Document*.

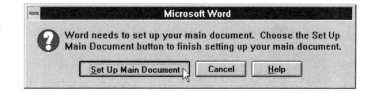

Figure 59. If you want to create a new data source, select *Create Data Source* from the *Get Data* drop-down list box (Figure 56). Then follow the steps from Figure 6 in the **Creating the Data Document** section earlier in this chapter.

Then click on the *Mail Merge Helper* button on the *Mail Merge* toolbar to open this dialog box. Now click on *Setup*.

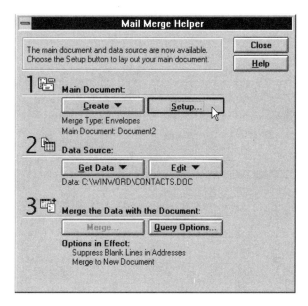

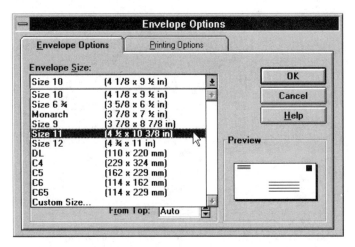

Figure 60. Both of these methods open the *Envelope Options* dialog box. On the *Envelope Options* tab, select an envelope size from the drop-down list box.

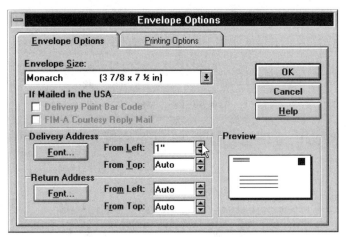

Figure 61. In the *Delivery Address* and *Return Address* sections, you can adjust the positions of the addresses by changing the *From Left* and *From Top* options.

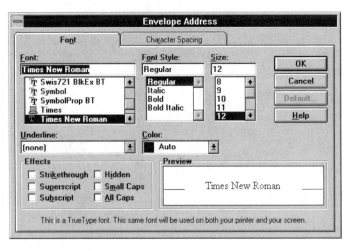

Figure 62. Click on the *Font* button to open the *Envelope Address* or *Envelope Return Address* dialog box, containing the *Font* and *Character Spacing* tabs, so you can change the formatting of the address text.

Figure 63. On the *Printing Options* tab, Word selects options based on the selected printer. If these options are not appropriate, change them. Click on *OK*.

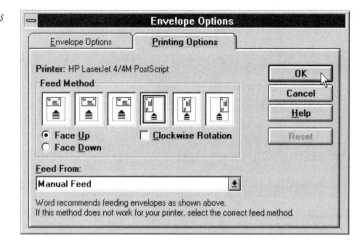

Figure 64. Then in the *Envelope Address* dialog box, choose the *Insert Merge Field* button and choose the appropriate merge fields from the drop-down list box. Include any punctuation to set up the address.

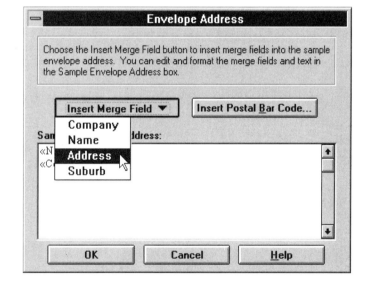

Figure 65. To insert a POSTNET bar code, click on the *Insert Postal Bar Code* button to open this dialog box.

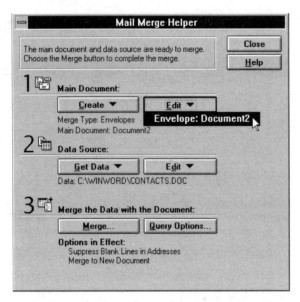

Figure 66. After closing the *Envelope Address* dialog box, Word opens the *Mail Merge Helper* dialog box. Under *Main Document*, choose *Edit*.

Figure 67. Word displays the envelope in *Page Layout* view.

If you have specified an address in the *Mailing Address* box on the *User* tab of the *Options* dialog box (see **Chapter 3**), that address is used as the return address. You can delete the return address if your envelopes have a preprinted return address on them.

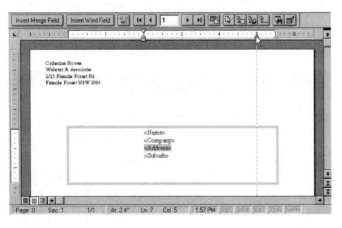

Figure 68. The merge fields are placed in a frame. You can adjust the address text by dragging the indent markers on the ruler.

Figure 69. When you are ready to print, click on the *Merge to Printer* button on the *Mail Merge* toolbar.

LABELS

Figure 70. In a new document, choose *Mail Merge* from the **Tools** menu (Figure 1) to open the *Mail Merge Helper* dialog box. Under *Main Document*, click on *Create* and choose *Mailing Labels* from the drop-down list box.

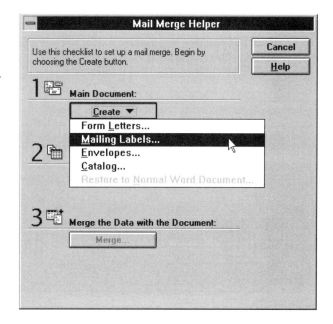

Figure 71. Choose *Active Window* in this prompt box.

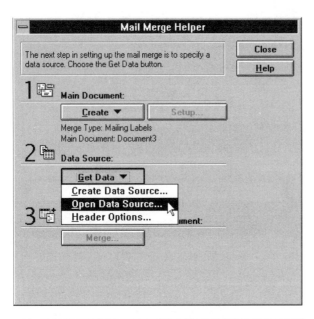

Figure 72. Then in the *Mail Merge Helper* dialog box, choose *Open Data Source* or *Create Data Source* from the *Get Data* drop-down list box (see Figure 56 in the **Envelopes** section earlier in this chapter for more information).

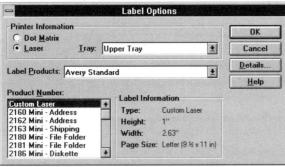

Figure 73. In the *Label Options* dialog box, choose the specifications for your printer and label type.

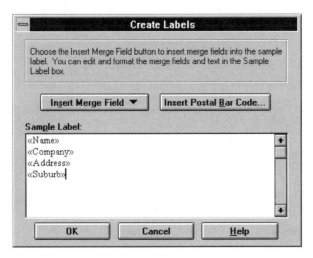

Figure 74. Word opens the *Create Labels* dialog box. This operates the same way as the *Envelope Address* dialog box (see Figure 64 in the **Envelopes** section).

Figure 75. In the *Mail Merge Helper* dialog box, click on the *Merge* button under *Merge the Data with the Document* (step 3).

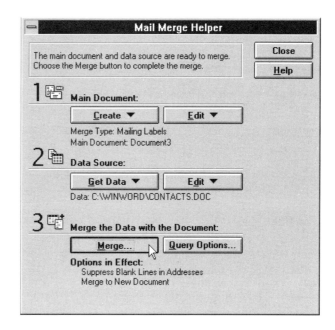

Figure 76. Then select options in the *Merge* dialog box (see Figure 44 under **Merging the Documents**, earlier in this chapter, for information).

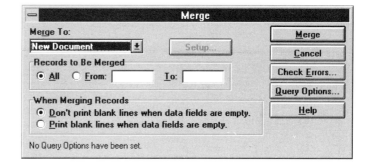

TABLES 17

CREATING TABLES

You use tables within Word for a number of reasons: laying out text and graphics in columns; displaying tabular data; or generally enhancing the look of the document. You can create and modify tables using the *Standard* toolbar or a **Table** menu command.

USING THE STANDARD TOOLBAR

Figure 1. Place the insertion point in your document where you want the table. Click on the *Insert Table* button on the *Standard* toolbar; a box grid drops down. Click again and hold the mouse button and drag the mouse down and to the right. Word displays the number of rows and columns you select at the bottom of the grid. Release the mouse button when you see the number of rows and columns you want.

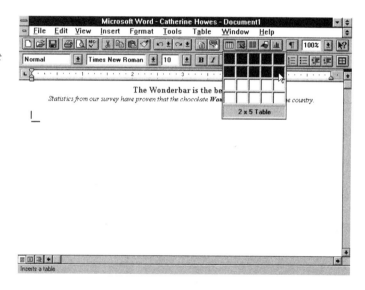

Figure 2. Word inserts a table and puts the insertion point in the first cell, ready for typing.

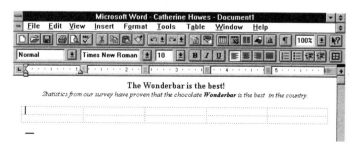

USING THE TABLE MENU

Figure 3. Alternatively, you can insert a table by selecting *Insert Table* from the **Table** menu.

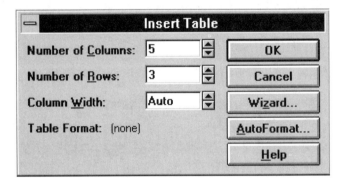

Figure 4. In the *Insert Table* dialog box, specify the number of rows and columns you need, as well as the column width.

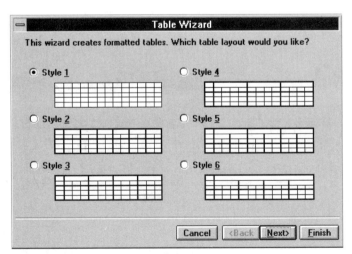

Figure 5. Click on the *Wizard* button to open the *Table Wizard* dialog box and have Word help you format the table. See **Chapter 7** for more information.

Figure 6. The *AutoFormat* button opens this dialog box. Select from the predefined layout styles (see Figure 42, under **Applying Borders and Shading to Tables**).

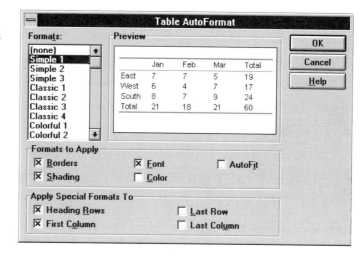

Figure 7. If you cannot see the table in your document, select *Gridlines* from the **Table** menu so you can see the outline of the table. The gridlines don't print.

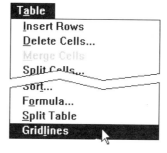

Figure 8. Within the table, each cell includes an end-of-cell marker, and each row an end-of-row marker. You can turn these on or off with the *Show/Hide* button on the *Standard* toolbar.

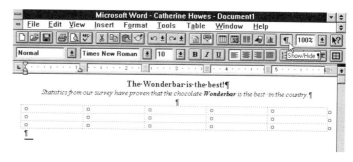

Figure 9. If you click the right mouse button on the table, Word displays a shortcut menu to select some common commands for tables.

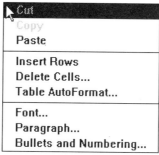

The·Wonderbar·is·the·best!¶
Statistics·from·our·survey·have·proven·that·the·chocolate ***Wonderbar*** *is·the·best··in·the·country.* ¶
¶

Chocolate Bar	¤	¤	¤	¤
¤	¤	¤	¤	¤
¤	¤	¤	¤	¤
¶

MOVING AROUND TABLES

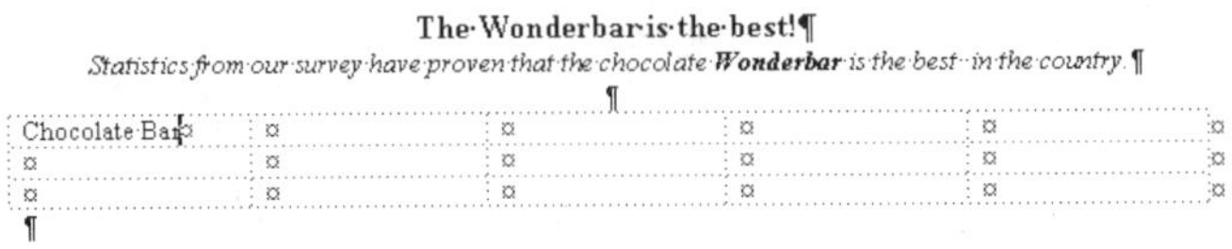

Figure 10. Word automatically positions the insertion point in the first cell of the table, where you can start typing in text. Text automatically wraps onto the next line when it reaches the end of a cell. You can also place graphics into table cells (see **Chapter 12** for information on importing graphics).

Keyboard Action	Result
Tab key	Moves to next cell
Shift+Tab	Moves to previous cell
Tab key at the end of a table	Creates new row
Alt+Home	Moves to first cell in current row
Alt+Page Up	Moves to top of cell in current column
Alt+End	Moves to last cell in current row
Alt+Page Down	Moves to last cell in current column
Up, Down, Left and Right arrows	Move to next cell in that direction
Ctrl+Tab	Inserts a tab

Figure 11. Use the Enter key to create a new paragraph within a cell. The Tab key creates a new row if the insertion point is in the last cell of a row. To insert a tab into a cell, use the Ctrl+Tab keys. The directional arrow keys move the insertion point in the direction you select. To place the text insertion point in a cell, simply click the insertion point in that cell. This figure displays the keystrokes required to move around a table.

SELECTING PARTS OF TABLES

Cell selection bar

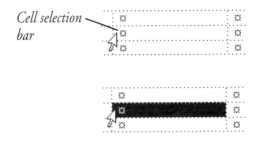

Figure 12. To select a cell, move the mouse pointer to the left of the cell until it becomes a right pointing arrow, click the mouse once in the cell selection bar.

Figure 13. To select a row, move the mouse to the left of the row you want to select. Click when the pointer becomes a right pointing arrow in the row selection bar.

Figure 14. To select a column, move the mouse pointer above the column you want to select. When the mouse pointer becomes a black down-arrow, click to select the column below.

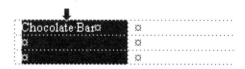

Figure 15. To select multiple cells, rows, or columns, hold the mouse button down and drag it across the cells you want to select.

Figure 16. You can also use the Table menu commands to select rows, columns, or the entire table. Make sure you add the insertion point to the relevant row or column before selecting these commands.

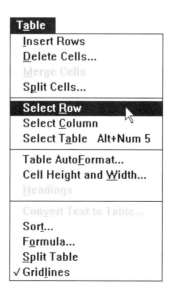

MODIFYING TABLES

ADDING CELLS, ROWS, AND COLUMNS

Before you insert a new cell, row, or column, you need to select an existing cell, row, or column.

Figure 17. Select the number of cells, rows, or columns you want to add.

With rows selected, click on the *Insert Rows* button to insert the same number of rows above the selected rows. (The *Tables* button on the *Standard* toolbar changes depending on what part of the table you have selected to insert.)

If you want to add a row at the end of the table, place the insertion point in the last cell of the last row and press the Tab key.

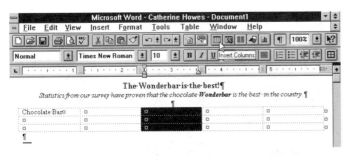

Figure 18. When you select columns and click on the *Insert Columns* button, Word inserts that number of columns to the left of the highlighted columns.

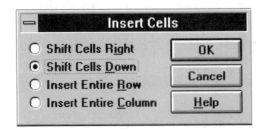

Figure 19. The *Insert Cells* button opens the *Insert Cells* dialog box when you select cells in a table. Choose whether you want to insert cells to the left of the selected cells, or insert rows or columns.

Figure 20. The first command in the **Table** menu also changes between *Insert Cells, Insert Rows, Insert Columns* depending on what you select. You can also choose these commands to modify the table.

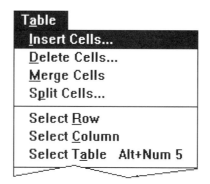

DELETING CELLS, ROWS, AND COLUMNS

Figure 21. Select the part of the table you want to delete. Then from the **Table** menu, choose *Delete Cells, Delete Rows,* or *Delete Columns*—the command that appears in the menu depends on what you have selected.

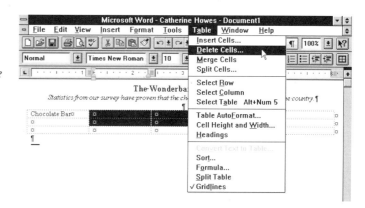

Figure 22. The *Delete Cells* command opens this dialog box. Choose from the options.

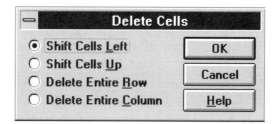

MOVING CELLS, ROWS, AND COLUMNS

You can move and copy selected parts of a table by using the *Cut, Copy,* and *Paste* commands on the *Standard* toolbar and **Edit** menu, or using drop-and-drag editing with the mouse, as you do with normal document text (see **Chapter 2** for more information).

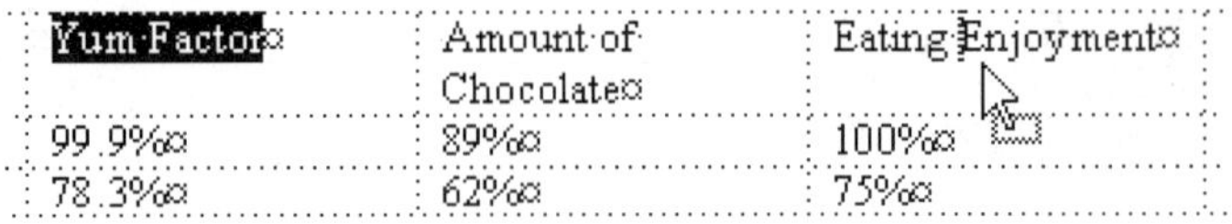

Yum·Factor¤
Amount·of·Chocolate¤
Eating·Enjoyment¤
99.9%¤
89%¤
100%¤
78.3%¤
62%¤
75%¤

Figure 23. Select the cells, rows, or columns you want to move. Place the mouse pointer over the selection so the arrow points to the left. Then drag it to a new position. The mouse cursor changes to the drag and drop cursor.

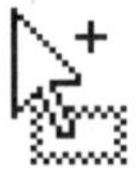

Figure 24. Hold down the Ctrl key as you drag to copy the selection. The mouse pointer looks like this.

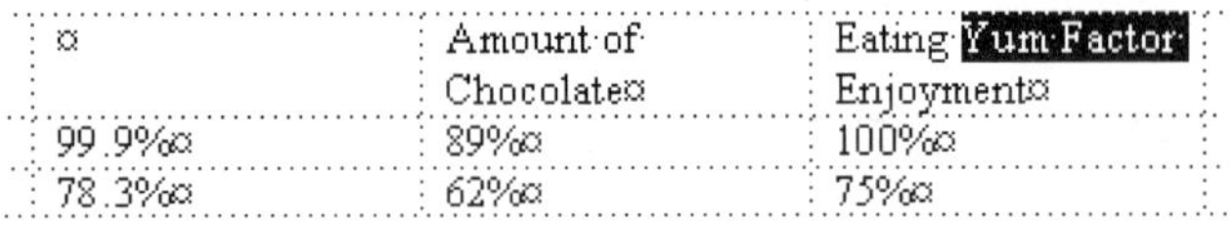

¤
Amount·of·Chocolate¤
Eating·Yum·Factor·Enjoyment¤
99.9%¤
89%¤
100%¤
78.3%¤
62%¤
75%¤

Figure 25. Release the mouse button to reposition the selected part of the table in the new location.

If you selected only the text within a cell, Word adds the text to the new location.

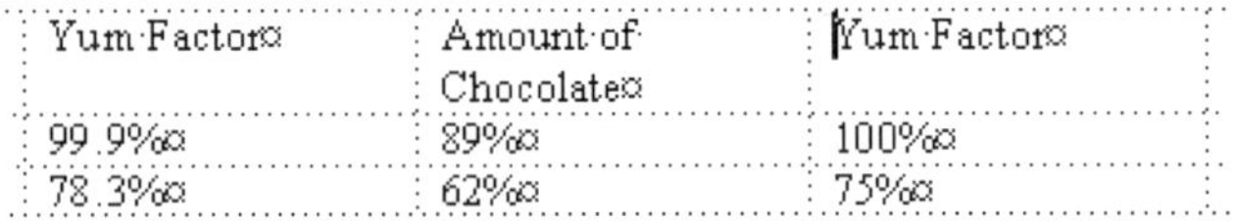

Yum·Factor¤
Amount·of·Chocolate¤
Yum·Factor¤
99.9%¤
89%¤
100%¤
78.3%¤
62%¤
75%¤

Figure 26. If you select the end-of-cell mark, the text you move replaces the existing text.

CHANGING THE SIZE OF TABLES

When you insert a table into a document without altering its size, Word applies the default size settings. You can, however, alter row heights and columns widths through the *Cell Height and Width* command in the **Table** menu. Alternatively, you can use the mouse with the ruler, or you can change the table directly with the mouse.

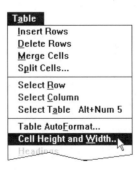

ROW HEIGHT

Table
Insert Rows
Delete Rows
Merge Cells
Split Cells...
Select Row
Select Column
Select Table Alt+Num 5
Table AutoFormat...
Cell Height and Width...

Figure 27. Select the rows for which you want to alter the row height and choose *Cell Height and Width* from the **Table** menu.

Figure 28. In the *Cell Height and Width* dialog box, you can change the indent of the selected row, the height, and the alignment of the row on the page. The *Previous Row* and *Next Row* buttons let you select the previous and next rows without having to close the dialog box.

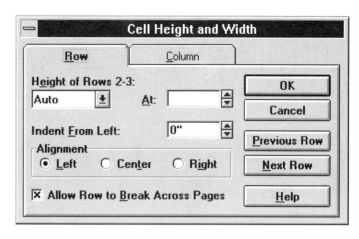

Figure 29. To change the height of the selected rows, select from the options in the *Height of Row* drop-down list box. *At Least* lets you choose a minimum row height value, which increases if the cell contents exceed it. *Exactly* is a fixed height; if the cell contains anything larger than this specified height, Word doesn't display or print it. *Auto* automatically adjusts to fit the contents of the cell.

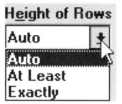

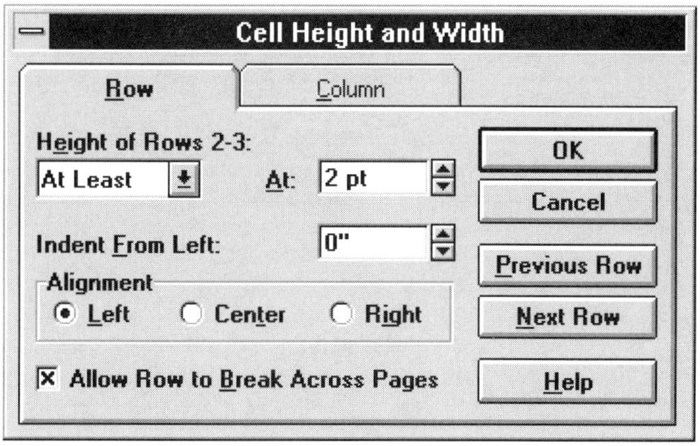

Figure 30. To get the right height, type it into the *At* text box, and select *OK*.

You can set every row of a table at a different height, but all cells within a row must be the same height.

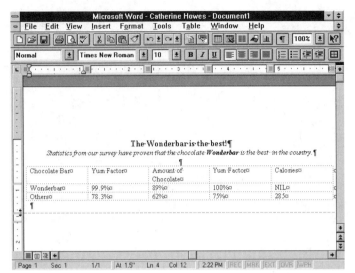

Figure 31. You can also change row height with the ruler in *Page Layout* view. Drag the row markers on the vertical ruler to change the height.

COLUMN WIDTH

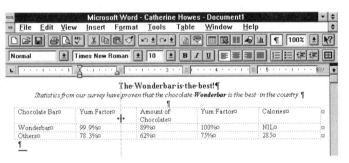

Figure 32. Put the mouse pointer over the column border until it becomes a two-headed arrow. Hold the mouse button down and move it to the left or the right, and release the button.

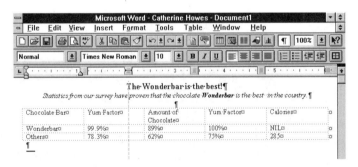

Figure 33. Alternatively, point to the marker on the ruler above the gridline you want to adjust, and click and drag the mouse.

Whether you use gridlines or the ruler to adjust column widths, Word resizes all columns to the right in proportion to their original width. The overall width of the table doesn't change.

If you hold down the Shift key while changing the size of a column, only the column to the right adjusts accordingly, and the overall width of the table doesn't change.

Figure 34. If you use the Ctrl key while dragging a column border, any columns to the right adjust so that they are all equal in width, without changing the overall table width.

Holding down the Shift and Ctrl keys while you drag adjusts the current column width without changing the other columns. The table widens to accommodate the change.

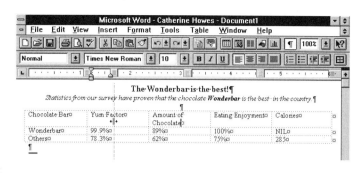

Figure 35. You can also change the column width of selected columns through the *Cell Height and Width* command in the **Table** menu. In the *Cell Height and Width* dialog box, select the *Column* tab.

You can define the width for the selected column, and the space between columns. The latter option refers to the usable space within a cell, similar to a left and right margin for each individual cell. (You can format the spacing of text in a cell the same way you do in your document, using the ruler and the *Paragraph* command in the **Format** menu.)

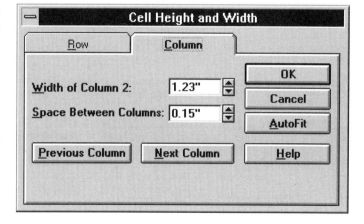

The *Previous Column* and *Next Column* buttons let you automatically select an adjoining column for modifications, without leaving the dialog box.

Click on the *AutoFit* button to have Word resize the selected columns according to the size of their contents.

FORMATTING TABLES

TEXT

You format text and apply styles in table cells as you do with normal document text. To insert a tab in a cell, you need to press Ctrl+Tab because the Tab key moves you between cells in a table.

SPLITTING TABLES

Figure 36. You can use the *Split Table* command in the **Table** menu for two operations. Firstly, if you inserted the table at the very beginning of your document, you won't be able to put the insertion point before it. However, if you put it in any of the cells in the first row and select the *Split Table* command, Word inserts a paragraph marker above the table and you can type with the *Normal* style.

Figure 37. You can also put the insertion point in a row, and choose the *Split Table* command to split the table above the row that the insertion point is in.

MERGING CELLS

Figure 38. You can merge adjoining cells together to create one large cell. Select the cells that you want to merge, and choose *Merge Cells* from the **Table** menu.

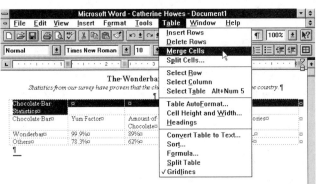

Figure 39. This joins the selected cells into one, long cell. Use this command to create headings in tables.

Chocolate Bar Statistics				
Chocolate Bar	Yum Factor	Amount of Chocolate	Eating Enjoyment	Calories
Wonderbar	99.9%	89%	100%	NIL
Others	78.3%	62%	75%	285

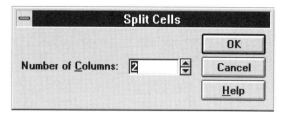

SPLITTING CELLS

Figure 40. Select the cell you want to split. Then choose *Split Cells* from the **Table** menu. In the *Split Cells* dialog box, specify how many columns you want to split the cell into.

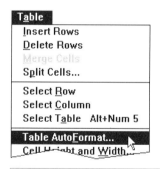

APPLYING BORDERS AND SHADING TO TABLES

If you want horizontal and vertical lines in your table, you need to apply borders.

Figure 41. Position the insertion point in the table and choose *Table AutoFormat* from the **Table** menu.

Figure 42. This opens the *Table AutoFormat* dialog box. From the *Formats* list box, select a design. Word displays its formats in the *Preview* box.

In the *Formats to Apply* and *Apply Special Formats To* sections, choose the options you want to apply to the table, then click on *OK*.

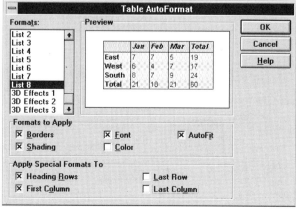

Figure 43. To add borders and shading to individual cells, use the *Borders* toolbar.

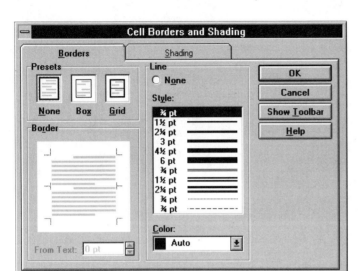

Figure 44. You can also choose *Borders and Shading* from the **Format** menu and use the options in the *Cell Borders and Shading* dialog box.

Spreadsheet Functions

In tables, you can perform calculations, create a graph, or set up a database.

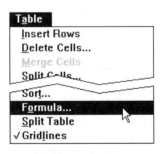

Figure 45. Click in the cell you want the calculation result to appear in, then choose *Formula* from the **Table** menu.

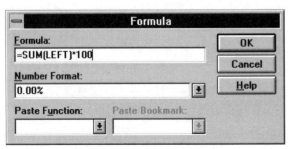

Figure 46. Word opens the *Formula* dialog box.

Word proposes an appropriate formula in the *Formula* text box.

Figure 47. To change the formula, delete the proposed formula (leave the equals sign). You can then type in a formula using cell references and mathematical symbols for a calculation.

Alternatively, you can select a function from the *Paste Function* drop-down list box.

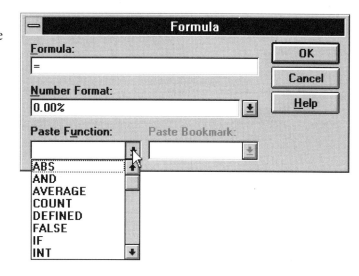

Figure 48. After Word inserts the function into the *Formula* text box, you need to type the cell references for the calculation between the parentheses. Use commas to separate individual cell references, and colons to indicate a range of cells.

Columns are named A, B, C, etc. from left to right; rows are numbered 1, 2, 3, etc. down the table.

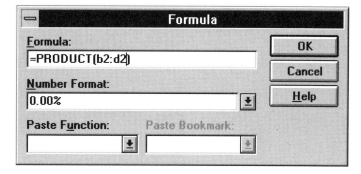

Figure 49. The *Number Format* drop-down list box lets you choose a different numbering format.

Choose *OK* to insert the result in the table.

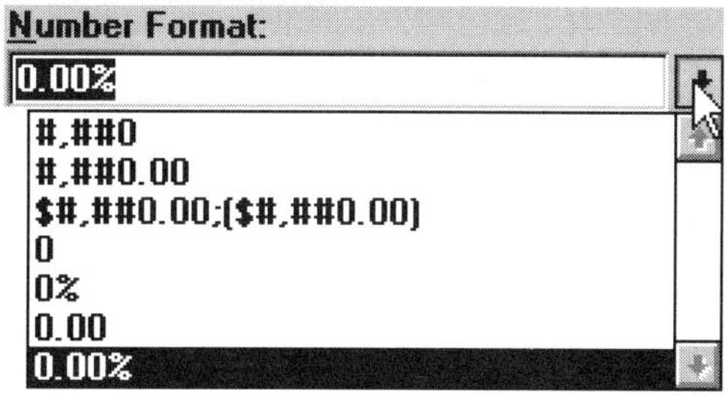

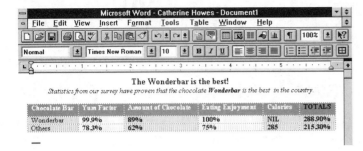

Figure 50. If you change the value of a reference cell that is in a calculation, you can update the result by selecting the old result and pressing F9.

See **Chapter 16** to see how you can use a table to store database information.

MICROSOFT GRAPH 18

INTRODUCTION

Microsoft Graph is an application within Word. You can use Graph to display numeric data as a chart, and insert this chart into your Word document.

Charts created in Graph become "embedded" objects in your document. This means that you can return to the original graph and datasheet at any time to edit it by double-clicking on the graph in your Word document.

STARTING MICROSOFT GRAPH

Figure 1. Before you start Graph, click in your document where you want the upper-left corner of the completed graph to appear. Then click on the *Insert Chart* button on the *Standard* toolbar.

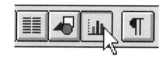

Figure 2. Alternatively, select *Object* from the **Insert** menu. The *Object* dialog box appears. From the *Create New* tab, choose *Microsoft Graph* from the list box, and select the *OK* button.

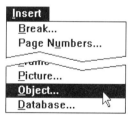

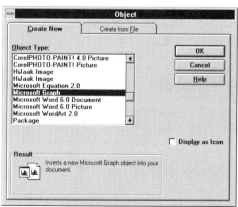

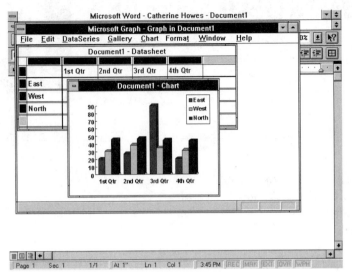

Figure 3. Both methods open Graph over your Word document. Two windows appear—the *Datasheet* window and the *Chart* window. By default, Graph already has data in the *Datasheet* window, and the data plotted as a graph in the *Chart* window. You can edit this data in the datasheet and replace the data with new data that you type in (or you can import information directly from other applications, such as Lotus 1-2-3, or Microsoft Excel).

Figure 4. You can maximize the Graph application window by clicking on the maximize button.

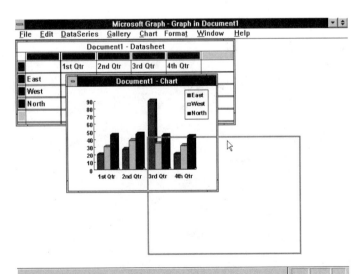

Figure 5. You can move the *Chart* window so it doesn't overlap your *Datasheet* window by dragging the title bar of the *Chart* window to a space on the screen. This way you can see both windows clearly at the same time.

THE DATASHEET WINDOW

Figure 6. Click anywhere in the *Datasheet* window to make it the active window.

   Graph divides the datasheet into 4000 rows and 256 columns, into which you can enter numbers and labels. Whenever you change the datasheet, Graph automatically reflects those changes in the chart.

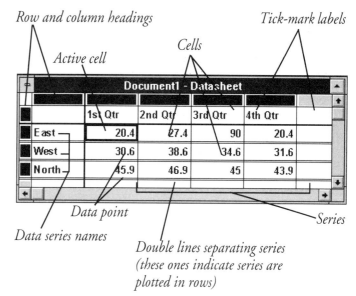

Row and column headings

Tick-mark labels

Cells

Active cell

Data point

Data series names

Series

Double lines separating series (these ones indicate series are plotted in rows)

SELECTING DATA CELLS

In the datasheet, you can select a single cell, a group of cells, or the entire datasheet. Cells are selected when they appear highlighted. Your commands and actions affect only cells that are selected.

Figure 7. When you put the mouse over the datasheet cells, it appears as a white cross. To select a single cell, click this pointer on the required cell.

		1st Qtr	2nd Qtr	3rd Qtr	4th Qtr	
	East	20.4	27.4	90	20.4	
	West	30.6	38.6	34.6	31.6	
	North	45.9	✛ 46.9	45	43.9	

Document1 - Datasheet

Figure 8. To highlight more than one cell, click and drag over the cells, then release the mouse. When you select more than one cell, the first selected cell appears with a black border and a white center; whereas the other cells are filled black. The white cell is the active cell. You can type new text in this cell without affecting the other cells.

		1st Qtr	2nd Qtr	3rd Qtr	4th Qtr	
	East	20.4	27.4	90	20.4	
	West	30.6	38.6	34.6	31.6	
	North	45.9	46.9	✛ 45	43.9	

Document1 - Datasheet

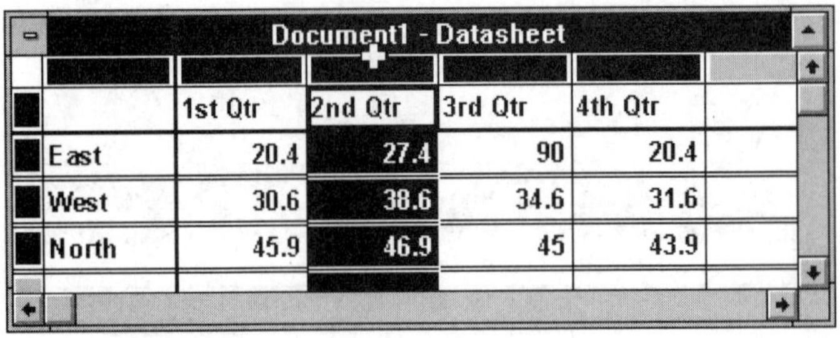

Document1 - Datasheet					
	1st Qtr	2nd Qtr	3rd Qtr	4th Qtr	
East	20.4	27.4	90	20.4	
West	30.6	38.6	34.6	31.6	
North	45.9	46.9	45	43.9	

Figure 9. To select an entire row or column, click on the corresponding heading box.

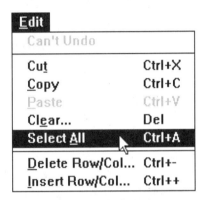

Edit

Can't Undo	
Cut	Ctrl+X
Copy	Ctrl+C
Paste	Ctrl+V
Clear...	Del
Select All	Ctrl+A
Delete Row/Col...	Ctrl+-
Insert Row/Col...	Ctrl++

Figure 10. To select the whole datasheet, choose *Select All* from the **Edit** menu.

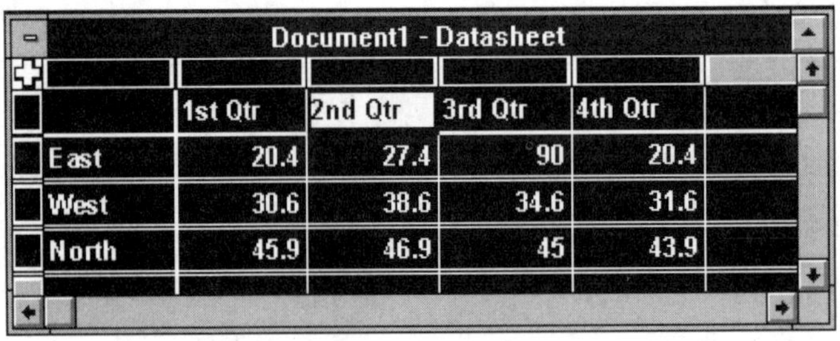

Document1 - Datasheet					
	1st Qtr	2nd Qtr	3rd Qtr	4th Qtr	
East	20.4	27.4	90	20.4	
West	30.6	38.6	34.6	31.6	
North	45.9	46.9	45	43.9	

Figure 11. Alternatively, you can click on the small blank square at the top left of the table, next to the column headings, to highlight the whole datasheet.

ENTERING AND EDITING THE DATASHEET

In the datasheet, you can type a name for each data series, a label (or category) for each group of data points, and a number to be plotted on the chart.

Figure 12. To enter data in a cell, select the cell you want to enter the data in. Then, type the data in the cell; or type a name if you have selected a labelling cell. The data you have typed appears in the active cell, and replaces any existing data in that cell.

When you have finished typing the text for that cell, press Enter or select another cell.

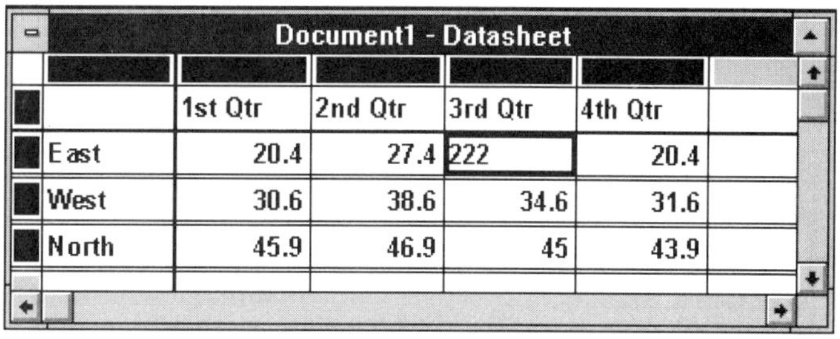

		1st Qtr	2nd Qtr	3rd Qtr	4th Qtr	
	East	20.4	27.4	222	20.4	
	West	30.6	38.6	34.6	31.6	
	North	45.9	46.9	45	43.9	

Document1 - Datasheet

Figure 13. You can also edit the contents of a selected cell by pressing the F2 key, or double-clicking on the cell you want to edit. Graph then displays the *Cell Data* dialog box. Edit the text in the text box, and click on *OK*.

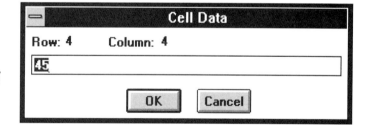

Cell Data

Row: 4   Column: 4

45

OK   Cancel

Figure 14. You can edit the text in the *Cell Data* dialog box the same way you edit in Word. This table outlines other editing methods for the *Cell Edit* dialog box, using the keyboard.

Editing a cell	
F2 or double-clicking on cell	Opens the Cell Data dialog box, so you can edit the contents of the active cell
Backspace	Opens the Cell Data dialog box and deletes the contents of the active cell
Ctrl+; (semi-colon)	Opens the Cell Data dialog box and enters the current date
Ctrl+Shift+: (colon)	Opens the Cell Data dialog box and enters the current time

ENTERING SERIES DATA IN ROWS AND COLUMNS

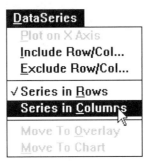

Document1 - Datasheet

	1st Qtr	2nd Qtr	3rd Qtr	4th Qtr
East	20.4	27.4	222	20.4
West	30.6	38.6	34.6	31.6
North	45.9	46.9	45	43.9

Double horizontal lines, indicating series plotted in rows

Figure 15. A data series is a row or column of data that Graph uses to draw data markers on a chart. You can decide whether the data series names are contained in the first row or first column, by choosing from the **Data Series** menu. Your choice affects how Graph plots the data on the chart.

DataSeries

Plot on X Axis

Include Row/Col...
Exclude Row/Col...

√ **Series in Rows**
Series in Columns

Move To Overlay
Move To Chart

Figure 16. By default, Graph enters series data in rows. Double horizontal lines divide each series on the datasheet. When *Series in Rows* from the **Data Series** menu is checked, Graph considers each row a data series, and each cell in that row to be a data point in that series.

If you want to enter series data in columns, choose *Series in Columns* from the **DataSeries** menu.

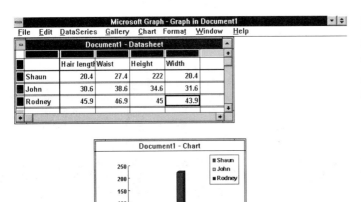

Microsoft Graph - Graph in Document1

File Edit DataSeries Gallery Chart Format Window Help

Document1 - Datasheet

	Hair length	Waist	Height	Width
Shaun	20.4	27.4	222	20.4
John	30.6	38.6	34.6	31.6
Rodney	45.9	46.9	45	43.9

Document1 - Chart

Figure 17. Type in data series names down the first column, and category names across the first row. Then, enter the data for each series across each row.

The category names you type in the first row of the datasheet appear along the *x*-axis of your chart; and the data series names from the first column appear in the legend, or along the *y*-axis of three-dimensional charts.

You should not enter names in the cell at the top left corner of the datasheet, because Graph does not use it when plotting data.

CHANGING COLUMN WIDTHS

You can adjust the widths of columns to suit the longest text or number that you have entered into the cells. You can make the columns in the datasheet as small as one character wide, or as large as 255 characters wide.

Figure 18. First, select the columns that you want to change.

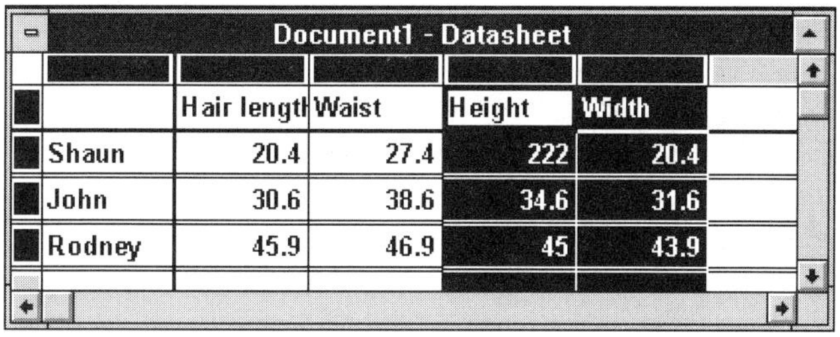

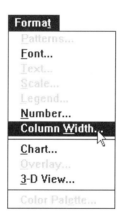

Figure 19. Then, select *Column Width* from the **Format** menu.

This opens the *Column Width* dialog box. By default, the *Standard Width* check box is selected. The size of the columns is nine characters wide.

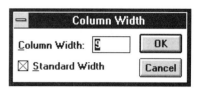

Figure 20. Type a number between one and 255 in the *Column Width* text box to indicate the width you want. Then, click on *OK* to close the dialog box.

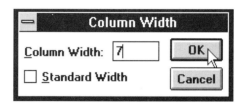

Figure 21. Alternatively, you can change column widths with the mouse. Place the mouse at the top right-hand edge of a column; the mouse pointer changes to a bar with a double-headed arrow. Drag this arrow left or right to adjust the column width.

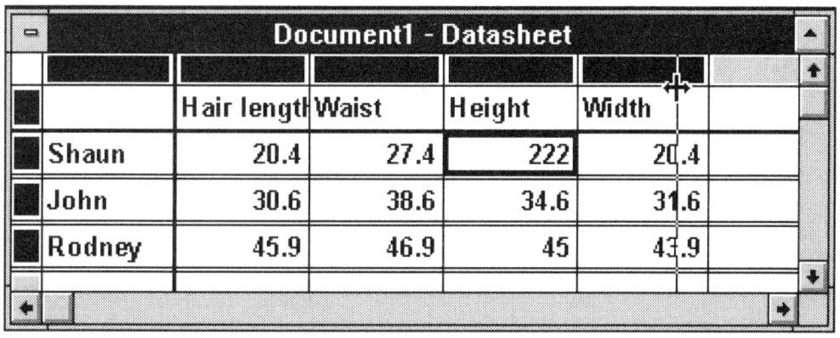

INSERTING AND DELETING ROWS OR COLUMNS

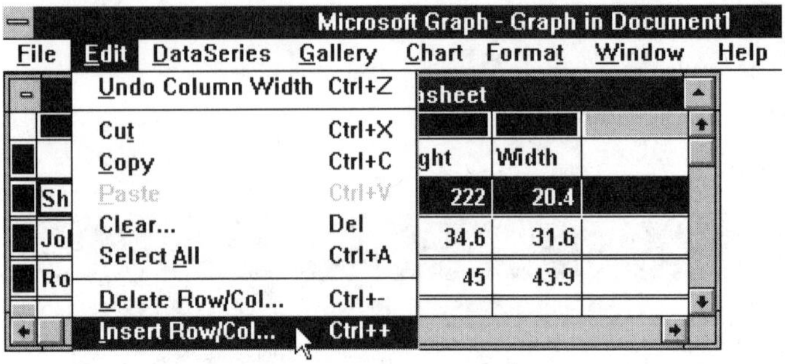

Figure 22. To insert a datasheet row or column, first select a whole row or column; or highlight a number of rows or columns by dragging with the mouse. Then, select *Insert Row/Col* from the **Edit** menu.

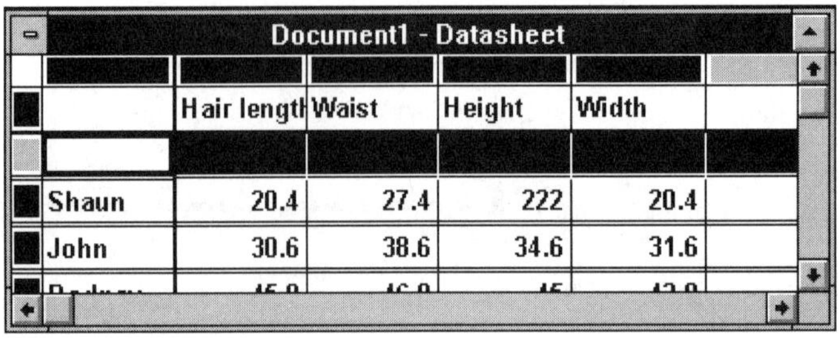

Figure 24. If you highlighted one row or column of the datasheet, Word inserts one row or column; if you selected three rows or columns, three go into the datasheet, and so forth.

Graph inserts new rows above the selected rows. Graph inserts new columns to the left of the selected columns.

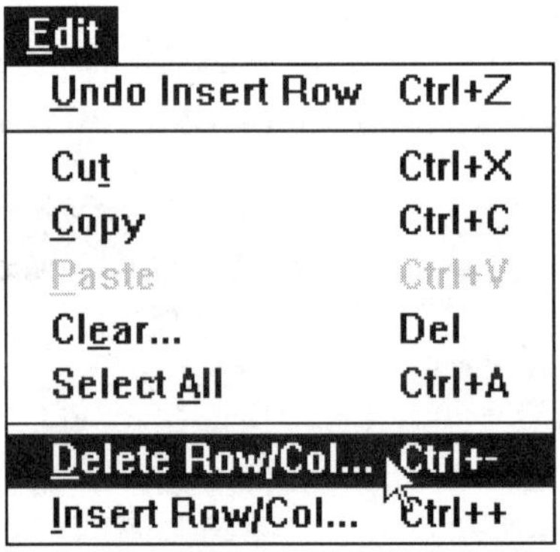

Figure 25. To delete rows or columns, highlight the required rows or columns and then select *Delete Row/Col* from the **Edit** menu.

Figure 26. If you selected only part of a row or column, and then selected the *Insert* or *Delete* command from the **Edit** menu, a dialog box appears. You can still insert or delete a row or column by clicking on the corresponding radio button.

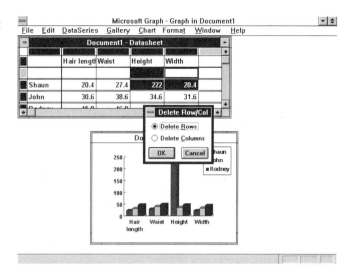

CUTTING, COPYING, AND PASTING TEXT

You can cut, copy, and paste the contents of cells, rows and columns the same way you do with text in Word (see Chapter 2).

Figure 27. For example, to move data on the datasheet, select any cells you want to move. Then, select *Cut* or *Copy* from the **Edit** menu.

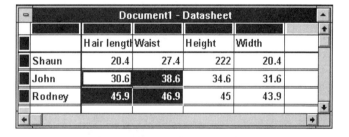

Figure 28. Then, select the cell where you want to insert the data, and choose *Paste* from the **Edit** menu.

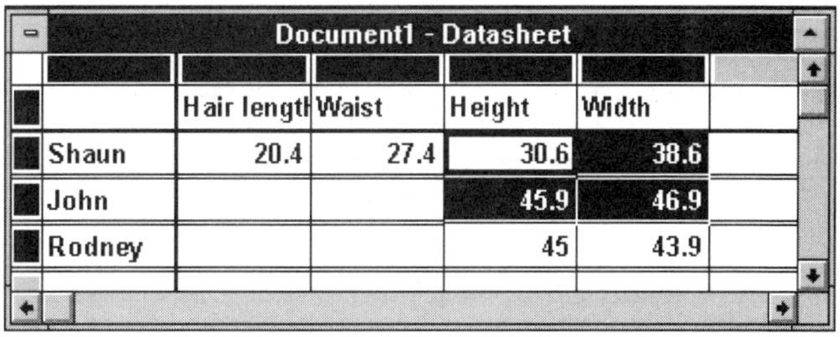

If you have cut data from more than one cell, Graph pastes the selected cells over a range of cells the same size.

If you paste your cut or copied data into any cells that already contain data, Graph replaces this, and the new data is reflected in the chart.

EXCLUDING AND INCLUDING CHART DATA

You can exclude rows and columns without deleting them from the datasheet. This lets you control what data appears on the chart.

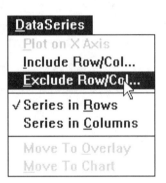

Figure 30. To exclude selected rows or columns, choose *Exclude Row/Col* from the **DataSeries** menu.

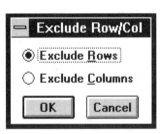

Figure 31. If you select only part of the row or column, Graph displays the *Exclude Row/Col* dialog box. Select the *Exclude Rows* or *Exclude Columns* radio button, and click on *OK*.

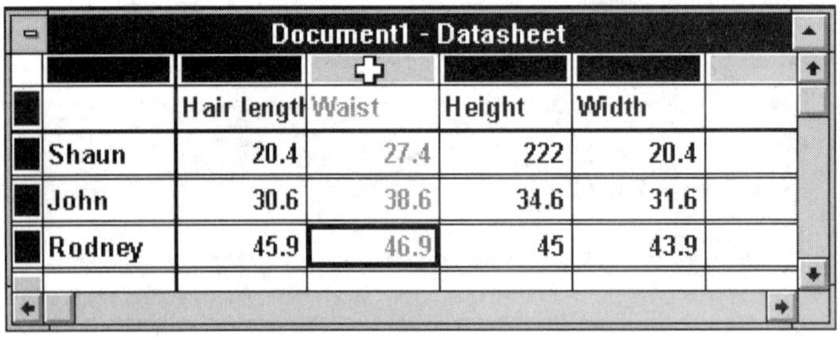

	Hair length	Waist	Height	Width	
Shaun	20.4	27.4	222	20.4	
John	30.6	38.6	34.6	31.6	
Rodney	45.9	46.9	45	43.9	

Document1 - Datasheet

Figure 32. Alternatively, you can double-click on a row or column heading to exclude that row or column.

Any row or column you have excluded appears dimmed in the datasheet.

Figure 33. To include rows and columns you have excluded, first select the rows and columns you want to include. Then choose *Include Row/Col* from the **DataSeries** menu.

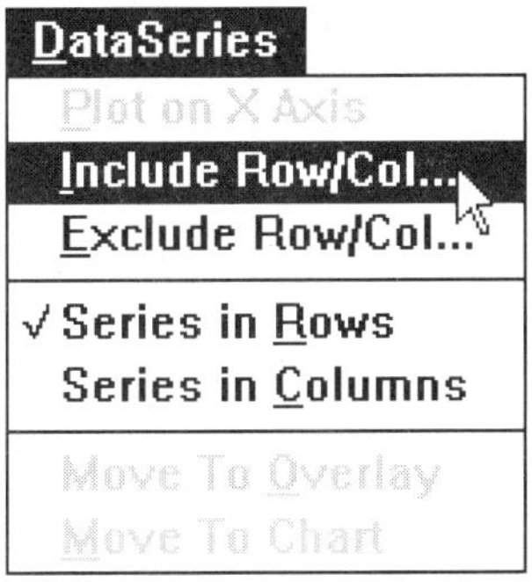

You can also include a row or column that you have excluded by double-clicking on the corresponding heading row.

These rows or columns on the datasheet now appear black and are plotted on the chart.

FORMATTING NUMBERS

With Graph, you can change the format of numbers in the datasheet to include symbols such as currency signs and percentages. How you format the numeric values in the datasheet determines how the tick marks appear on the chart axis.

Figure 35. Select those cells you want to format, or select the entire datasheet by clicking on the small blank square at the top left of the datasheet. Then select *Number* from the **Format** menu.

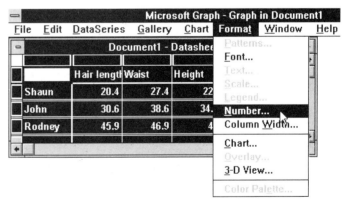

Figure 37. If you selected the whole datasheet, Graph displays this dialog box. Click on *OK*.

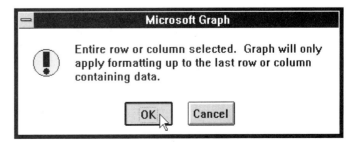

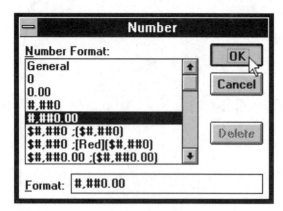

Figure 38. The *Number* dialog box then appears. From the *Number Format* list box, select a format. (*General* is the default format.)

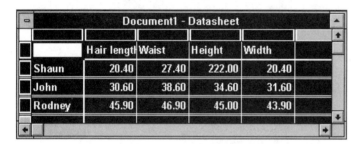

Figure 39. When you click on *OK*, Graph formats the numbers on your datasheet.

THE CHART WINDOW

Figure 40. Once you have entered all the labels and numbers into the datasheet, you can concentrate on changing the chart window.

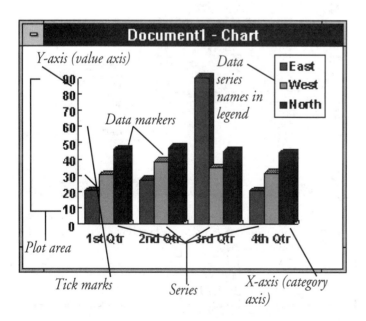

Figure 41. To make the chart window active, either click on it, or select *Chart* from the **Window** menu.

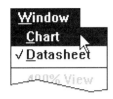

TYPES OF CHARTS

Figure 42. The sample chart may not show your information to its best advantage, so you can change the style of chart. Graph offers 12 types of charts—seven two-dimensional and five three-dimensional. These charts are listed in this table.

Chart types and uses	
Area	Shows how values change in proportion to the total over a period of time. Similar to a line chart, but emphasizes magnitude of values, rather than flow of time and rate of change. (The 100% option shows relationships to the whole.)
Bar	Shows individual figures at a specific time, or draws comparisons among items. Similar to a column chart, but the vertical orientation places less emphasis on the flow of time. (The stacked and 100% options show relationships to the whole.)
Column	Shows variation over a period of time, or draws comparisons among items. (The stacked and 100% options show relationships to the whole.)
Line	Shows trends or changes in data over a period of time. Similar to an area chart, but emphasizes flow of time and rate of change, rather than magnitude of values. Often used for stock quotes.
Pie	Shows the relationship of parts to the whole. Can contain only one series of data.
XY (Scatter)	Shows relationship or degree of relationship between numeric values in different groups of data. Useful for finding patterns or trends and for determining whether variables are dependent on or affect one another.
Combination	Shows related data that is measured in different units (up to four axes can be used in this chart); useful for comparing two different kinds of data or juxtaposing series to show correlations that you might not otherwise recognise.
3-D Area	Shows a 3-D view of an area chart. Emphasizes the sum of plotted values, and separates series into distinct rows to show differences between the series.
3-D Bar	Shows a 3-D view of a bar chart. Emphasizes values of individual figures at a specific time or draws comparison among items.
3-D Column	Shows a 3-D view of a column chart. Emphasizes comparison of data points along two axes (a category axis and a series axis) so you can compare data within a series more easily and still view data by category.
3-D Line	Shows lines in a chart as 3-D ribbons. Makes individual lines easier to view, particularly when they cross, while still showing all series in one chart for comparison.
3-D Pie	Shows a 3-D pie chart, with height to the slices. Places additional emphasis on the data values that are in front.

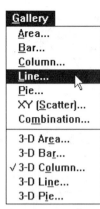

Figure 43. By default, Graph plots new charts as 3-D column charts. To change the chart type, choose the **Gallery** menu. The option that has a check mark beside it is the style that is active. Then, choose one of the chart options.

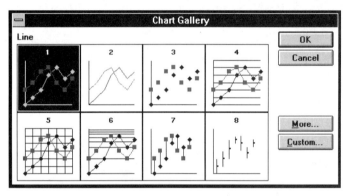

Figure 44. This opens the *Chart Gallery* dialog box which displays a range of formats for that chart type. Click on the *More* button to view more choices. Then, select from the built-in formats for that chart type.

Click on *OK* and your new chart appears in the chart window of Graph.

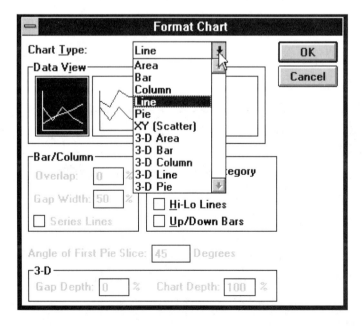

Figure 45. Changing the chart type replaces any formatting, such as patterns and gridlines, that you have applied to your chart. So you should select a chart type before you customize it.

If you have already formatted your chart and you want to change the chart type but retain the formatting, choose *Chart* from the **Format** menu (or click on the *Custom* button in the *Chart Gallery* dialog box). This brings up the *Format Chart* dialog box. Select the chart type you want from the *Chart Type* drop-down list.

Figure 46. You can also use the commands in the *Format Chart* dialog box to format the chart data markers. The available formatting options vary for each chart type you select.

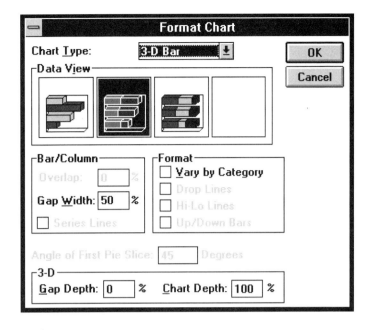

CHANGING THE SIZE OF THE CHART WINDOW

Figure 47. Unlike the datasheet window, the chart window doesn't have a maximize button, but you can make this window larger. Place the mouse over the outer border of the chart window; the mouse pointer changes to a double-headed arrow. Drag in the direction of the arrows to adjust the size of the chart window.

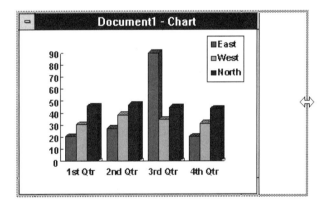

Figure 48. Release the mouse button; Graph changes the size of the chart and reformats the axes, text, and other chart elements to match the new size.

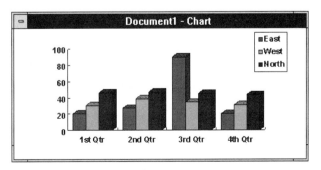

ADDING TITLES

You can add a chart title, and titles for the axes to make all the information clearer. You can also add *attached* or *unattached* text to a chart. Attached text items are titles attached to a chart item, such as an axis or a data marker. You cannot move attached text separately from the chart item. Unattached text can be added anywhere on the chart, which is useful for creating subtitles or comments.

ATTACHED TEXT

Figure 49. To add titles to your chart, select the *Titles* command from the **Chart** menu.

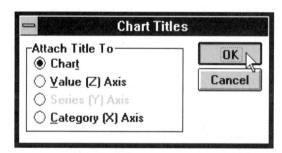

Figure 50. In the *Chart Titles* dialog box, select the type of title you want to add to your chart. Then click on *OK*.

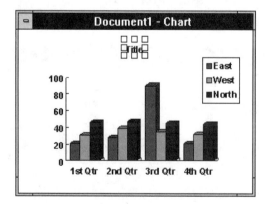

Figure 51. An "item" appears on the chart screen with white handles around it.

Figure 52. Add the title text then press the Esc key, or click anywhere away from this item.

You can insert line breaks by pressing Enter.

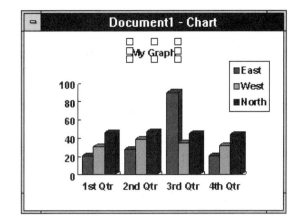

Figure 53. To display data labels, values, or percentages on the chart, choose *Data Labels* from the **Chart** menu (see Figure 49).

Graph now opens the *Data Labels* dialog box. Select the label you want displayed by clicking on the radio button. Choose:

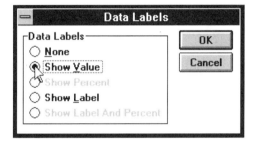

- *None* to remove all existing data labels from the chart.
- *Show Value* to display the value above each data point.
- *Show Percent* to add percentages to each slice of a pie chart.
- *Show Label* to display the category name above each data point in each series.

Figure 55. Click on *OK* to close the *Data Labels* dialog box, and apply the changes to your chart.

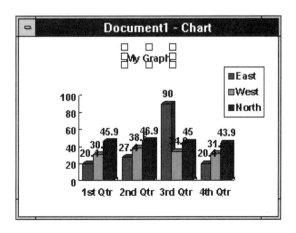

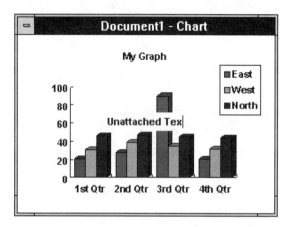

UNATTACHED TEXT

Figure 56. To add extra text, first make sure nothing else is selected in the chart (press the Esc key to deselect all items). Next, type the text. As you type, the text appears in the center of the graph.

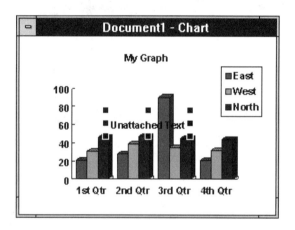

Figure 57. When you have finished entering text, press the Esc key, or click the left mouse button outside the newly entered text item. Black handles appear around the text.

SELECTING CHART ITEMS

Each time you want to edit, format, or move a chart item, you must first select it.

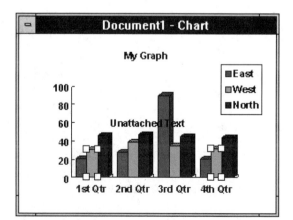

Figure 58. When you select chart items or attached text, Graph marks them with white handles.

Click on a chart item to select it. You can also press the arrow keys on the keyboard to select an item; keep pressing the keys until the desired item becomes selected.

Figure 59. When you select unattached text, Graph marks it with black handles.

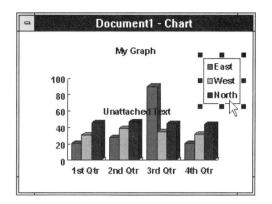

MOVING AND RESIZING ITEMS

Before moving and resizing items on the chart, you need to select them. The white squares surrounding attached text indicate that you cannot move or resize the text directly with the mouse. If unattached text is surrounded by black handles, this indicates that you can move, resize, and format the item with the mouse.

Figure 61. First, select an item with black handles. As you move the mouse pointer over the top of unattached text, the mouse pointer changes to an I-beam.

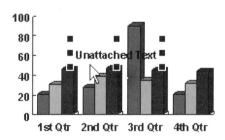

Figure 62. The I-beam pointer lets you click the insertion point into the text. Then you can retype, insert, and delete characters as you desire. Press Esc when you have finished; press Esc again if you want to deselect the text.

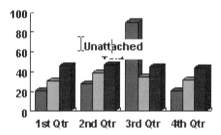

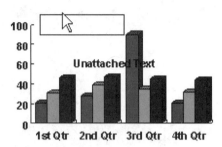

Figure 63. The arrow pointer allows you to drag the item to a new position.

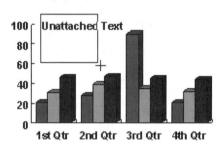

Figure 64. The crosshair pointer allows you to change the size of the item by dragging on one of the black handles.

THE LEGEND

The legend of a chart identifies what the data markers show. The text in the legend is either the data series or the category names on the datasheet. To change the legend text, you need to edit the datasheet. You can format this text, as well as the legend box border and area, and change where the legend sits.

Figure 65. If the legend is not visible, select *Add Legend* from the Chart menu.

Figure 66. To move the legend to a new position, select it.

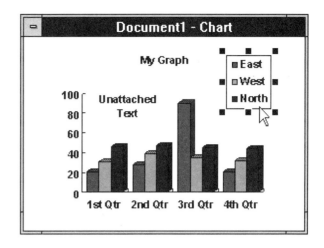

Figure 67. Then, to position the legend, drag it anywhere in the chart.

If a line appears, this means that Graph will move the chart to accommodate the legend's new position. The line shows where the top of the chart will be.

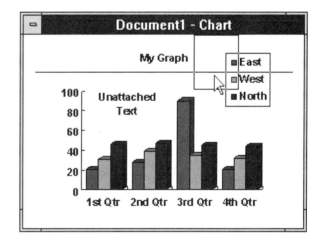

Figure 68. Alternatively, you can select *Legend* from the **Format** menu to display the *Legend* dialog box. Under *Type*, click in a radio button to select an option for the legend's position, then click on *OK*.

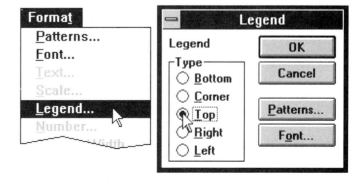

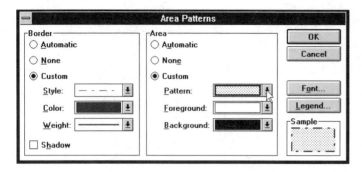

Figure 69. From the *Legend* dialog box, you can also format the legend. Click on the *Patterns* button to opens the *Area Patterns* dialog box.

Select from the drop-down lists to determine the *Border* and *Area* patterns. The *Sample* box shows your choices.

Click on the *Font* button in the *Legend* dialog box, or the *Area Patterns* dialog box, to bring up the *Chart Fonts* dialog box.

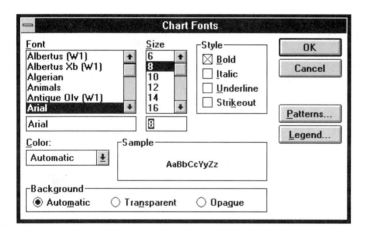

Figure 70. In the *Chart Fonts* dialog box, you can set the font, size, style, color, and background settings of the text.

The *Area Patterns*, *Chart Fonts*, and *Legend* dialog boxes are interrelated. Whatever dialog box you are in, you can access the other two dialog boxes.

Figure 71. To delete the legend from the chart, select *Delete Legend* from the **Chart** menu.

FORMATTING CHART CHARACTERISTICS

You can change individual parts of your chart, such as the font and size of the chart title, and the colors of the bars in the chart. You need to select these different areas in your chart before you can make changes.

A chart item is selected when it has handles around its boundaries. If the handles are black, you can drag this item to a new position, or you can resize it. If the handles are white, you cannot change the size or position directly. Then select a command from the **Format** menu and select from the options in the corresponding dialog boxes.

Note: A shortcut to making changes to chart items is to double-click on the item with the mouse—Graph opens the appropriate dialog box to change its appearance.

ADDING GRIDLINES

Gridlines extend from the axis values and categories across the plotting area to the data markers. The gridlines help guide your eyes to read the chart. You can add gridlines that correspond to either major or minor tick marks on the axes. You can also format the line color, style, and weight separately for the major and minor gridlines.

Figure 72. To add gridlines to your chart, select *Gridlines* from the **Chart** menu. This brings up the *Gridlines* dialog box. The options in the dialog box vary depending on whether your chart is two- or three-dimensional. Select the check boxes for the gridlines you want to display, or clear the check boxes for any gridlines you do not want to display and click on *OK*.

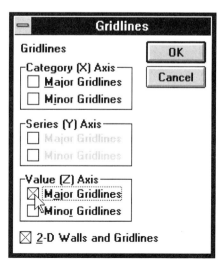

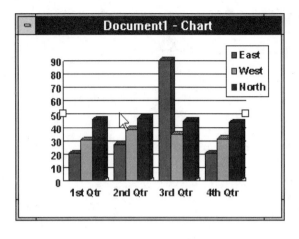

Figure 73. To format gridlines, double-click on a minor or major gridline.

Alternatively, select a gridline and choose *Patterns* from the **Format** menu. Both methods open the *Line Patterns* dialog box.

When you select a gridline, it is marked with white handles. You only need to select one major or minor gridline for an axis to affect all other major or minor gridlines for that axis.

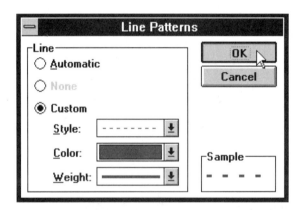

Figure 74. In the *Line Patterns* dialog box, select the formatting options from the drop-down menus. The *Sample* window shows you what your choices will look like.

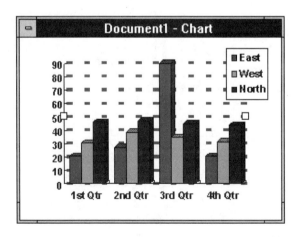

Figure 75. Click on *OK*. Word then applies your changes to the chart.

RETURNING TO WORD

Figure 76. To return to Word, select *Exit and Return to Document1* from the **File** menu. (Note that *Document1* in our example could be replaced by the name of your document.)

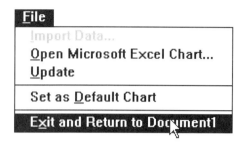

Figure 77. Word displays a confirmation dialog box asking if you want to update your document by adding this chart, select *Yes*.

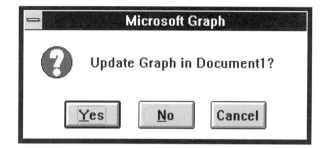

Figure 78. Your chart is now placed in your document.

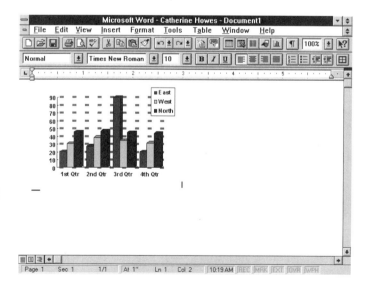

Since your graph is an embedded object, you can double-click on the chart in your Word document, and the chart and datasheet windows open, allowing you to make any further changes to the chart.

For information on resizing and positioning your chart in your Word document see **Chapter 10** and **Chapter 13**.

Index

U

Undo and Redo buttons   30
Undo command   85
User Info options   53

V

View options   51
viewing formats of paragraph   76
viewing multiple columns
   Normal view   89
   Page Layout view   89
   Print Preview   90
views
   Full Screen view   152
   Master Document view   148
   Page Layout   89
   Page Layout view   149, 171
   Print Preview   82, 87, 153, 160
   Zoom command   150

W

white space   137
widow   66
wizards   117, 308
   built-in   118
word count   139
Word screen 1
wordwrap   15
WYSIWYG   141

Z

Zoom command   150, 155